BETWEEN FRONTIERS

BETWEEN FRONTIERS

Nation and Identity in a Southeast Asian Borderland

Noboru Ishikawa

NUS PRESS
SINGAPORE

OHIO UNIVERSITY PRESS
RESEARCH IN INTERNATIONAL STUDIES
SOUTHEAST ASIA SERIES NO. 122

OHIO UNIVERSITY PRESS
ATHENS

First Published by:

NUS Press
AS3-01-02, 3 Arts Link
National University of Singapore
Singapore 117569

Fax: (65) 6774-0652
E-mail: nusbooks@nus.edu.sg
Website: http://www.nus.edu.sg/nuspress

ISBN 978-9971-69-355-8 (Paper)

Ohio University Press, Athens, Ohio 45701
www.ohioswallow.com

First published in the United States of America in 2010 by:

Ohio University Press
The Ridges
Athens, Ohio 45701

EAN 978-0-89680-273-5 (pb)

Printed in the United States of America

Ohio University Press books are printed on acid-free paper ∞ ™

18 17 16 15 14 13 12 11 10   5 4 3 2 1

Library of Congress Cataloging-in-Publication Data available

Ishikawa, Noboru.
[Kyokai no shakaishi. English]
Between frontiers: nation and identity in a Southeast Asian borderland / Noboru Ishikawa.
p. cm. — (Ohio University research in international studies. Southeast Asia series; no. 122)
Includes bibliographical references and index.
ISBN 978-0-89680-273-5 (pb: alk. paper)
1. Boundaries. 2. Nation-state. 3. Nationalism—Malaysia—Sarawak. I. Title.

JC323.I8513 2009
320.5409595'4—dc22   2009042171

Cover: Untitled painting by Yuichiro Shibata.

Contents

List of Tables

List of Figures

List of Illustrations

List of Abbreviations

BPS	Barisan Pemuda Sarawak
BIMP-EAGA	Brunei Darussalam-Indonesia-Malaysia-Philippines East ASEAN Growth Area
BERJASA	Barisan Anak Jati Sarawak
CCO	Clandestine Communist Organization
FELDA	Federal Land Development Authority
LDR	Lundu District Report
LDQR	Lundu District Quarterly Report
NEGARA	Parti Negara Sarawak (PANAS)
NKKU	Negara Kesatuan Kalimantan Utara (Unitary State of North Kalimantan)
PGRS	Pasukan Gerilya Rakyat Sarawak (Sarawak People's Guerrilla Force)
PKI	Parti Komunis Indonesia (The Communist Party of Indonesia)
PRB	Parti Ra'ayat Brunei (Brunei People's Party)
SG	The *Sarawak Gazette*
SG-LDMR	Lundu District Monthly Report, The *Sarawak Gazette*
SGG	The *Sarawak Government Gazette*
SUPP	Sarawak United People's Party
TKI	Tenaga Kerja Indonesia (Indonesian Labor Force)
TNKU	Tentra Nasional Kalimantan Utara (North Kalimantan National Army)

Acknowledgements

The length of the acknowledgements which follows is indicative of the great personal debts I accumulated in the course of my research and book writing.

Firstly I dedicate my sincere gratitude to the people of Telok Melano, Telok Serabang, and Sematan. They allowed me to live in their midst to ask questions, and they patiently discussed things with me at great length. All the villagers, to whom I am very grateful, appear anonymously in this book, however, my adoptive mother deserves special mention. I am very much indebted to Puan Rabinah Sahari and her family.

Scholars, government officials, and friends in Malaysia and Indonesia contributed this book. I am grateful to Awang Hasmadi Awang Mois for his introduction of the Sarawak Malay community. Thanks also go to Napsiah Mahfoz, Peter Kedit, Tafik Abdullah, Sanib Said, Daniel Chew, Sim Ah Hua, Jayl Langub, Abdul Rashid Abdullah, Mohammed Tazuddin Junaidi, Ik Pahon, Syed Junaidi, Fariastuti, Riwanto Tirtosudarmo, Adrian Lapian, Michael Leigh, James Chin, Wan Zawawi Ibrahim, Poline Bala, Awang Mois Pengiran Marali and his family, Mawardi Rivai, Abdi Nurkamil, Ichsan Prihatin, and their family, Kazue Sakai, Anna Ng, and Yuji Asou.

Special thanks are due to the help I received from librarians and archivists; Suria Bujang, Tan Yang Hiok, Hadiah Abang Anuar, Entrie ak Kadir, Busman Jeli, Lily Sia, Nurul Aida Adris, Nora Safiee (the Sarawak Museum Library), Mona Lohanda (the Arsip Nasional Jakarta), Ali Musa (the National Library, Jakarta), Ben Abel (Cornell University Library), and Yumi Kitamura (CSEAS Library, Kyoto University).

Field research in Sarawak (1993–94, 2002, 2006, 2007) was conducted under the auspices of the State Planning Unit, Chief Minister's Department, the State Government of Sarawak (SPU), and the Sarawak

Museum, and financially supported by the Japanese Government Scholarship for Asian Studies (1993–94) and Grants-in-Aid for Scientific Research from the Japanese Ministry of Education, Culture, Sports, Science and Technology (2002, 2006, 2007). Fieldwork in Indonesia (2002, 2006, 2007) was carried out under the auspices of the Lumbaga Ilmu Pengetahuan Indonesia (LIPI) and funded by Grants-in-Aid for Scientific Research from the Japanese Ministry of Education, Culture, Sports, Science and Technology.

This book is partially based on my dissertation submitted to PhD Program in Anthropology, Graduate School and University Center, City University of New York. I thank my committee members; May Ebihara, Eric Wolf, Mervyn Meggitt, Glenn Petersen, Delmos Jones, and Shamsul A.B. I am especially indebted to May Ebihara, Eric Wolf, and Shamsul A.B. who made me what I am as an anthropologist and a fieldworker. I am also grateful to Sydel Silverman, Jane Schneider, and Thomas Burgess for their advice and encouragement.

Takashi Shiraishi, Lesley Potter, Victor King, James Warren, Anna Tsing, Sidney Mintz, Eric Tagliacozzo, Donna Amoroso, Caroline Hau, Patricio Abinales, Wil de Jong, Chris Baker, Awang Hasmadi Awang Mois, Jayl Langub read my manuscript in its embryonic form either entirely or partially. Their advice and suggestions were invaluable. I also benefited from the conversations with Dave Lumenta and Saki Murakami. Two anonymous reviewers improved this book. All errors of fact and interpretation are, of course, my own responsibility.

I contracted intellectual debts in Japan. Makio Matsuzono, Seiichi Muratake, Eikichi Ishikawa, and Takenori Noguchi first taught me social anthropology. Kazuo Ohtsuka, Motomitsu Uchibori, Teruo Sekimoto, Etsuko Kuroda, Tsuyoshi Kato, Takashi Sugishima, Kiyoshi Nakamura, and Makoto Tsugami meticulously read the Japanese version of my manuscript either entirely or partially and gave comments.

My colleagues at the Center for Southeast Asian Studies, Kyoto University, provided me with a stimulating setting for research, writing and exchange of ideas. I am grateful for my association with one of the innovative centers for area studies, where researchers strive to cross the lines of demarcation that separate the various social and natural science disciplines from one another.

I had an opportunity to be affiliated with Asia Research Institute, National University of Singapore as a visiting research fellow. During the last stage of revisions, I benefitted from the exchange of ideas with Anthony Reid, George Souza, Geoffrey Wade, Mario Ruten, Rodolphe

De Koninck, Patrick Daly, Mike Feener, Wu Xiao An, Kwee Hui Kian, David Hill, Mika Toyota, Erman Erwiza, Thung Ju Lan, Atsushi Ota, Natasha Hamilton-Hart, Reynaldo Ileto, Goh Beng Lan, Stan B-H Tan, Liu Hong, and Shapan Adnan.

There are many helpers, who operated computers, processed words, charts and photographs, and drew maps. I wish to thank Masami Nishio, Dave Lumenta, Tran Thi Que Ha, Aya Tanaka, Tomoko Kawai, Noriko Tabata, Yumi Kato, Kumi Okunishi, Gaku Masuda, and Kimiya Kitani for their fine work.

I am grateful to my friends in New York City, who taught me how to see, listen, and think. Special thanks go to Yuichiro Shibata, Teruo Nakamura, and Hiroshi Sasaki.

The present volume has a twin brother/sister among Japanese-speaking readers. Through the accumulation of individual papers originally written in Japanese, which were transformed into English chapters of this book as well as the English chapters turned into Japanese ones, simultaneous book making in both languages was possible. What was intriguing to me is that I could not appropriately translate my writing, word for word, either from Japanese to English or vice-versa. Subsequently I wrote two books with identical contents. The Japanese version was published in 2008 as *Kyōkai no Shakishi: Kokka ga Shoyū o Sengensuru toki* from Kyoto University Press. Beyond geographical barriers, this book will be brought to many parts of the world. My deepest thanks are due to Paul Kratoska (NUS Press) for his scholarship and editorship in turning a book making into a global project. I am also grateful to Gerald Jackson (NIAS Press).

I wish to record my gratitude to my parents and parents-in-law for their unfailing support through the years. A special note of thanks must go to my father, Hiroyoshi Ishikawa, who taught me first how to look at the world in sociological terms.

Finally I owe the greatest appreciation to my wife, co-fieldworker, and foremost critic, Mayumi, who gave unstinting support at every stage of research and book writing. Without her, this study could not have been imagined. In Tokyo, New York City, Sarawak, West Kalimantan, Jakarta, Singapore and Kyoto, in trying and happy times, she was always there. To her this book is dedicated in gratitude and admiration.

A Note on Currency

When the symbol $ is used, this refers to the currency in Sarawak under the Brooke colonization. The colonial Sarawak dollar was equivalent to the Straits dollar and pegged to sterling at the rate of 2 shillings and 4 pence. The symbol M$ denotes the Malaysian ringgit.

Introduction

Border Zones

This book deals with a set of questions about the construction and evolution of the nation-state. Research on this much studied topic has long recognized and examined differences between insiders and outsiders, between the domestic and the foreign, and the self and the other. Far less attention has been devoted to borderlands, the transitional areas that lie between them. National borders are notional lines on a map and on the ground that provide a sharp demarcation between two territories, and two sovereignties. They also lie at the heart of what can be called border zones, areas on both sides of a border where the proximity of a place that is different in matters such as currency, laws, citizenship, and commodity prices has a profound influence.

The questions examined here could be asked about a myriad of borders around the world, with parallel but not identical answers. The border zones used as a case study in the discussion that follows run across the western part of the island of Borneo and separate the Malaysian state of Sarawak from West Kalimantan, Indonesia, two regions that are culturally similar but have vastly different economic, political and historical circumstances. Through this case study, the book will consider whether the geo-body of the nation-state really inscribes spatial and temporal boundaries on people's mental maps, and what kind of national order emerges when the state attempts to enforce its claims to territoriality. In addition, the book considers what organizational features the state requires to maintain its dominion, and how people strategically situate themselves, as members of local communities, nations, and ethnic groups within a social field designated as national space. The answers proposed here derive not only from present relations but also from the last 140 years of history in western Borneo, when social relations based on maritime and riverine networks were transformed

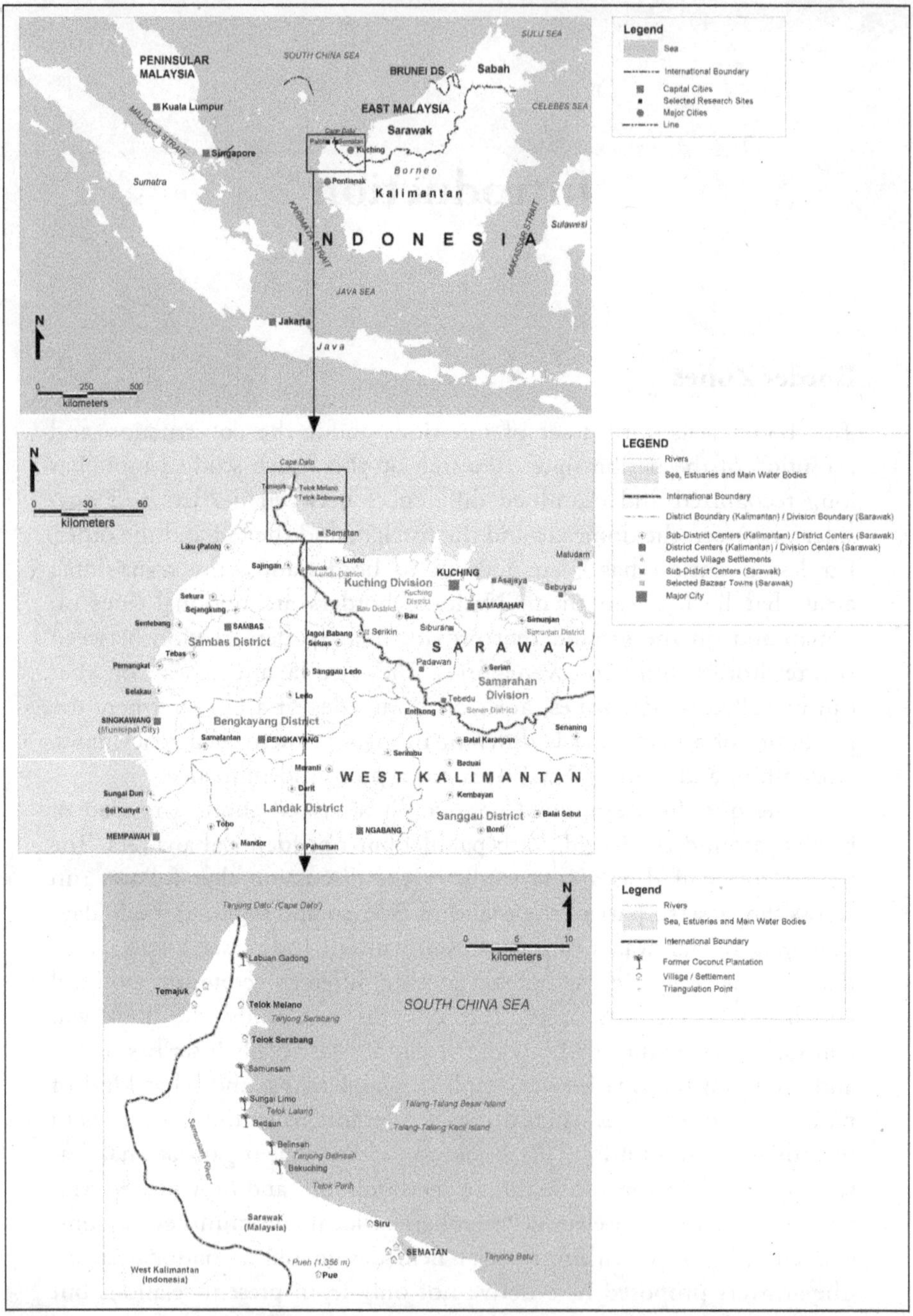

Fig. 1 Research Sites

through the colonial imposition of a state boundary and further reconfigured by postcolonial nation-states.

A Hyphen between Nation and State

In a sense this study arises from a hyphen, the small and often disregarded piece of typography that appears between the words "nation" and "state". The habitual use of the term "nation-state" to describe a specific form of state, one that governs the territory of a particular nation, creates an impression that nation and state are inevitably and perpetually intertwined. The automatic usage of this conceptual linkage complicates dealing with the relationship between the terms.

"Nationalism" has been one of the most effective concepts in post-war academic writing for exploring the relationship between nation and state, and, as the ideological alibi of the territorial state, the principal justification and vehicle for assigning populations collective status as members of nations. Nationalism is a contentious abstraction, but scholars have generally treated the nation as something "imagined", "fashioned", and "disseminated" (Anderson 1991, Bhaba 1990, Chatterjee 1986, Gellner 1983, Balakrishnan 1996, Smith 1971, cf. Lomnitz 2001). The nation, in these formulations, exists in the mind, in printed matter, on school maps, and is represented by symbols such as flags and national anthems. The state, by contrast, is a piece of institutional machinery with a clear-cut spatial boundary that provides a location for the nation. The nature of the imagined community (Anderson 1991), the narrativity of nations (Bhabha 1990), and the colonial logics of nationalist discourse (Chatterjee 1986) have been engaged to explore how nations were formed out of communities of citizens in territorially defined nation-states, who share collective experiences through reading books, pamphlets, newspapers, maps and other texts (Anderson 1991, Thongchai 1994).

The Nation-State Underfoot

This study focuses on something much more concrete, the physical presence under people's feet rather than an abstraction in their minds. Rather than discussing the iconology of nationalism, it deals with the social, economic, and political processes involved in the making of national space, looking at the construction and evolution of national boundaries and national space, along with state power and societal responses to it.

I define "national space" as a social field within which people are represented as a single collective social group. Throughout this study, national space serves as an analytical interface where nation and state are contested, and as a point of articulation that links a particular social group with a political association holding effective dominion over a geographic area. State territory and national space are by no means necessarily identical, and each has a distinct history, constituency, and set of interests.

Ever since Max Weber described the nation-state as "a compulsory association claiming a monopoly on the legitimate use of physical force within a given territory" (Weber 1958: 77), territoriality has been a basic prerequisite for the nation-state. This definition leads to treatment of the organizational development and spatial formation of the state as two separate processes. Foucault and the theorists of new geography have pointed out that meta-narratives provided by modern social theorists concentrate on processes of temporal change, while keeping spatiality constant (Foucault 1980, Lefebvre 1991, Harvey 1996, Soja 1989). The processes through which the territoriality of the state is recognized and the nation spatially arranged within a prescribed territory are taken as established theoretical facts rather than a proposition to be examined (cf. Vandergeest and Peluso 1995, Migdal 2004).

Studies of international politics have likewise paid scant attention to the social processes of national territorialization. The modern nation-state is treated as an amalgam of sovereignty, nation, and territory, a concept rooted in the 1648 Treaty of Westphalia. The processes involved in the creation of national territoriality have been conflated with descriptions of treaty ratification in the history of world politics.

The insertion of spatial considerations into a consideration of the genesis of the nation-state provides the vantage point for the present study, which considers national space as a social field in which practical policy implementation and the response of society take much clearer shape than is the case with abstractions such as "nationness" and "nationhood".

National Space and Borderlands

A borderland provides a useful perspective from which to examine the genesis of state territoriality, the evolution of national space and the relation between the two. Residents of border zones deal on a daily basis with the most concrete manifestation of the nation-state — its territorial boundary, and for people in this situation the nation-state is an everyday reality rather than the subject of ideation and imagination. Questions of identity and "location work" (Appadurai 1996) can have far-reaching consequences, and quotidian decisions about the affiliation of people and things are deeply associated with the position of people as villagers, members of ethnic groups, and nationals of geo-bodies, all of which put political, economic, and socio-cultural grids upon them.

The borderland under study has long been a social interface between paired political systems: the Brunei and Sambas sultanates, the white rajahs of Sarawak and the Dutch colonial government, the post-war British colonial administration in Sarawak and Indonesian West Borneo, and independent Malaysia and Indonesia. At one time a major mercantile crossroads, the zone has become an obscure peripheral area separating modern national territories. In many ways, the region represents the history and social formation of island Southeast Asia in microcosm, and this study is particularly concerned with its social, economic, and cultural incorporation and exclusion (cf. Cole and Wolf 1974, Heyman 1991, Kearney 1991, Sahlins 1989).

Flows and Interfaces

Like lines in mathematics, national boundaries occupy no space. They "occur where the vertical interfaces between state sovereignties intersect the surface of the earth.... As vertical interfaces, boundaries have no horizontal extent...." (Muir 1975: 119). In theory the full sovereign power of the state extends to this imaginary line, and there it stops completely. In practice, the space around the border becomes a special field, a threshold that accommodates a series of social, economic and cultural flows from one national arena into another, a zone where things are no longer what they were, but not yet what they will be. Located at out-of-the-way places in the national territory, borderlands function as liminal zones where the nature of things is inevitably transformed by the proximity of an alternative system. Crossing national boundaries between economically weak nations and nations that are well-off alters the value of commodities and of labor. Because boundaries create, channel, truncate, and regulate flows of people, goods, capital, ideas and practices, institutional and organizational forms, and technologies, border zones are an excellent arena for examining the genesis of transnationalism and its relation to the state.

As a liminal space, a borderland is both part of and distinct from the territorial state. Victor Turner wrote that such spaces provided for "the liberation of human capacities of cognition, affect, volition, creativity, etc., from the normative constraints incumbent upon occupying a sequence of social statuses" (Turner 1982: 44). The state's governmentality and the agency of individuals are both highly visible at the territorial margin. Boundary demarcation is a matter of national importance, but a borderland is a non-state space where the authority of government is constantly repelled by local residents, not as a political act but as part of daily life (Scott 2009). Relationships along a border escape conventional state-society oppositions as well as the subsuming of state into society (cf. Migdal 1988, 2001).

At issue are the national order of things and the response of borderland residents to the state's inscription of territoriality and mobilization of labor, the formation of an ethnically segmented national society, the singularizing of national affiliations of people and commodities through immigration and customs regulations, and the formation of social identity grounded in the spatial demarcation of administrative villages, ethnic communities, and the national territory. The use and deliberate infiltration of the international boundary through kin networks, contraband commodity trade, trans-border flight from indentured labor, shifting cultivation beyond national territory, and dual identity formation figure in these processes, and appear in historical as well as ethnographic sources.

The examination of state-society relationship in a Bornean borderland is highly relevant to the general process of nation-state making. Theory generated from a thinly populated, primary jungle-girded ecological niche with an extremely porous border presents a view of state-society relations, with close parallels throughout Southeast Asia and elsewhere, where populations have long been non-sedentary, non-territorial, and "transnational" in nature.

Uneven Expansion of the Nation

Scholars discussing nation-making have long pondered the state project of incorporating and homogenizing people under state territorialization. However such constructionism often lacks critical attention to social dislocation, peripheralization, and fragmentation. Due attention to social heterogeneity is conducive to a better understanding of the social process of nation-making.

One of the issues at stake is the identity of those who live within a nationally bounded dominant social order where they are marginalized. How did a border village become an isolated enclave? Why are the villagers regarded neither as authentic members of their ethnic group nor as citizens? How do they acknowledge "national space" and "village space"? This book describes how the borderland residents consciously locate as well as dislocate themselves in such national and ethnic categories in a community geographically distant from the center of the state, isolated from the waves of urban-based political mobilization and the dissemination of the national order of things (cf. Tsing 1993, 1994).

The heterogeneity or the uneven expansion of the nation is often overlooked in the study of the making and unmaking of nations. This issue can only be handled by simultaneously taking chronology and space into consideration. As Eric Wolf pointed out, "differences in location and timing, as well as in the nature of socio-cultural segments and their activity systems, would render the process of national incorporation uneven. It is more likely that the outcome would favor the rise of heterogeneous social arrays than the development of homogeneous national or sub-national totalities" (Wolf 1999: 12). In the study of the genesis and spread of national space, the homogeneity of the nation tends to be a common premise. Nationalism, nationness, and nationhood are presumed to diffuse as modular forms from one place to another. We are fully aware, however, that even culture, the hallmark concept of anthropology, is not shared equally. Neither is the nation.

Micro-area and Micro-history

In this book, I try to avoid writing about things of which local people are not aware, or of things far removed from their lifeworld. The study is thus micro-oriented in terms of its geography, compared to numerous studies where researchers often hop around a geo-historical arena (sometimes as vast as a nation-state and beyond) to find and narrate facts related to their topic. Unlike subject-oriented historians, who are less concerned with the relationships between places on which events take place, anthropologists tend to stick to a social field where entanglements of social relations seem to be tangible and observable through fieldwork. I am not pursuing a functional whole, but a spatial unit is fundamentally necessary for thick description in time and space. Instead of hopping around the sea of archival documents, either arbitrarily divided by administrators or grouped together by file makers, this study cherishes the primordial feeling of historical one-ness of a micro-area, much as anthropologists in the heyday of functionalism enjoyed their closed social field of analysis. However, this village ethnography is transnational. By looking at a village at the edge of the state territory, I deal with a social space whose frame of reference goes beyond the conventional analytical limits of a community, a nation-state, or an empire.

My ethnographic project is also micro-history-oriented. I treat archival documents as fieldnotes, and field research as the study of the most recent layers of spatially bounded local history. During two years of field research in the borderland of western Borneo, I gained practical knowledge of and a feeling about the places, communities and people recorded in historical documents. My internalization of local history through being on the spot made me better understand the words of colonial officers and the memories of elder villagers. All anthropological monographs dealing with the "ethnographic present" are destined to be historical documentation as time goes by. In this sense, there should be no categorical as well as ontological difference between anthropology and history, and this book recognizes no practical distinction between the two.

For the reconstruction of regional history of the borderland, I utilized the following archival materials. The *Sarawak Gazette* (1841–1941), Colonial Office Files (CO 144, 531, 874, 974), Memorie van Overgave, West Borneo (Westerafdeling van Borneo) and Mailrapporten. Oral interviews were conducted in Malay, Dayak, and Chinese communities in Sematan Sub-District, Lundu District, and Kuching, East Malaysia as well as in Sambas Malay and Bugis communities in Temajuk, Paloh, Sambas, and Pontianak, West Kalimantan, Indonesia.

In the field, I became familiar with the names and locations of mountains, rivers, bays, and communities mentioned in the *Sarawak Gazette* and other documents, and whenever I revisit historical documents on the borderland I can envision the landscapes and the physical features of the area. I have experienced the extreme roughness of South China Sea during *landas* monsoon season and the feeling of relief that comes after passing raging waves at Cape Dato, which marks the border between Indonesia and Malaysia; I have savored the tranquility of the coastal waters in Malaysian territory off the cape, the sense of security of Serabang Bay where pirates from the Sulu Archipelago and Bugis merchants from Pontianak once came for fresh water and shelter. I am familiar with the barren landscape of former coconut

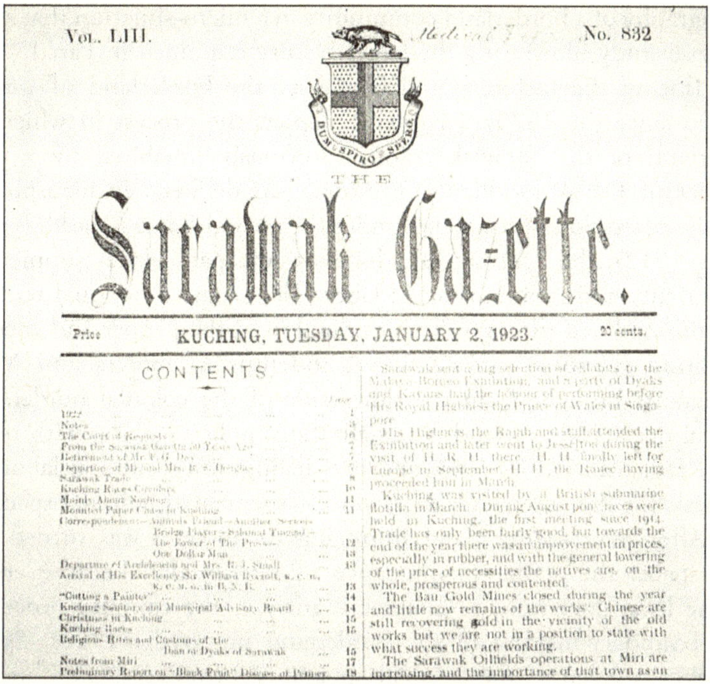

Vol. LIII. No. 832

THE

Sarawak Gazette.

Price KUCHING, TUESDAY, JANUARY 2, 1923. 20 cents.

CONTENTS

	Page
1922	1
Notes	3
The Court of [illegible]	6
From the Sarawak Gazette 50 Years Ago	7
Retirement of Mr. [illegible]	7
Departure of Mr. and Mrs. [illegible]	7
Sarawak Trade	8
Kuching Races [illegible]	10
Mainly About [illegible]	11
Mounted Paper Chase in Kuching	11
Correspondence—[illegible]—Bridge Player—[illegible]—The Power of The Press—One Dollar Man	12
Departure of Archdeacon and Mrs. [illegible]	13
Arrival of His Excellency Sir William [illegible], K.C.M.G. in B.N.B.	13
"Cutting a Painter"	14
Kuching Sanitary and Municipal Advisory Board	14
Christmas in Kuching	15
Kuching Races	15
Religious Rites and Customs of the Iban or Dyaks of Sarawak	15
Notes from Miri	17
Preliminary Report on "Black Fruit" Disease of Pepper	18

[illegible] Sarawak [illegible] exhibits to the [illegible] Exhibition, and a party of Dyaks and Kayans had the honour of performing before His Royal Highness the Prince of Wales in Singapore.

His Highness the Rajah and staff attended the Exhibition and later went to Jesselton during the visit of H. R. H. there. H. H. finally left for Europe in September, H. H. the Ranee having proceeded him in March.

Kuching was visited by a British submarine flotilla in March. During August pony races were held in Kuching, the first meeting since 1914. Trade has only been fairly good, but towards the end of the year there was an improvement in prices, especially in rubber, and with the general lowering of the price of necessities the natives are, on the whole, prosperous and contented.

The Bau Gold Mines closed during the year and little now remains of the works. Chinese are still recovering gold in the vicinity of the old works but we are not in a position to state with what success they are working.

The Sarawak Oilfields operations at Miri are increasing, and the importance of that town as an

Illus. 1 The *Sarawak Gazette* (January 2, 1923)

plantations at Labuan Gadong, now infested with wild boar, the difficulty of locating an international boundary between a Malaysian and an Indonesian village, the narrowness and steepness of paths through which the Dutch Sambas peasants once carried rubber sheets smuggled for sale to Sarawak merchants, the darkness of the old secondary forest where the Chinese communists hid themselves. In short, I know what Malay traders, Chinese coolies, Bugis migrants, Dayak swidden cultivators and communist guerrillas experienced over the course of the history of the borderland, and these landscapes, sensations, and memories remain with me now, internalized as everyday experiences and informing my writing.

Chapter Contents

This book consists of two parts with contrasting but constitutive focal points of investigation. Part I examines macro-level historical dynamics of the borderlands in southwestern Sarawak, while Part II presents an ethnography of a borderland community in a micro-situation that serves as a case study illustrating the larger history examined in Part I.

Tracing the historical trajectories of the borderland of western Borneo since the 1870s, Chapter 1 depicts the process in which the hinterland of the Sarawak colony, previously inhabited by a small number of Dayak swidden cultivators, was deliberately incorporated into the possession of the state. Under the second Rajah Charles Brooke (1868–1917), the Sarawak kingdom saw the parallel development of territoriality and mobilization of labor. The enclosed national territory was commodified through the introduction of the pepper and coconut plantation economy, with Chinese indentured laborers and Malay immigrants brought from the other side of the colonial border. The judicial declaration of land nationalization, policy making with regard to the redistribution of land, and marshaling of agricultural labor laid the basis for the emergence of ethnically segmented national space.

After *terra nullius* (land belonging to no one) was turned into state space, the actual maintenance of territoriality became crucial for the local government. Chapter 2 analyzes the complex process of state boundary-making in the borderland up to the 1920s. Special attention is given to the colonial apparatus introduced in an attempt to control and confine the cross-border movements of mobile people and commodities.

While the primary focus of the first two chapters falls within the national territory, the third chapter expands the analytical arena to embrace a social milieu extending beyond the borderlands of western Borneo, examining the structural features that joined the hinterland with the larger political economy of Southeast Asia and beyond. Rubber booms in the 1920s, the implementation of the International Rubber Regulation Agreement (IRRA), and subsequent illicit trans-border trade provide examples of the way the empire enclosed economic space and of the response of border society.

The hinterland communities of southwestern Sarawak adjacent to the Dutch border remained rubber smuggling points until security arrangements and alliance structures associated with the Cold War violently transformed daily life. Cross-border links based on illicit trade and kinship were suddenly broken owing to the military confrontation (*Konfrontasi*) between Indonesia and the newly-formed Malaysia and a communist insurgency. The international boundary became rigid and impenetrable. It became the site of military clashes, and traditional cross-border symbiosis ceased to exist in everyday life.

The second part of the book considers the simultaneous process of a village and a nation making from the perspective of a Sarawak community called Telok Melano, where the village boundary coincides with the national border. The goal is to substantiate the macro history presented in Part I with an ethnographic account based on fieldwork in a Malay community. Oral history accounts collected through my period of fieldwork connect the ancestors of present-day residents with events described in archival documents.

How was a social group at the edge of the state territory socio-culturally and economically drawn into as well as excluded from the national space? Chapter 4 explains the historical process of marginalization of Telok Melano peasantry starting in the 1880s. The chapter shows how Malay coconut cultivators from the Sambas region of Dutch West Borneo became stranded on the Sarawak frontier where they were bound to an unproductive ecological niche as the state tightened its control over the movement of people and commodities. The demise of the Malay entrepreneurship deprived plantation-workers-cum-villagers of the means of commodifying agricultural produce, and Malays living in Telok Melano turned to subsistence farming of hill rice, adopting slash-and-burn agriculture.

Exclusion from plantation agriculture and subsequent engagement in swidden cultivation set the borderland Malays apart within the Sarawak Malay ethnic category. While slash-and-burn agriculture is an important ethnic indicator for the up-river Dayaks, the Malay swidden cultivators are considered unfit for ethnic orthodoxy of the Malays traditionally engaged in maritime trade and fishery. Chapter 5 looks at the issue of ethnic displacement by comparing two Malay ethnic constructs, the one that of the Malay aristocracy situated in the state capital of Kuching and the other that of Telok Melano peasantry on the territorial periphery.

How was the neighborhood of Telok Melano spatially transformed into a village compound as well as a national territory in the border zone? The chapter that follows examines the history of a moving boundary in the borderland to explore the way in which everyday spatial recognition along the boundary relates to the emergence of social identities. The discussion centers on the relationship between nationalism and village communalism.

The presence of another nation-state across the border has had a powerful effect on residents of Telok Melano. Independence and *Konfrontasi* brought about a series of misfortunes, including deaths, burnt homes, and evacuation. The liberation of Sarawak from British colonialism violently inscribed a national boundary on the mental maps of villagers. Nationality divides local residents, yet transnational interaction remains strong and even indispensable for the survival of communities on both sides of the border.

The value attached to commodities and labor changes as they move from an economically weak country to one with a strong economy. Through the observation of daily social relations between Telok Melano and an Indonesian migrant community established across the border, Chapter 7 examines this phenomenon in relationship to the structural osmotic pressure generated between Indonesia to Malaysia.

Based on recent fieldwork in communities on both sides of the border, the eighth chapter re-examines the changing nature of border society. As the economic gap between Indonesia and Malaysia widened after the Asian economic crisis of 1997, a situation clearly manifested in the depreciation of the Indonesian rupiah against Malaysian ringgit, Indonesian borderlanders abandoned their own economic community to sell agricultural produce, natural resources, and labor on the Malaysian market for Malaysian currency.

With the opening of ten official entry points along the border between East Malaysia and Kalimantan, the flows of commodity and labor from Indonesia to Malaysia have increased. Once uncontrollable borderlands are now domesticated and endowed with new meanings, and the border area has become an important social field for state ventures such as economic zones and industrial estates. Proximity to the border is considered an advantage to procure inexpensive labor force and abundant natural resources from the neighboring country. The two governments that share the border are characteristically tolerant of illicit but locally sanctioned flows of laborers and goods, and are engaged in developing newer forms of regional economic cooperation beyond national boundaries.

The borderlands of western Borneo today provide an example of the articulation of the organizational power of the state and the structural power of transnational capitalism. The final chapter concludes the examination of 140 year borderland history by exploring the relationship between nation-state and transnationalism. The discussion looks beyond conventional models of state-society juxtaposition and societal inclusion of the state and proposes new perspectives on the construction of national space and the simultaneous deconstruction of a state boundary under transnational modernity.

PART I

From Sultanate Frontier to National Periphery

CHAPTER ONE

The Geo-body in Transition

Spatial Turn in Southeast Asia

The emergence of territorial states in Southeast Asia was a grandiose process of social change, marking a total transformation from the "pre-modern" to the "modern". To understand the nature of the transformation, it is crucial to focus on four processes involved in the spatial turn under Western colonialism.

The first is the emergence of an ideology in the West that provided a rational for the possession of colonial space. A new and exclusive relationship between a state and a colony required an ideological basis, conceptually turning tropical territories into "no man's land" (*terra nullius*). Then through judicial declarations of land nationalization, *terra nullius* became an imaginary national space that had no civilized society, and vast tracts of uncultivated "waste" land fell under colonial governance.

The second process required for the colonial state to realize its national space was actual policy-making with regard to the redistribution of land and the marshaling of labor for cultivation of cash crops and exploitation of natural resources. Land laws, labor ordinances, and immigration acts created a social field where the usufruct of land was distributed to peasants and entrepreneurs. Plural societies, where multiple ethnic groups were mobilized for plantation and mining sectors are typical byproducts of colonial engineering. The nationalization of space and the mobilization of labor operated in tandem to make *terra nullius* a capitalist production site and a mercantile exchange sphere.

Thirdly, the nationalization and legal redistribution of land were followed by the actual implementation of policies, and the last phase was the reaction of local society to the colonial apparatus that evolved in connection with the construction of national space.

The relationship between state and society at work in a newly created space is geographically as well as historically specific, and subject to local variation based on timing and location. The next two chapters attempt to empirically interrogate the above-mentioned four processes, using a maritime borderland zone of colonial Southeast Asia as a case study.

Colonizers who expanded their dominance over the Malay world beginning in the eighteenth century attempted to transform the region's vast riverine-maritime complex into discrete state possessions that were to a large extent arbitrary creations.[1] The land, whether primary jungle or swidden in fallow, was declared to be state property and made subject to redistribution, even though people had cultivated it or collected forest produce from it for generations. Colonial administrators saw no concept of private ownership in the East, identifying only rights of usufruct over communal land. Furthermore, they regarded their predecessors — the local rulers — as barbaric Asiatic despots and, on this self-righteous basis, claimed the sole right to possession and allocation of land. Stamford Raffles, a founding father of Singapore, for instance, considered sultans and local chiefs petty tyrants, who siphoned off the fruits of their people's industry through a tributary system (Raffles 1830: 151–2).

The production of colonial space was also legitimized by social evolutionary thinking, then a dominant ideology of the European bourgeoisie. Karl Marx thought the lack of land ownership and existence of despotic monarchies to be common characteristics of Asia. Many other Western social thinkers saw Eastern absolutism as comparable to Western feudalism, a stage prior to where they placed themselves in a linear developmental process. These ideologies provided colonizers with a justification, as both leaders on the evolutionary ladder and social reformers for transferring power from local rulers to colonial governments. When local rulers were removed by the newly established administrations or placed under the rubric of indirect colonial rule,

[1] From the "age of discovery", the claim to take possession of native land has been ritualistic. European landfall in the Caribbean in 1492, for instance, was accompanied by a series of "ceremonies and juridical formalities to take possession of the island, making the declarations that were required, and which at more length are contained in the testimonials made there in writing" (Greenblatt 1991: 55). For Columbus, taking possession seems to have been principally the performance of a set of linguistic acts: declaring, witnessing, and recording.

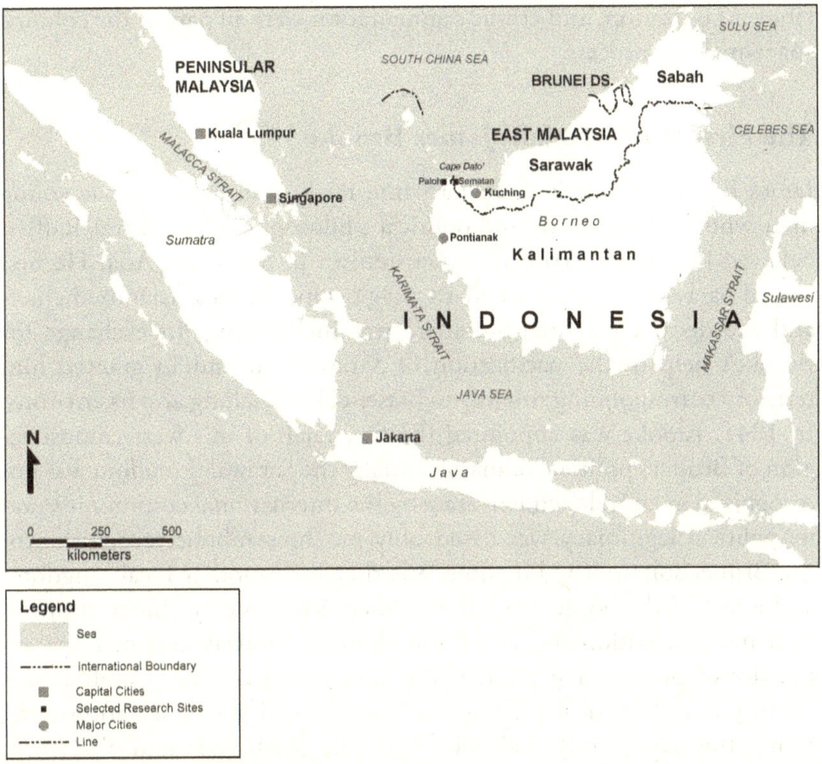

Fig. 2 Malay Maritime World

ownership of and control over territorial space was also transformed. The colonial government became the supreme landlord with the prerogative to allocate land and to tax both the people who labored and the goods produced within its bounded territory.

The colonizing of space proceeded concurrently with the process of mobilizing labor and reconfiguring pre-existing relations between man and nature. Flora in the colony was vastly altered for commercial agriculture, labor was assembled through in-migration, and land was allocated for cultivation. This reconfiguration of colonial space led to the emergence of an ethnically segmented peasant society: both foreign and domestic indentured laborers planted commercial crops in the plains; natives in the interior engaged in shifting cultivation and collection of jungle produce; and mobile sea-faring peasants found an economic and habitational niche on the coast. Ownership and allocation of land, labor mobilization, and ethnic segmentation were all part of the colonial space-making process.

The First White Rajah, James Brooke

James Brooke, the first so-called white rajah, was an ambitious young man who, influenced by the political philosophy of Stamford Raffles, believed in British territorial expansionism in Southeast Asia. He first visited Sarawak in 1839, when a struggle between local Islamized chiefs and the decaying Brunei Sultanate was intensifying. In exchange for Brooke's help in the pacification of Sarawak, the sultan granted him territory corresponding roughly to present-day Kuching and its environs. In 1841, Brooke was appointed the first rajah of this westernmost region of Brunei's political domain. Initially the Sarawak kingdom was not recognized as an independent state by the international community, and its political legitimacy was based only on the symbolic recognition of the Brunei sultan. The kingdom was therefore another local kingdom, and it lacked the borders and the politico-economic machinery features of a modern nation-state. The kingdom of Sarawak retained characteristics of pre-colonial polities, but under Brooke rule it embraced a century-long historical process that transformed it into a nation-state, laying the basis for British colonized rule (1946–63) and a place in independent Malaysia.

The situation of Sarawak was far from unique. Many Western colonial governments were not in fact extrinsic to local society. Colonial administration retained pre-existing political systems. In Southeast Asia, not a small number of colonial governments resembled traditional kingdoms, dynasties, and religious communities both structurally and operationally. The port state of Melaka as governed by the Portuguese, and later by the Dutch East India Company, operated according to the principles of statehood in Southeast Asia. According to Ricklefs, the kings of Batavia regarded the Dutch East India Company as just another kingdom (Ricklefs 1974: 27).

The same is true of Sarawak. From the viewpoint of Islamized sultans, local Malay chiefs, Muslim traders (*nakoda*), Dayak leaders (*orang kaya*), and leaders of Chinese communities (*kongsi*), the first rajah of Sarawak was another newly emergent local lord.[2] The essential

[2] In this book Dayak means a member of a group of indigenous peoples inhabiting parts of Borneo, including the Iban, the Orang Ulu, and the Land Dayak.

power of his kingdom came from the charismatic nature of the rajah himself. When on expedition, James Brooke was portrayed as a brave war leader fighting rebellious pagan tribes such as the Iban and the Kayan. When in Kuching, the capital of Sarawak kingdom, the rajah's daily routine was to come to the royal palace under the shade of a yellow umbrella, a symbol of the cosmological power and dignity of Malay rulers.[3]

Like other kingships in Southeast Asia, the Sarawak succession followed a patrilineal line, passing from James to his nephew Charles Brooke, and thence to Charles' son Vyner. Under James, the Sarawak government consisted of a small number of British and native officers. In 1841, it was run by four white officers and two Malay officers; the numbers slowly grew to 30 British and 15 Malay officers by 1884, but even at the turn of the twentieth century, white officers numbered less than 50 (Naimah 1999). As in a traditional Southeast Asian state, the officers — both British and Malay — formed an unstable entourage surrounding the rajah. Each of his subordinates maintained a relationship with the rajah based on the exchange of salary and loyalty, and the state's governmental organization was an extension of such dyadic relations. But Rajah Brooke was also white, British, and Christian. The neighboring colonial powers did not regard him in the same light as other local chiefs at the margin of their territory, but had certain expectations of governance in line with European models.

Rajah Charles Brooke as a Supreme Landlord of the Tropics

The near absence of registration or administrative instructions on land before 1871 has been well documented (Porter 1967: 17–31). Under James Brooke, Sarawak was still in political turmoil, at war with the Iban and other natives in the interior, and the first rajah was in no position to implement land reform and agro-economic policies. The situation changed after the coronation of Charles Brooke, whose reign would mark the economic transformation of Sarawak through the expansion of regional trade with Singapore and the early development of export-oriented commodity production.

According to Porter, "Charles Brooke was bold and more practical than his uncle and the effect of his confident approach to his duties

[3] For the detailed analysis of political history of Sarawak under James Brooke as a "man of prowess", see Walker 2002.

began to be seen almost immediately after he assumed responsibility for administrative government" (Porter 1967: 32). Charles Brooke implemented nation-building by improving land administration and mobilizing labor, both crucial to promoting commodity production. Charles immediately proposed a comprehensive land regulation that was passed unanimously by the Supreme Council and announced in the *Sarawak Gazette* on January 21, 1871. The first and basic land law of Sarawak made all "unoccupied and waste" land the property of the Sarawak government, available for commercial production, and liable for reversion to the state if left uncultivated:

> 1. All unoccupied and waste lands the property of Government, required for agricultural purposes, beyond the township and with the exception of such tracts as may be reserved or disposed of by Public Sale, shall be granted to applicant at the words mission pleasure of the Government in Fee simple for $1 per acre or on lease of 900 years on payment of 50 cents per acre, with an annual quit rent of 10 cents per acre...
> 2. Persons taking land on lease of 900 years to have the option after the expiration of 3 years, of purchasing the land in Fee simple on payment of the additional sum of $ 1 per acre...
> 3. All lands granted whether upon lease or in Fee simple, are liable to revert to the State, in the event of one-fourth not being cleared and brought under cultivation or otherwise made use of for pasturage, or building purposes within 10 years of the period of possession...
> 4. All mortgages, upon land to render them legal, must be duly registered...
> 5. Squatters will have no actual right to the land, but in the event of the Government taking over such lands the temporary possessors will receive compensations for their plants, arbitrarily fixed by two or more persons, nominated by Government: all buildings run up on such lands are to be limited in value to $25, and to be liable to be called upon for the payment of rent and taxes.
>
> [Items 6-13 omitted.]
>
> (*SG*, January 24, 1871: 39)

The government's aim in claiming possession of land was to establish its sole right to distribute it to cultivators of commercial crops. To support this goal, a series of detailed agrarian policies were drawn up to encourage the cultivation of gambier and pepper, which commanded a good price in the international market at the time. Gambier, used for dyeing, was usually planted together with pepper for economic and ecological reasons.[4] But their cultivation did not yield long-term plantation sites. Gambier processing required large amounts of firewood, while pepper quickly exhausted the soil. In the search for firewood and fresh soil, planters moved inland to clear virgin or secondary forest in fallow.

In 1872, a government proclamation assured Chinese planters that "they shall have land free of all payments and to any extent, if they engage to bring it under cultivation however gradually"; that "no tax shall be levied on exports of gambier or pepper for the first six years"; and that "the Government will engage to allow gambier and pepper gardeners to have salt and tobacco free of duty on the spot for the term of six years". Anticipating the socio-economic form the gambier-pepper plantations would take, the regulation granted "the leading Chinaman of each river ... power from Government to exercise authority over coolies". The government also promised to enforce social control, maintaining that "coolies who stipulate to serve masters for certain periods will be obliged by the law to do so or incur punishment" and pledging "to assist to recover runaway coolies and in all other ways to assist the planters in accordance with the rules of justice" (*SG*, June 17, 1872: 47).

In 1876, the government announced 99-year land grants of "1,000 fathoms square"[5] at nominal rents, on the condition that "a proper course of farming and bona fide system of gambier and pepper cultivation be carried out". Freedom from export duty was extended another four years — or ten years in the case of "persons coming to Sarawak and there opening gardens with their own capital (that is without advances from Govt.)" — and taxes thereafter were promised to be light. Signaling the relative scarcity of labor, the government also undertook to provide "free passages from Singapore to Kuching for all Towkays and coolies intending bona fide to cultivate gambier and

---

[4] The reasons for the co-cultivation of these plants are: (1) gambier produced refuse that manured pepper vines; (2) the sale of fast-growing gambier provided an income before the pepper matured for harvest; and (3) gambier plants required little attention compared to labor-intensive pepper production, thus their demands were complementary rather than competitive.

[5] 1 fathom = 6 feet.

pepper in Sarawak"[6] (Porter 1967: 38–9). In the same year, the rajah allowed sago cultivators to obtain title to their land, as well as those who produced rice, coconuts, or other "native culture", provided the land was at least 1/2 to 1 mile from the townships.

The decade of the 1870s was thus a formative period in the development of Sarawak's agricultural landscape. Charles Brooke and his government took active measures to promote cash crop production through the transformation of virgin and secondary forest and the immigration of agricultural laborers. Unlike large-scale plantation industries developed by European planters in British and Dutch colonies, the expansion of cash crop agriculture in Sarawak was left largely in the hands of Chinese entrepreneurs.

Lundu District's Encounter with Brooke Colonization

Lundu District, 1,870 square kilometers situated in the western corner of the First Division,[7] is an area with a long history of Brooke colonization. Lundu, one of the oldest administrative districts under Brooke administration, occupied a portion along an extremely porous international boundary with Netherlands East India. The borderland area was divided by the low mountain ridge running from Cape Dato on the coast to Mt. Raya in the interior. On the Sarawak side, rivers such as the Lundu, Tuba, and Serikin ran into the South China Sea. On the Dutch side, the Sambas, Landak, and Sparan rivers ran down to the plain. Marked only by this watershed, the boundary between the Brooke territory of Sarawak and Dutch Sambas originated in and coincided with the frontier that separated the Brunei and Sambas sultanates.

The district became part of Sarawak in 1841 when it was granted to James Brooke by the sultan of Brunei. For the Brookes, this district was a relatively unproblematic colonial territory compared to the Second Division (the Batang Lupar, Saribas and Kelakah districts), where they faced ongoing Iban resistance. It was Lundu where the first fort was established in the early 1870s, functioning as a training station for young British officers in their first years of duty, from whence they transferred to outstations further afield.

[6] "Towkay" (*taukay*) is a common word of Hokkien origin, meaning the head of a firm or shop.

[7] The First Division comprised of current divisions of Kuching, Samarahan, and Sri Annam.

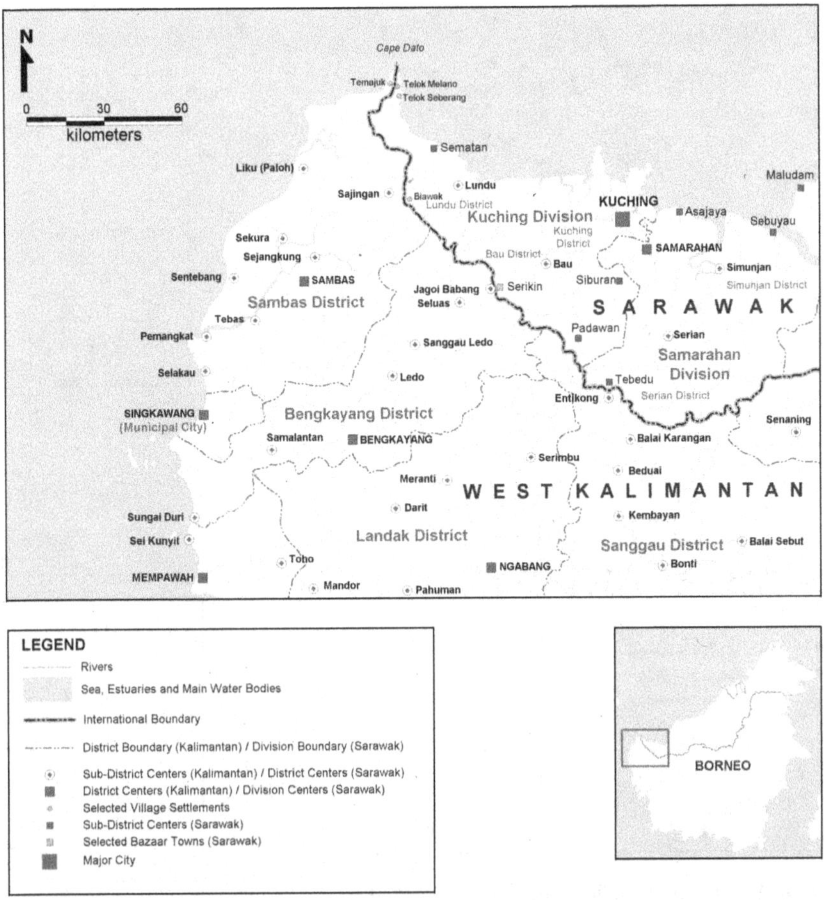

Fig. 3 Sarawak (Malaysia) and West Kalimantan (Indonesia)

Long before the Brookes came to power, the Lundu region had been under the jurisdiction of the chief of the Lundu Dayaks. The chief collected levies on commodities such as beeswax and edible bird's nest, and imposed fines if fruit trees were destroyed on the premise that they were planted by the chief's ancestors (*SG*, May 1, 1882: 31). One of the earliest accounts of Lundu is found in a travel journal written by Spenser St. John, who left a vivid description of a longhouse there in the 1860s:

> No village in Sarawak is blessed with greater prosperity than this. The old Orang Kaya, being of a most determined character, has reversed

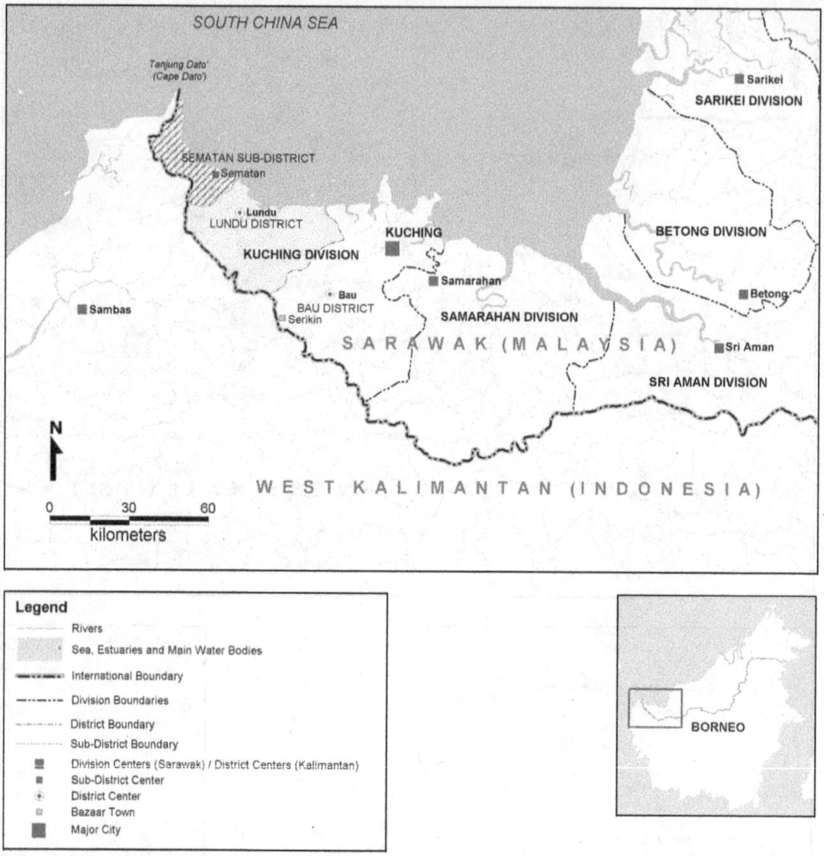

Fig. 4 Lundu District and Sematan Sub-District

> the usual order of things; and the Malays, instead of being the governors, are the governed. Having for years been little exposed to exaction, they are flourishing and exhibit an air of great contentment (St. John 1862: 8).

During the reign of the second rajah, however, Dayak rule was completely abolished. On March 23, 1882, Brooke government officials arrived with a proclamation from Charles Brooke that deprived the Lundu Dayak chief of all jurisdiction over his subjects (*SG*, May 1, 1882: 31). Unlike other outstations relatively free from the rajah's interference due to lack of communications, the First Division and its officers were henceforth under close supervision:

> There was a European Resident and his two European assistants, who were responsible for the administration of the First Division which surrounded Kuching. Resident of the First Division was the highest post in the Sarawak Civil Service. Under Charles Brooke this was a post of great trust and confidence. The Resident in Kuching was usually called upon to give advice on matters affecting other Divisions or the country as a whole. Often he was placed in charge of the government when the rajah was absent. However, the Resident of the First Division was usually unable to administer Kuching or the First Division without the rajah's continuous interference (Ward 1966: 94).

The government's economic policy and its effect at the local level were therefore most apparent in the First Division, and Lundu was one of the first places where new agro-economic policies were implemented. The district functioned as an experimental area for the new cash crops of pepper, gambier, coffee, and coconut. As a result, Lundu District was quickly transformed from a local consumption agro-economy to one based on export-oriented cash crop production.

The development of export agriculture in Lundu was also encouraged by the rapid growth of the Singapore commodity market during the latter half of the nineteenth century. Two years before the coronation of Charles Brooke in Sarawak, the 1869 opening of the Suez Canal significantly boosted worldwide trade. Within five years, the value of Singapore's trade increased by 154 per cent[8] (Moore and Moore 1969: 371). Singapore was the regional center for interoceanic trading vessels — Bugis *pinisi*, Chinese *junks*, and European steamships — that cruised the South China Sea during the northeast and southwest monsoon. Cape Dato, at the western tip of Lundu District, was located in the heart of the trading network that linked Singapore, the west coast of Dutch Borneo, Sarawak, and Brunei.

Charles Brooke's government targeted Singapore Chinese merchants (*taukay*) for migration and investment in the district. According to the *Sarawak Gazette* of June 17, 1872:

> The last Royalist [steamship] brought us a number of Chinese Taukays from Singapore and Rhio with the professed purpose of looking for land suitable for gambier and pepper planting. They returned to Singapore by the same steamer, and before leaving

[8] From $58,250,915 in 1868 to $89,632,235 in 1873.

> expressed themselves much satisfied with what they saw. Free passages were granted them by Royalist, and Heartsease conveyed them to Lundu and back. It is their intention to form a company in Singapore in which Sarawak merchants would join (*SG*, June 17, 1872: 46).

During the reign of James Brooke, a large number of Chinese had come to Sarawak's First Division, finding work in the Bau goldfields and in Kuching to the southwest, or settling in farming communities in and around Kuching, Bau, and Lundu (Porter 1967: 28). They are assumed to have fled Dutch Borneo where Chinese gold miners were at war with the Dutch throughout the 1840s and 1850s (Chew 1990: 21–2). In Lundu District, St. John had noted "about 200 Chinese working on gardens extending over about a hundred acres of ground, and neatly planted with various kinds of vegetables, among which beans and sweet potatoes appeared most numerous". According to him, Chinese agricultural products were not exported, but mainly sold within regional markets for local consumption by "the sago growers and workers of the rivers to the north" (St. John 1862: 8).

The district was an open gate to immigration into Sarawak from across the border and the region, supplying the important labor reserves for the expansion of Lundu's plantation economy. Within a decade of Charles' accession, numerous Chinese estates had been established. One district officer reported that "the scheme for planting gambier and pepper now in process of trial with the Chinese will, if fairly successful, provide a good starting point, from which to initiate a wider plan of introducing the cultivation of the same and the other products among the Malays and Dayaks" (*SG*, December 8, 1877: 85).

Throughout the 1880s, Lundu residents and new settlers were quite responsive to the new production system, but success brought its own problems. A district report of 1887 stated that "land disputes and collisions between Chinese gardeners and Dayaks are somewhat constant and from the number of pepper gardens opened all around Lundu such disputes will increase" (*SG*, July 1, 1887: 121). New land regulations also caused a great deal of confusion in Lundu, where residents had previously managed their swidden fields according to customary law.

The officer stationed at Lundu was thus kept busy explaining the land regulations to the local people. He reported that, "I sent all these men into Court and explained to them Land Regulations and the system of permits to open and to extend gardens and gave orders that no clearing was to be made without application to the Government authorities at the Fort" (*SG*, July 1, 1887: 121). Despite these efforts, land continued to be cleared without reference to the government, which prompted Rajah Brooke to issue the following order in 1889:

> Whereas it has come to my knowledge that land lying at the foot of Lundu mountain is being appropriated by Malays under pretense that it has been given or sold to them by Dayaks. I hereby make known to all denominations of people living in Lundu that any-one clearing land lying between Lundu River and Gading Mountain and planting on it without permission from the Government does so at his own risk; and in the event of such land being required by the Government will receive no compensation (*SG*, January 1, 1889: 7).

In June 1893, opening gardens without application to the district office became an offense subject to a fine. Three months later, the Police Court recorded two cases of breach: in one, a Chinese planter was fined $5; in the other, a Dayak was ordered to pay court costs for felling jungle without a permit (*SG*, September 1, 1893: 146).

The purpose of land regulation was twofold: to grant land to planters and to reclaim land in the event it was left uncleared and uncultivated. Officers stationed at Lundu Fort were responsible for granting land and for transferring previously granted but unused land to other planters. The *Sarawak Gazette* of the 1890s provides a glimpse into the continuing confusion and daily routine of an officer in Lundu:

> A good deal of my time has been taken up with surveying gardens in the vicinity. Principally marking out land for which permits have been granted. Sibuyaw Dayaks living at Lundu have been given land between Simuning and S'Kati, the land has been laid out in a way that will give them plenty of space for extending, and the allotments, numbering fifteen, join each other. The Dayaks have been given to understand that they will receive no other land if they fail to give this every attention or allow it to become a field of "lalang" [weeds]. The soil is exceedingly good, and the land, covered with young jungle, of their own choice (*SG*, October 2, 1893: 163).
>
> Between Sompa and Rambungan a good deal of land of out here has been given to Malays for coconut planting but none has yet got beyond planting a small patch with watermelons. All permits however are given on the understanding that if no real work is done in six months, the land may be granted to others (*SG*, October 1, 1898: 195).

> A good many permits have been issued to Malays for coconut planting, but none appears to have done anything yet. As this land has been especially reserved to Malays for two years, and none have yet done anything, I shall now grant permits to Chinese to plant if any should wish to do so (*SG*, December 1, 1898: 224).

As a result of the land and labor regulations, new cash crop fields mushroomed. An officer who inspected various upriver and coastal areas of Lundu reported that seventy gardens containing some 60,000 pepper vines had been opened in 1889.

Table 1 The Average Number of Pepper Vines/Garden

Area	*No. of Gardens*	*No. of Vines*	*Vines/Garden*
Jangkar	11	9,000	818
Siberis	2	1,000	500
Serayan	6	5,000	833
S'Larat	11	5,500	500

Source: *SG*, September 2, 1889.

Between 1893 and 1895, as many as 293 land permits were issued in the district (*SG*, Dec. 2, 1895: 220). The majority of applicants were Chinese, along with a small number of Dayaks from groups such as the Sibuyow, Jagoi, Selako, and Larah. The Malays in the district, however, were virtually unrepresented in mainstream agricultural development until the mid-1890s, when Malay settlers began to be involved in copra (dried coconut) production. This led to dramatic growth in the Malay population in Lundu and the Sematan coast leading to Cape Dato.

The Development of Plantation Economy

Lundu's plantation economy was based on ethnically differentiated modes of crop production. The differences stemmed mainly from the way labor was mobilized for the operation of agricultural estates. Chinese plantations were owned by merchants from Singapore, Pontianak and Kuching who employed coolies from Dutch Borneo. Dayak cultivation was family managed, with labor rarely involving more than a single longhouse or group of kinsmen. Malay plantations were opened by Malay merchants from Sambas and other coastal areas in Dutch Borneo. The Malay peasants from Sambas region worked under the leadership of Malay and Bugis ship captains (*nakoda*)-turned-merchants. Except for a small number of Dayak and Malay laborers employed at Chinese-owned fields (*SG*, November 1, 1893: 173, Lockard and Graham 1992: 28), Lundu's plantation industry was based on this ethnically segmented labor organization.

Chinese *Taukay*-owned Pepper and Gambier Plantations

According to the census of 1889, the Chinese population in Lundu was 947, with a male/female ratio of 5:1 (765 males and 182 females). Most were indentured laborers from Dutch West Borneo working on pepper and gambier plantations. Chinese planters, taking advantage of the special incentives offered by the Sarawak government, cultivated cash crops "by living on the premises or putting coolies in charge" (*SG*, August 1, 1899: 261).

Table 2 The Population of Lundu District (1889/1898)

Ethnic Group	*Male*	*Female*	*Total 1898*	*Total 1889*	*+/–*
Chinese	629	168	798	947	–150
Malays	737	659	1,396	1,023	373
Sibuyau	429	436	865	844	21
Silakow	366	333	699	804	–105
Larah	135	120	255	333	–78
Various	61	66	127	149	–22

Source: *SG*, August 1, 1898: 166.

The terms "plantation", "garden", and "estate" were used interchangeably in Lundu District reports to describe Chinese-owned cultivated fields. The size of the fields and the number of laborers employed varied significantly. Pepper gardens recorded in 1893 ranged from 3 to 8 hectares.

Table 3 The Size of Pepper Gardens

Planter	*Cultivated Land*	
Wa Ha, Liam Kim	160 fathoms sq.	(8.29 ha)
Seng Ha, Ah Low	100	(3.24 ha)
Ngo Wa, Ah Low	130	(5.48 ha)
Kim Eng, Hop Pan	150	(7.29 ha)
Liang Heng, Ah Jew	100	(3.24 ha)

Source: *SG*, October 2, 1893: 163.

Gardens with more than 1,000 vines would have required a labor force well beyond that of a household, especially during harvest season. The *Sarawak Gazette* reported that in Sematan Sub-District, there were 37 gardens with more than 100 vines. "The number of vines on the said plantations amount to 50,250, and the aggregate number of labourers employed on the same appear to be 81 males" (*SG*, July 1, 1893: 114). One Pontianak Chinese had employed 28 coolies to clear 600 acres for a coffee plantation that was one of the largest in the district (*SG*, April 1, 1895: 66–7).

The larger plantations under the management of wealthy *taukay* merchants with multiple holdings were often described as "firms" or "kongsi",[9] independent units patterned after clan-based organizations in China (*SG*, April 1, 1895: 66). The *Sarawak Gazette* in 1892 recorded the sale by public auction of the property owned by the Ban Hin Long firm, comprising seven pepper gardens with more than 5,500 vines, two shop houses in Lundu bazaar, and one dwelling house in Kuching (*SG*, August 1, 1892: 143). Large plantations had on-site clerks for daily operations and obtained special permission from the government to allocate *arrack* (hard liquor made from rice) and opium to their indentured laborers. They were equipped with accommodation facilities for coolies, as indicated by the inspection report of a colonial officer who "visited Bong Keh Sam's coffee plantation at S'nibong and found that a substantial building with bilian [ironwood] shingles was in the course of construction for the accommodation of his coolies, half of the building finished was occupied by the coolies. The coolies numbering twenty-eight I found to be in good health. Six of their number who had been giving trouble received punishment" (*SG*, April 1, 1895: 67).

It is difficult to reconstruct how these plantations operated due to the scarcity of reliable archival materials but the following extract from a report by the Resident of Lundu District indicates how labor was mobilized. Bound to plantation owners by advance payment, Chinese coolies were forced to sell the pepper seeds they cultivated to the estate owners who had advanced them money at a price far below their fair market value.

> A bad system of opening gardens is in vogue, a system which is bad all round, doing good to neither Towkay nor coolie and eventually ending in the loss of the garden opened up.

[9] For a discussion of *kongsi* organization in Sarawak, see Daniel Chew (1990).

> The system is based on what is the invariable custom in the East, i.e., the advance of wages and other sums of money before any work has been done to warrant such payment. In this way any broken down coolies can relieve his immediate wants by clearing a few fathoms of jungle, putting in young pepper vines, and then borrowing money on the security of his garden, with a promise to sell all his crop to the mortgagee at a price considerably below market value, the mortgage in the mean-time supplying him with food till vines bear. By this time he is hopelessly in debt on account of his original advance, now swelled by the value of the provisions he has meanwhile been supplied with by the Towkay (*SG*, June 1, 1889: 77).

Pepper cultivation was a speculative enterprise, subject to sudden ups-and-downs in market price. Planters in Lundu District tried to insulate themselves by keeping dried seeds in stock when the price was low. Well-connected merchants, however, had a great advantage over the growers:

> As I find the pepper planters here have been getting very low prices for their pepper, in some cases less than half the price current in Singapore, I now put a notice in bazaar every fortnight showing the prices current in Singapore in the hope that it will enable them to get better prices from their Taukays (*SG*, August 1, 1899: 261).

The government's priority lay in securing revenue from taxes levied on export commodities. It therefore focused on ensuring the smooth operation of Chinese plantations. This is best seen in the distribution of agricultural produce in local markets, an issue of major concern to Chinese plantation owners. A number of coolies secretly sold crops to Chinese merchants outside Lundu bazaar rather than to their own employers:

> Apparently in the Lundu district one or more Towkays has over reached himself and the harm of this not only affects himself but also the district, by unsettling a part of its population and laying them open to great temptation to dishonesty in the way of fraudulently selling crop to those who are not entitled to it, from which it is but a step to robbery and other crime (*SG*, June 1, 1889: 78).

District officers tried to contain the illicit marketing of commodities by restricting distribution channels to local networks based on patron-client (*taukay*-plantation worker) relations. In spite of their efforts, the illicit sale of crops by coolies and their arrests regularly featured in Lundu officials' monthly reports:

> ... two cases in which Chinese have been arrested for bringing pepper for illicit sale from Simpadi, Lee Kai Juh in the employ of Messers, Tap Soon Seng of Kuching, and Sio Chang and Ah Siam in the employ of Messers, Ghee Soon & Co. In the former case the purchaser has been brought to light but he is at present in Kuching (*SG*, September 1, 1893: 146).
>
> ... two Chinese had been arrested during my absence, found bringing pepper to Lundu from Simpadi for illicit sale (*SG*, October 2, 1893: 163).

Sales of agricultural produce outside the patron-client relationship continued to be subject to prosecution by the government, and Chinese laborers were deprived of maneuverability in profit making.

The Encroachment of Dayak Swidden Fields

Dayaks, especially Selakos who had newly migrated from Dutch West Borneo, repeatedly complained about the Lundu chief's claim on land and forest produce (*SG*, May 1, 1882: 31). The abolition of the sovereign powers of the Lundu Dayak chief by Charles Brooke in 1882 was initially welcomed by local residents but after the Brooke government was in control, a fundamental transformation in the Dayak way of life began to take place.

Unlike Chinese and Malays who migrated to Lundu in response to economic opportunities under the Brooke government, most of the Dayaks living there had been engaged in swidden rice agriculture there for a long period of time. The land regulations of the Brooke government deprived them of customary rights to the secondary forest, curbing their ability to use land for swidden cultivation outside their existing domain (Hong 1987: 40). The new government's claim on the land formerly under customary tenure caused great confusion in Lundu. The government felt confident that the regulation would be beneficial, reporting in 1893:

> The Sibuyau Dayaks do not seem to appreciate the land regulations, having always looked upon land in this neighborhood as their own property. The permit system I feel sure will encourage the natives in bringing the soil under regular culture for they now seem to understand that reckless felling of jungle is prohibited (*SG*, September 1, 1893: 146).

However, just two years later, the *Sarawak Gazette* printed this document:

> Some Sibuyau Dayaks are claiming that they had been unjustly fined by the Court for breaches of land regulations, in felling forest for planting without taking our permit (*SG*, December 2, 1895: 220).

The revised land regulations announced in 1893 gave further recognition to commercial "squatters", who "could be dealt with leniently" or permitted "to take out title" on the land they occupied. The commercial squatters were, in effect, given legal title to land cleared and then "abandoned" by others. Considering that Dayak swidden cultivators left their fields in long fallow, the regulation gave planters secondary forest that had been cleared by Dayaks. In this sense, the order was the government's deliberate attempt to curtail Dayak shifting cultivation and customary tenure.

Dayaks in Lundu were brought into cash crop production relatively early in the colonial era, in what was probably an inevitable response to land encroachment by the Brooke regime. Though their adjustment initially was involuntary, some Dayaks in Lundu became quite active in the development of the export-oriented plantation economy. Their gardens flourished, according to many colonial officers who inspected them:

> I was struck with the appearance of the pepper cultivated by Silakau Dayaks though not on a large scale, what there was equaled Chinese (*SG*, February 1, 1893: 26).
>
> ... the pepper planted by these Selakau Dyaks seemed to be doing exceedingly well, and they deserve great credit for the way some of them keep up their gardens (*SG*, January 2, 1894: 10).

The average size of Dayak plantations was much smaller than that of the Chinese. The average number of pepper vines per garden owned by Dayaks ranged from 350 to 450, which could have been managed by a family unit, as compared to the Chinese average of 980–1,400 vines per estate.

There were exceptions, however, and in 1895 the *Sarawak Gazette* mentioned one Selako planter who owned more than 3,000 pepper vines in Sematan (January 2, 1895: 11). To maintain 3,000 pepper vines required intensive labor, especially in weeding and harvesting, and was well beyond the capacity of an individual domestic group. There

Table 4 The Number of Pepper Vines and Gardens (Chinese and Dayak Gardens)

Area	*No. of Gardens*	*No. of Vines*	*Vines/Garden*
Simatan [Sematan]			
Chinese	29	28,500	983
Dyaks	10	4,500	450
Lundu			
Chinese	91	127,700	1,403
Natives	8	2,800	350

Source: *SG*, April 1, 1895: 66–7.

is, unfortunately, no historical documentation on the Dayak mode of large-scale commercial cultivation at the turn of the century.

Nakoda Entrepreneurs and Malay Coconut Plantations

Malay commercial activities on the coast of Lundu District were part of a larger trading network that encompassed the east coast of Riau, Singapore, the Natunas, Sarawak, along with ports such as Sambas, Menpawah, and Pontianak in West Dutch Borneo. The coastal area between Lundu and Cape Dato was directly linked to commercial hubs in Java and Singapore by the trading networks of Sambas Malay and Bugis *nakoda* merchants. According to a British observer:

> There was a string of Malay trading settlements, along the coast of Borneo on the South China Sea side, from Tg. [Cape] Dato at the northern side. The archipelago-wide trade was in the hands of local Malays and Bugis who sailed in prahu of 800 to 1,200 pikul burden, carrying from 40 to 60 men each.[10] These boats made two voyages a year. Each consignment, according to the individual size of the vessel, was worth for 2,000 to 8,000 Spanish dollars annually (Moor 1837: 13).

Even after James Brooke came to power, Malay trading activities survived for a time, linking Pontianak and Brunei via Cape Dato, with Sematan and Lundu port functioning as important strategic points connecting West Dutch Borneo and Sarawak. From the mid-nineteenth

[10] 1 pikul = 60.48 kg.

century, *nakoda* trading activity expanded as *nakoda* merchants engaged in the timber business in the Lundu coastal district in response to rising demand for timber in Singapore, and employed Sambas Malays as coolies and carpenters. In the early 1890s, the *Sarawak Gazette* recorded substantial contact between *nakoda* and Lundu officials in connection with the timber trade and ship-building: the *nakoda* asked for monopolies on certain types of timber (especially *tengar* bark and *piñaga* wood) and jungle produce; the Brooke government ordered them to pay export duty on each shipment to Singapore and Java, and Sambas Malays to pay tax on each *sampan* (boat) they built (*SG*, February 1, 1893: 26; September 1, 1893: 146; December 1, 1894: 208; April 2, 1894: 56; August 1, 1895: 144; December 2, 1895: 220). Logging activities by *nakoda* on the coast between Lundu and Cape Dato, as well as on major riverine areas such as Kuala Lundu, Kuala Sematan, and Kuala Samunsam, facilitated the later development of coconut plantations in the area (see Fig. 9).

The *nakoda* merchants thrived on their maritime as well as riverine trading, but the establishment of the Brooke regime and the influx of Chinese *taukay* traders caused their commercial activities to decline. As Sanib Said pointed out, the Sarawak government took decisive measures to deprive Malays of economic power:

> One of the important steps taken was to close the source of production as well as the market to Malay traders. This involved breaking the mutual dependence between Dayaks and the Malay traders. This was achieved by a resettlement policy implemented by the formation of a fort system in every major river settlement.... Hence movement of population could easily be observed and controlled. The fort, always manned by one or two European officers and a Kuching Malay Native Officer, then acted as the strategic and administrative center of the river system.
>
> In turn, the Malay traders were encouraged to take up subsistence farming round the fort. The result was that the Malay community living in that river system would be under constant observation from the Government, and they had no alternative but to concentrate on mere passive and sedentary occupations (Sanib 1985: 21–2).

Losing their commercial supremacy to Chinese capital, *nakoda* traders finally turned to agricultural production to survive under the Brooke regime. Unlike Chinese and Dayak peasants, Malays in the district did not participate in inland pepper cultivation, continuing instead to plant coconuts and some bananas on the coast. In January

1894, the amount of pepper produced for export in Sematan reached 1,122 pikuls (67,881 kg), but not a single pepper garden was registered under a Malay name (*SG*, March 1, 1894: 41).

Since the cultivated interior of Lundu and Sematan had already been exploited by Chinese and Dayak pepper planters, it was difficult for *nakoda* traders to enter these industries, when they turned to agricultural production. Moreover, pepper prices on the international market had often collapsed, making the crop unattractive, but Sambas *nakoda* (Malay and possibly Bugis merchants), long engaged in coconut planting in coastal districts of Dutch West Borneo, had the necessary expertise to open coconut plantations. Copra was a low profile export that hadn't undergone any dramatic price increases on the international market. Figure 5 shows the price fluctuation of pepper and copra exports in Kuching Foreign Trade Returns from January 1890 to December 1900. The percentage of pepper and copra exports during the same period is shown in Figure 6; the sharp ups-and-downs of pepper exports reflect price fluctuations. Compared to pepper, copra was insignificant in Sarawak's international trade returns, but it provided a stable income for coastal populations. The formation of a

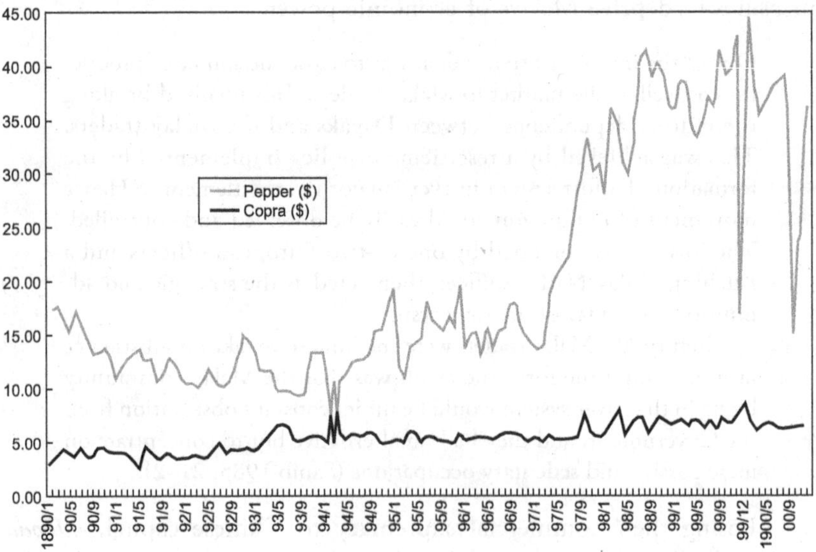

Fig. 5 Price Fluctuation of Pepper and Copra Export in Kuching Foreign Trade Returns from January 1890 to October 1900

Source: *SG* Kuching Foreign Trade Returns, 1890–1900.

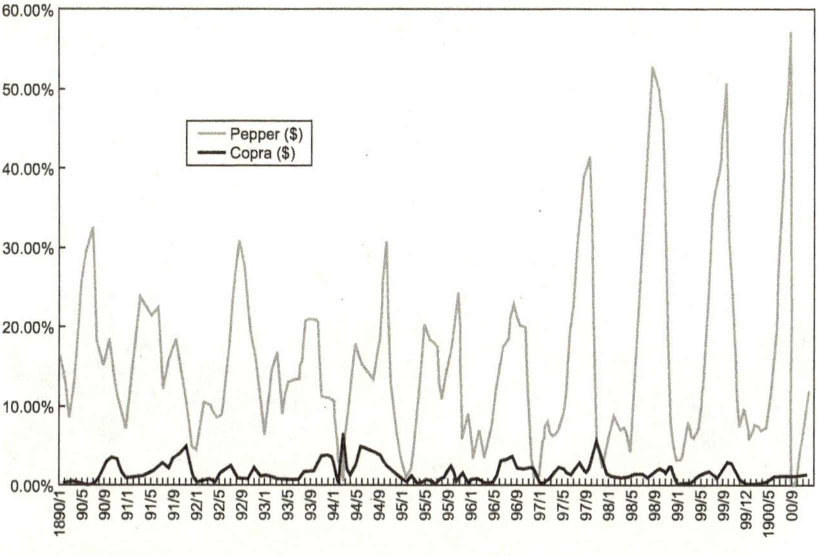

Fig. 6 Percentage of Pepper and Copra Export in Kuching Foreign Trade Returns from January 1890 to October 1900

Source: *SG* Kuching Foreign Trade Returns, 1890–1900.

coconut plantation belt on the frontier coast near Cape Dato encouraged Malay migration from Sambas and its vicinity in the 1890s.

Opening a new coconut plantation along the previously uninhabited coast required substantial inputs of labor. Besides clearing virgin forest, weeding and copra production — to harvest, husk, and dry seed — were all labor-intensive. *Nakoda* plantation owners brought Malays across the Sarawak/Dutch Borneo border to serve as estate caretakers and laborers, providing their necessities during the settling-in period. These workers were accompanied by a wider community that included children and grandchildren, traditional medicine men (*bomoh*), midwives (*bidan*), and carpenters (*tukang*).

The majority of the *nakoda* held the title *haji*, and many were literate.[11] The ability to read and write *jawi* (an adapted Arabic alphabet

[11] Lundu District office recorded following names of *nakoda* traders who registered coconut estates: Tuanku Jin, Haji Taha, Haji Matarip, Haji Usin, Haji Sleman, Nakoda Hitam, Haji Matsalleh, and Taip. Except for Tuanku Jin of Sungei Cina (origin unknown) and Haji Sleman (a Sarawak man married to a Natuna woman), all were either from the Dutch West Borneo coast or the Natuna Islands.

Illus. 2 The remains of a coconut plantation on the Sematan coast

for writing the Malay language) was important in applying to open coconut gardens under the land regulations (registration forms were available in Jawi, English and Chinese). Individually, *nakoda* routinely developed more than one plantation, moving between Sambas and Sarawak to bring additional labor. The resulting increase in the Malay population of Lundu District coincided with a decrease in the male Chinese population, who had been employed on experimental tobacco estates in the late 1880s (see Table 2). The government said the increase in the Malay population was due "partly to immigration from Sambas and partly to natural increase as families of five and six children are very common among the Malays here", and found it "very satisfactory" (*SG*, August 1, 1898: 166).

Plantations and *kampung* (villages) occupied the same land, a characteristic of the Malay mode of cash crop production. Plantations of greatly varying sizes aggregated at river mouths such as Bakuching, Belingsah, Bedaun, Sungei Limo, Kuala Samunsan, Telok Serabang, and Telok Melano. Colonial officers reported in 1898 that "the whole coast from S. Blinsah to Telok Milano [Melano] has now been practically taken up for cocoanut planting" (*SG*, July 1, 1898: 142) (see Fig. 9). The plantations filled the coastal area to about 300 meters from the ocean front:

> [Between Kuala Sematan and Kuala Blungai] there are altogether 17 plantations aggregating a little over 1¼ mile in length and averaging about 400 yards deep (*SG*, August 1, 1899: 261).
>
> Between S. Puguh and Simatan [Sematan] there are about half a dozen cocoanut plantations made by Malays. These clearings extend for 1¼ mile along the beach with a depth of 300 or 400 yards, they are fully planted up and the cocoanuts are doing very well (*SG*, January 3, 1899: 11).

Village organization in the plantation belt gradually shifted from loosely structured aggregates of several coconut plantations to administratively independent communities with village heads. By 1899, six *kampung* were established with officially appointed *tua kampung* (village heads) and a *penghulu* (district head): Belinsah, Bedaun, Sungei Cina, Simunsam, Serabang, and Telok Melano (see Fig. 9). By the end of the nineteenth century, *nakoda* from Dutch Borneo were incorporated into Sarawak's government-backed plantation economy. Malays had maintained their community-based labor organization under the leadership of the *nakoda*, and migrated to new plantations, which became their home villages.

In this coastal area of western Borneo, the emergence of nation-bound economic spaces signaled the decline of Malay maritime supremacy. European colonialism generated new center-periphery dynamics, and the area was transformed from the hub of pre-colonial *nakoda* commercial networks to the margin of a modern national territory. Malay commercial networks were segmented and compartmentalized by a new colonial boundary of Sarawak and Dutch West Borneo. The economic policies of the Brooke government broke down Malay commercial dominance by supporting Chinese commercial activities as well as the production of agricultural commodities. The Malays suffered a sharp economic downturn as the *nakoda* class gradually lost its preeminence in trade and moved into the sedentary agriculture in the frontier region of Sarawak.

Spatial Assemblage and Labor Mobilization

Victor King has stated that "the Brooke Raj did not have the personnel, finances, skills, nor the desire to carry through substantial social, economic and political transformations in Sarawak" (King 1990: 113). Charles Brooke himself was aware that his government's efforts at economic development were far from satisfactory. He admitted as much after four decades in power:

> I do not flatter myself when I say that I have tried my best to advance agriculture, but I have most signally failed, and am, in consequence, much disappointed. Nevertheless, I still entertain hopes that the time for its development is not far distant, and I am prepared to take any pains, to receive any amount of advice and to undergo any trouble if only I can see my way to successfully spread gardens and plantations in the place of our vast jungles (Bampfylde and Baring-Gould 1909: 302).

Commodities produced on plantations in places such as Java and British Malaya brought profit to colonial governments and foreign entrepreneurs. Compared to what British and Dutch colonizers achieved elsewhere, the degree of socio-economic transformation in Sarawak was rather disappointing for Brooke and his officers, and leads to the observation that Sarawak slumbered peacefully under the eccentric despotism of white rajahs, who were dedicated to the preservation of virgin forest.

This statement certainly is not an accurate description of the frontier district of Lundu at the turn of the twentieth century, because the shift to an export-oriented economy brought fundamental change to the social demography and political economy of local communities. The advent of Chinese indentured laborers, the encroachment of Dayak swidden agriculture, and the formation of coastal Malay plantation-cum-villages were the results of social engineering deliberately carried out by the Sarawak government. Between the 1870s and the 1890s, the period in which Charles Brooke's agro-economic policies took effect in local areas such as Lundu, the Sarawak economy's basic structure

Table 5 The Breakdown of Export Items in 1886 as a Percentage of Total Export Value

Items	*Share (%)*
Forest products	8.0
Minerals	9.7
Cultivated products and manufactured goods	52.9
Maritime products	0.6
Imports re-exported	8.8

Source: *SG*, May 12, 1887: 78–9.

changed. In 1871, export items listed in the government's annual report were limited to *gutta percha*, Indian rubber, beeswax, *trepang* (holothurian), sago, gold, rice, camphor, and bezoar stone, most of which are jungle produce rather than cultivars, but by 1886 jungle produce accounted for only 8 per cent of the total value of exports (*SG*, May 12, 1887: 78–9).

The frontier region of Lundu gradually transformed its natural resource-dependent economy based on the sale of jungle produce to an export-oriented cash crop economy during Charles Brooke's reign, coinciding with the growth of the Singapore commodity market and the acceleration of world trade. In this most sparsely populated agricultural frontier, featuring tracts of inaccessible primary jungle, the expansion of the cash crop economy would not have been possible without state intervention. Chinese, Dayaks, and Malays responded in their own ways to both the new agro-economic policies and the demand of the world commodity market.

The Geo-body in Transition

This chapter has shown how the Brooke government treated the hinterland of the Sarawak kingdom, previously occupied by a small number of Dayak swidden cultivators, as *terra nullius*, unoccupied land, and made it state property, thereby transforming its economy. The territory was subsequently commodified through the introduction of pepper, gambier, and coconut cultivation, which relied on the labor of Chinese coolies and Malay immigrants brought from Dutch Borneo. The importation and mobilization of migrant workers led to the formation of an ethnically segmented agricultural society in the borderland, while territorial enclosure turned mobile people into sedentary agricultural laborers.

The emergence of this state-bound, agricultural space caused a significant decline in the fortunes of one ethnic group in particular. Malays enjoyed maritime supremacy when western Borneo was the hub of pre-colonial commercial networks. The expansion of trading networks by the *nakoda* merchant class had in fact been a major element in the Malay maritime world of Southeast Asia. In that world, western Borneo was a crossroads for peoples and commodities, linking Sarawak, the western part of Dutch Borneo, Brunei, the Philippines, the Malay Peninsula, the Great Natuna Islands, Singapore, Sumatra, the Riau Archipelago, and Java.

European colonialism generated a new center-periphery dynamic. The Malay commercial network was segmented by the colonial boundaries of Sarawak and Dutch West Borneo. The economic policies of the Brooke government demolished Malay commercial dominance by supporting new Chinese mercantilism and the production of agricultural commodities. As a result, Malays suffered economic dislocation, in which the maritime *nakoda* class gradually lost its preeminence in trade.

With government incentives, Chinese capital was invested for the development of plantations based on contracts between coolies and *taukay* entrepreneurs. The government controlled the movement of agricultural produce from coolies to *taukay* in order to secure tax revenues. For Dayaks, a series of land regulations brought fundamental transformation to agriculture in the region as the government's encroachment of secondary forest previously managed under customary law restricted swidden agriculture and associated migratory patterns. Their mode of production became more sedentary, and traditional hill rice cultivation gradually achieved a symbiosis with export-oriented commodity production. The development of Malay coconut plantations was closely related to traditional *nakoda* activities in the region, which were in decline. Malay and Bugis adventurers from Sambas, Dutch Borneo, then tried their luck on the frontier of Sarawak, adopting a mode of production based on patron-client relations between *nakoda* traders and mobile peasants. The establishment of Malay plantations led to the emergence of numerous peasant communities along the frontier coast.

These three distinctive modes of production, as well as the spatial assemblage of Chinese, Dayaks, and Malays, consolidated an ethnically segmented peasant society in the Lundu hinterland. Although they differed in organization, size, and the commodity cultivated, each ethnic group experienced a single absolute forcibly imposed by the colonial authority — the nationalization of frontier land previously occupied by the Lundu Dayak chief and his kinsmen.

The creation of national space through labor mobilization led to the formation of a new plural society. In the next chapter, I will discuss the apparatus necessary for this achievement, paying special attention to state attempts to confine cross-border flows of people, goods, capital, ideas, and practices.

CHAPTER TWO

Inscribing a Boundary at the Imperial Margin

The kingdom of Sarawak gradually established itself as a full-fledged territorial state by inscribing a boundary within the border zone between Sarawak and Dutch West Borneo. Following the formation of a multi-ethnic labor market for the cultivation of crops in Lundu District, the maintenance of national space became a crucial policy issue for the local governance, and the authority tried to control the mobility of commodities and the flow of labor into and out of the territory. The following discussion first looks into how the colonial government tried to turn a fuzzy frontier into a linear international boundary and considers to what extent it succeeded in inscribing a colonial divide on the imperial margin between the British and Dutch Empire.

Sarawak Kingdom and *Mandala*

Modern nation-states can be distinguished from pre-colonial indigenous polities by qualitative differences in their territoriality. The mature state should be most easily recognized within the framework of political geography, where "frontier" and "boundary" have been coherently, or at least routinely, distinguished. Pre-nation-state polities are identified with the former, and nation-states with the latter. In other words, the linear boundary, rather than the unbound frontier, defines a nation-state. Benedict Anderson characterizes the religious communities and kingdoms that preceded modern nation-states as "cultural systems", arguing that the Christian, Islamic, and Buddhist worlds existed before, beyond, and without regard to, the territorial framework of nation-states (Anderson 1991).

The Anglo-Dutch Treaty of 1824 began to transform the fuzzy political realm of traditional polities into the precisely bounded territories of two European empires. The transfer of Bencoolen in Sumatra to the Dutch and Malacca on the Malay Peninsula to the English divided maritime Southeast Asia into two domains: one north and one south of Singapore. Arbitrary as it was, this division was useful in settling claims in Sumatra and Malaya. But it was of little use on the island of Borneo, where the frontier between the Sambas and the Brunei sultanates was more important in forming the boundary between colonial empires. In coastal western Borneo, at approximately the same latitude as Singapore across the South China Sea, the frontier between the two sultanates was based on the natural watershed of a central mountain ridge. In the process of colonial division that followed 1824, the interface between the British and Dutch territory in this region remained fuzzy, not linear, a political buffer zone. It was in this porous social space that a British ex-officer of the East India Company established his own kingdom and became a white rajah in 1841.

Prior to the establishment of colonial nation-states, polities with unbounded territories existed on and around the island of Borneo, as elsewhere in the region. Indigenous Islamic polities, such as Brunei, Sambas, Ketai, Pontianak, and Banjarmasin were surrounded by numerous smaller indigenous chiefs. These traditional polities are often referred to as *mandala*, or circles of kings (Heine-Gelden 1956, Wolters 1982). The *mandala* polity as a prototype of indigenous political systems in Southeast Asia is said to have the following characteristics. The domain of the *mandala* is under the influence of a charismatic man of prowess, whose territorial reach expands and contracts in accordance with the waxing and waning of his power. The fringe of the political domain becomes fuzzier as the distance from the central orbit of power becomes greater. A related prototype is Tambiah's *galactic polity*, wherein the interface between kingdoms is like the fringe of a galaxy where more than one symbolic power domain crosses and overlaps (Tambiah 1976).

Spatial Models and Agency on the Ground

General discussions of the transformation of political space from a zonal frontier to a linear boundary tend to be based on static and typological models. As debates on the transition from feudal society to the modern nation-state in Western Europe have shown, these models are based on an *a priori* presumption that the frontier of the traditional indigenous polity is an evolutionary precursor of the boundary of modern nation-states. This understanding, however, has undergone revision in recent years.

One historian of Europe, Peter Sahlins, has pointed out in a study of boundary making between France and Spain in the Pyrenees that the pre-modern geo-body coexisted with the modern nation-state, and the traditional zonal frontier was compatible with the boundary of the nation-state. Of the credibility of evolutionary models of territoriality, he wrote:

> Applied to the historical experience of state formation in Europe, and in particular to the paradigmatic example of France, the models fail to explain much of anything. As a schema, it ignores two critical dimensions of political boundaries: first, that the zonal character of the frontier persists after the delimitation of a boundary line; and second, that the linear boundary is an ancient notion. As a historical description, the model falls dramatically short of the evidence (Sahlins 1989: 4).

Likewise, in the Malay world of Southeast Asia, boundary engraving by modern nation-states did not instantaneously alter indigenous social formations. Most notably, traditional indigenous polities became part of the apparatus of indirect colonial rule.

To examine the dynamism of historical moments concealed in static models, a processual approach is needed to understand the priority of state-society dialectics over static models of political space. In this regard, recent discussions of the genesis of national space in Southeast Asia fall short because they pay limited attention to the geo-historically specific process of spatial transformation under nation-states. Benedict Anderson and Thongchai Winichakul, for instance, focus on map making and the map's inscription onto the mental schemata of the nation as a powerful geo-political logo (Anderson 1991, Thongchai 1994). As discussed by Thongchai, the emergence of modern geography in Thailand contributed immensely to the internalization of national space. The reproduction and spread of the map as an icon of nation through the development of print capitalism was regarded as a central device for the realization of national space.[1]

[1] Anderson further identifies the "census" and the "museum" as part of the apparatus for imagining the nation. The census enables the state to produce a cadastre for taxation and conscription through the quantitative grasp of subjects, while the museum authenticates national history and domesticates ethnicity under the state.

What studies of the spread of the iconography of the geo-body lack is attention to geographically specific historical processes in which various segments of society on the ground accept, ignore, reject and strategically appropriate the authority's imposition of a spatial grid. The arguments of Thongchai and Anderson, with their focus on the spread of nationalism, revolve around the creation of a national society receptive to the geo-body of the nation-state, but not around the genesis of national space *per se*. They discuss the emergence of people who have access to national maps and the ability to read them. As an aspect of modernization, the spread of print capitalism and national education in geography produces an educated mass that is responsive to the national map as a symbol of the nation, and shapes the formation of a national society. However, it is also necessary to consider the political economy of space production and the process of policy implementation by the state and the dialectic between state and society. What is the social agency exercised by real people doing real things on the ground? How do people come to terms with, use, and even abuse the spatial division imposed on them by external political machinery? To the metropolitan educated mass, logos may provide a way to imagine the nation. To people at the periphery, however, the international boundary is a reality, and they consciously negotiate a threshold between "here and there", "we and they", and "our nation and their nation".

Border Realization and the Naturalization of Peoples

Two simple but basic questions provide a starting point for this discussion. How did Sarawak try to realize its territoriality in the transformation from kingdom to colonial state? And how did people respond to inscription of colonial boundary on the ground?

The story of the state's boundary-making in the borderland of Lundu District up to the 1920s is complex. The state sought to control inflows and outflows of people and goods across the porous colonial border: the cross-border movements of mobile people such as Chinese coolies, Dayak swidden cultivators, maritime Malay merchants and migrants, and of dutiable commodities such as salt, muskets, *jelutong* (natural rubber), ironwood, and *engkabang* (illipe nuts). The state in a sense naturalized people and commodities, seeking to make them its property through immigration, naturalization, and taxation policies. Such policies not only defined the national affiliation of people and

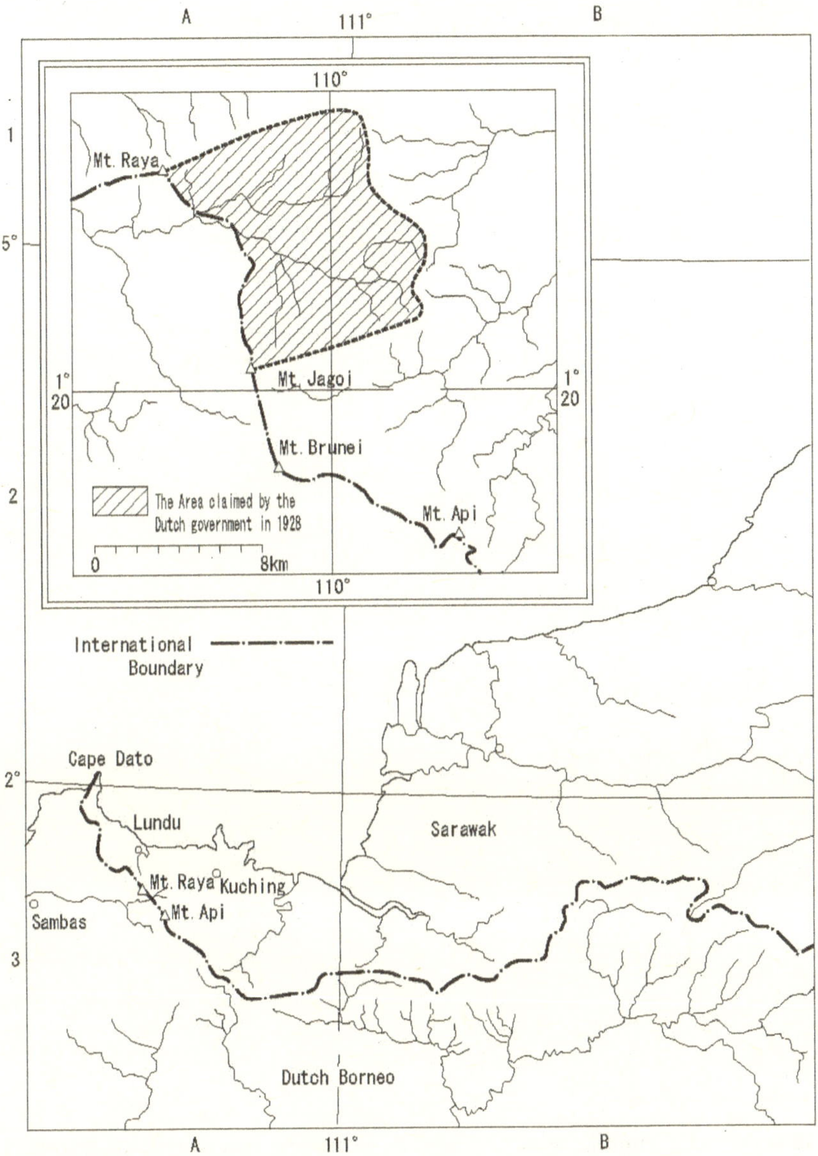

Fig. 7 The Borderland of Lundu District

commodities, but were indispensable for the formation and maintenance of state territoriality.

People move, and in doing so often cross national boundaries carrying with them capital, marketable commodities, ideas, and diseases.

86 6

een afstand van vierhonderd vijftig meter tot een punt op den Goenoeng Api, waar een pilaar is geplaatst; vandaar volgt de grens de waterscheiding afwaarts in ongeveer Z.W. richting over een afstand van zeshonderd vijftig meter tot een punt, waar een pilaar is geplaatst; vandaar in een richting ongeveer W. ten N. over een afstand van zevenhonderd meter tot een punt op het voetpad van het astronomisch station Goembang naar Siding, waar een pilaar is geplaatst; vandaar het voetpad volgende in eene over het algemeen N.O. richting over een afstand van vijfhonderd meter tot punt Batoe Aoem, waar een pilaar is geplaatst; vandaar in een rechte lijn loopende ongeveer N.W. ten N. tot de eerste rivier, een zijtak van de Odong rivier, een afstand van zeshonderd meter; vandaar den zijtak op den rechteroever volgende in eene over het algemeen W. richting tot de samenvloeiing met de Odong rivier, waar een pilaar is geplaatst; vandaar in een rechte lijn loopende ongeveer N.W. tot een punt op den linkeroever van de Tring rivier, waar een pilaar is geplaatst; vandaar in eene over het algemeen N.W. richting tot een punt op den linkeroever van de Toepijem rivier, waar een pilaar is geplaatst; vandaar in eene over het algemeen N.N.W. richting tot een punt op den rechteroever van de Pon rivier, waar een pilaar is geplaatst; vandaar den bergrug volgende in eene over het algemeen W. ten N. richting tot een punt op den linkeroever van de Meroemo rivier, waar een pilaar is geplaatst; vandaar over de Meroemo rivier tot een punt op haar rechteroever, waar een pilaar is geplaatst; vandaar de waterscheiding volgende in eene over het algemeen N.W. richting tot het triangulatie-station Goenoeng Broenai, waar een pilaar is geplaatst.

Van het triangulatie-station Goenoeng Broenai loopt de grenslijn ongeveer N.N.W. in een rechte lijn tot het Goenoeng Djagoei (Poko Pajoeng) triangulatie-station, waar een pilaar is geplaatst op het punt waar deze rechte lijn het voetpad tusschen Billeh en Djagoei Babang snijdt.

Van het Goenoeng Djagoei (Poko Pajoeng) triangulatie-station volgt de grenslijn den rechteroever van de Boewan rivier (welke binnen vijftig meter van bovengenoemden pilaar ontspringt) in eene over het algemeen N. richting tot haar samenvloeiing met de Berenas rivier, op welk punt een pilaar is geplaatst. Pilaren zijn eveneens geplaatst op den rechteroever van de Boewan rivier bij het punt waar zij wordt gekruist door het voetpad tusschen Setaäs en Siloewas en waar zij wordt gekruist door het voetpad tusschen Setaäs en Goenoeng Raja. Van het samenvloeiingspunt

Illus. 3 The administrative correspondence on the boundary demarcation between Mt. Api and Mt. Raya in Lundu District (Mailrapporten 1928)

States seeking to realize territoriality oppose the free flow of people and their belongings, and try to make people sedentary and singularize their affiliations. Why is the state so often an enemy of mobile people and things? Is there something primordial about the state's desire to fix people and things geographically and suppress flows and movements? (cf. Scott 1998, 1999).

Colonial Sarawak under the second rajah is a prototype of modern state control of people. While the reign of the first rajah was notable for the absence of regulation over the economy and society of the state, the reign of the second rajah clearly manifested territorial encroachment characteristic of the embryonic phase of a sovereign state. The state regulated local transnationalism through passport controls, provisions for the arrest of criminals from across the border and the seizure of run-away coolies, prevention of border-crossing during outbreaks of epidemic disease, control of the opium trade, and prohibition of cross-border swidden cultivation as well as identity politics in matters of naturalization, registration of marriages, and prohibition of bigamy by non-Sarawakian subjects. Correspondence between district officers and Rajah Charles Brooke recorded in the *Sarawak Gazette* contains lively accounts of state-society tensions as manifested in the social maneuvering of borderland residents and the state's policies to circumscribe national space.

Migratory Dayaks and the Head Tax

One of the first recorded border disputes between Sarawak under the reign of Charles Brooke and the Netherlands Indies in West Borneo occurred over the affiliation of the Dayaks who engaged in swidden cultivation in the border area. Both governments claimed as their subjects the Jagois (a group of Land Dayak residing in upper Sarawak) and thus the right to collect their head tax. As early as 1874, the Committee of Administration of Sarawak and the Dutch authority discussed border crossing by Jagoi Dayak (*SG*, May 16, 1874: n.p.) and the demarcation of the Sarawak-Sambas boundary (*SG*, July 24, 1874: n.p.). The issue was not settled at the time and occasionally resurfaced, as in this case recorded a decade later:

> The Sultan [of Sambas]'s object is undoubtedly, to absorb the Jagui [Jagoi] tribe, one of the largest tribes of Land Dayaks in upper Sarawak, and he has already demanded and received revenue from a portion of this tribe. Considering that the boundary between this portion of Sarawak and Dutch Borneo was years ago determined by Netherlands and Sarawak officials, the Sultan's claim is somewhat irregular, and, consequently, the Committee of Administration has refused to acknowledge it.... It is not only the Jagui farming

Fig. 8 Serikin/Jagoi Babang Border

> ground that the Sultan now seeks to obtain but also a portion of the Jagui villages; were he successful the whole of this tribe would be compelled to become subjects to Sambas (*SG*, Aug. 1, 1884: 80).

The affiliation and farming practices of the migratory Jagoi population continued to be discussed as late as the 1930s, and involved high-level officials in both Kuching and Pontianak, the respective capital cities, and those concerned seem to have paid scant attention to the international boundary that divides them.

> The Dayaks in the Jagoi area appear to have taken rather more trouble with their farming this year than formerly, but to the west of Jagoi farming land is scarce, and the inhabitants have been compelled to plant their padi over the border; several families have for this reason moved to Kampong Babang in Dutch territory (*SG*, December, 2, 1935: 228) (see Fig. 8).

From the beginning of Brooke rule, identifying subjects was important, even in the sparsely populated mountain region of southwestern Sarawak, because the head tax contributed substantially to district revenue. In 1892, for example, the Dayak head tax constituted 39.4 per cent of the total revenue for Lundu district, followed by court fees and fines (34.7 per cent), the exemption tax (17.1 per cent), licenses (4.6 per cent) and assessments (4.2 per cent) (*SG*, May 1, 1893: 78). However, neither the territorial affiliation nor the permanent presence of these swidden cultivators seems to have been a critical issue for either government. As long as head tax was paid, mobile Dayaks were allowed to engage in shifting cultivation in both Sarawak and Dutch Borneo.[2]

> The Jagoi Land Dayaks are growing very short of land for farming purposes, and are anxious to take up land across the Dutch border, where there is a large area of old jungle available. They were informed that permission for them to do this would have to be obtained from the Netherlands Indies authorities, and that in any case, if they farmed over the border, they were liable to find themselves paying two separate sets of taxes (*SG*, April 1, 1935: 51).

Apart from the payment of head tax, authorities were indifferent to Dayak mobility because the Dayaks were not involved with the commercial estates, where control of labor was a significant feature of their operations. For those workers, most of them Chinese or Malay, state surveillance took different forms. In the plantation belt between Lundu and Cape Dato, control over the national affiliation of agricultural laborers became ever tighter as securing and mobilizing a labor force became more important.

---

[2] Wadley (2003) looks at the history of internal territorialization in West Kalimantan with special focus on the interplay between state-created and local boundaries between 1865 and 1979.

Chinese Indentured Laborers and Opium

Unlike indigenous Dayaks, Malays and Chinese in Lundu District were migrants from outside Sarawak's territory; from the 1870s onward, they constituted the major agricultural workforce in the district. As discussed in Chapter 1, Malays and Chinese exhibited two distinct modes of labor mobilization and organization. Many Chinese entrepreneurs and agricultural laborers moved to Sarawak from Dutch Sambas. Under a government policy aimed at boosting cultivation of cash crops, Chinese planters were exempted from land rental fees as well as export duties on commodities. In 1898, the Chinese population in Lundu was still predominantly male, consisting of 765 men and 182 women (*SG*, August 1, 1898: 166). Most were contract laborers working on pepper and gambier plantations, and they were often bound to plantation owners by advance payments.

The Sarawak government's opium monopoly played an important role in retaining Chinese coolies within its territory and tying them to their employers. The government provided opium to Chinese firms under strict supervision. Estate operators (*taukay*) advanced opium to laborers in exchange for their future harvest of pepper and gambier. The state therefore condoned and profited from opium smoking by coolies. The Rajah also allowed Chinese entrepreneurs to open gambling dens and distill local spirits (*arrack*). Together, opium, gambling, and alcohol bound coolies to plantations through debt. The *Sarawak Gazette* of 1894 vividly documented the effect of this system on coolies, who, "when in a despondent frame of mind, [had] a tendency to go bad altogether, spending their last cent on opium or gambling and finally putting an end to a wretched existence by suspending themselves from the rafters of their *bangsal* [warehouse]" (*SG*, January 2, 1894: 56).

Opium, gambling, and *arrack* are familiar items in the history of commercial agriculture and mining in colonial maritime Southeast Asia. For both British Malaya and the Dutch East Indies, control of opium distribution was the backbone of the colonial economy (Trocki 1990, Rush 1990). Although much smaller in size than these colonial empires, Sarawak also made maximum use of human addiction to narcotics. In this sense, the kingdom of Sarawak was very much part of the colonial enterprise in Southeast Asia.

These circumstances notwithstanding, Chinese laborers often ran away, jeopardizing the government's goal of making the borderland an agricultural zone. The escape of indentured Chinese laborers under contract was regarded as a most serious offence, and the national boundary played a significant part in the apprehension of runaway coolies. For instance, the government introduced a passport system in 1876 as part of an effort to prevent fugitive coolies from reaching Dutch Borneo. The following government order on passports was reprinted frequently in the *Sarawak Gazette*:

> It is hereby directed that, for the better apprehension of runaway criminals and coolies under contract, each individual or head of party shall before leaving the Sarawak territory for Sambas take out a pass from the Government office at either Kuching, Paku, Simunjan, or Lundu; these passes are to be shown to the Dayak chiefs through whose villages the party may have to pass; and that in the event of any individual being found without a pass, he shall be apprehended and brought as a prisoner by the Dayak chief to Kuching (*SG*, June 24, 1876: 3).

Throughout the 1890s, government officers stationed at Lundu Fort were kept busy reporting cases of runaway coolies and their subsequent arrest. On March 10, 1894, for example, six coolies escaped from the Bong Keh Sam plantation into the jungle. They remained free for two weeks until they were captured by "a party of Malays" whom they had asked "to take them to Sambas". The report noted that "[t]hese men must have traveled a considerable distance ... and it is a wonder they didn't perish in the attempt" (*SG*, April 2, 1894: 56). In another case, a Sibuyau Dayak "picked up [a Chinaman] in the Sekembal River in distress. The Chinaman gave his name as Tan Ah Ngo and said he was on his way to Simatan. On inquiry it was discovered that he was a Sinkeh cooly in the employment of Fong Chu a timber worker, and that his real name was Lee Ah Jee. He received a short sentence of imprisonment and has since been returned to his employer" (*SG*, January 2, 1894: 10).

Dutch authorities across the border also restricted the movement of people crossing without passports and detained Sarawak subjects in its territory:[3]

---

[3] I tried my best to locate the colonial information on the Dutch borderlands adjacent to Lundu District, examining administrative documents such as Memorie van Overgave, West Borneo (Westerafdeling van Borneo) and Mailrapporten. It turns out, however, that the correspondence on the borderlands was kept in

> Lee Lip and Lee Young, who have for many years traded with Dayaks in the vicinity of Pengkalan Ampat, both Sarawak and Netherlands Borneo, were lately arrested by one Abang Mat at Sunkong, in Netherlands territory. Lee Yong has been detained, but Lee Lip was permitted to return. All their trade goods were seized. Lee Lip claimed that the Abang acted because they did not have passports provided by Kuching (*SG*, May 1, 1885: 42).

At the turn of the century, therefore, the border with Dutch Borneo functioned as a one-way valve, letting laborers enter but preventing them from leaving. When coolies absconded from pepper and gambier gardens, they were found and reprimanded, not only by plantation operators but also by government officials, both keen to secure labor for the nascent plantation industry in Lundu.

Coastal Malays and the Politics of Naturalization

Malays in Lundu district who opened coconut plantations on the coast, as mentioned in Chapter 1, did not participate in the inland cultivation of pepper and gambier. This new enterprise encouraged Malay and Bugis migration from Dutch Sambas, leading to the formation of numerous coastal communities between Lundu and Cape Dato in the 1890s. In the case of the Chinese, labor contracts, debt, and government surveillance and enforcement kept the labor force in place. Malay migrants who settled on the coast near the border, however, were only loosely tied to their *nakoda* planter-patrons. The government's mechanism for ensuring their permanent settlement operated in the sphere of marriage, family, and kinship.

Government policies regarding the Malays were intended to perpetuate conjugal ties and filial relations among Malay migrants in Sarawakian territory. Under the Charles Brooke administration, the supreme council of Sarawak government met to establish a law on civil marriage. On May 1, 1871, the body decreed that "no registration of

---

Netherland only if the information mattered in diplomatic relations. Substantial numbers of pages were devoted to the detailed descriptions on the official treaties and diplomatic agreements with the Sarawak government. As a result, the information on the Dutch border qualitatively differs from the detailed social history of borderlands of Sarawak, which I resorted for the construction of local and regional history.

marriage will be permitted, if either party has been previously married either in or out of the territory of Sarawak, unless a legal divorce has been obtained and can be produced or provided". Bigamy by non-Sarawakians was of particular concern to the authorities, and married migrants from Dutch Borneo were not permitted to take on another spouse in Sarawakian territory. Moreover, the government specifically prescribed a migrant's duty to maintain the welfare of his family in Sarawakian territory: "Should the husband at any time desire to leave the territory of Sarawak, he will be bound to provide for the maintenance of his remaining wife and children, and in the event of his not having sufficiently done so in the opinion of the Court, the Court will be justified in transferring the whole or part of the husband's property to his wife and children" (*SG*, May 12, 1871: 68). If a migrant failed to provide necessary support to his family members in Sarawak, the government also authorized the dissolution of his conjugal tie.

As seen in many monthly administrative reports sent from Lundu to Kuching, District Officers were busy dealing with the family matters of Malay migrants from across the border:

> On the 16th, Kaya, a daughter of Inchi Ahmat of Poi [Pue], complained that her husband Haji Talip an Islander had left her for eleven months without any maintenance. Haji Talip is now in Sambas and apparently has no intention of returning. Kaya has since been granted a divorce (*SG*, January 2, 1895: 11).
>
> On the 11th the Hon'ble the Acting Resident held Court. Haji Omar a Sambas Malay was sentenced to six months imprisonment he having represented to Tan Ahmat, that he was a freeman and had no wife in Sambas, on the strength of which he was allowed to marry a Lundu woman; it is now proved by Sergeant Bloto that Haji Omar escaped from Sambas goal about six months ago and has a wife and family there (*SG*, August 1, 1896: 101).

The most important duties of local Malay leaders such as *tua kampung* (village headman) and *penghulu* (district head), aside from collecting the head tax, were registering and reporting marriages. The prohibition of cross-border bigamy and institutionalization of family support in Sarawakian territory were part of a state project to create "Sarawakians". Under civil law, patrilineal filiation and birthplace determined the nationality of children. Those born in Sarawak territory to a Sarawakian father were recognized as Sarawakian. The maintenance of national affiliation of the family was crucial because the household was the basic unit for reproducing future generations of Sarawakians.

The Sarawak government was also keen to naturalize individual migrants in its territory. In 1900 the government announced the "Order of Naturalization of Aliens", which allowed immigrants from Dutch Sambas and other non-Sarawakian territories to apply to obtain Sarawakian nationality. Those who had been in Sarawak for more than five years and wished to remain there permanently were eligible to submit an application under the naturalization ordinance. Male applicants had to submit detailed information, including age, birthplace, father's name, father's birthplace and occupation, mother's name and birthplace, marital status, wife's name, wife's parents' names, number of children and their sex, current address, occupation, and length of residence in Sarawak. After an affidavit was submitted, the applicant took an oath in front of Rajah Brooke and in that way became Sarawakian (*SG*, August 1, 1900: 146).

State intervention in the realm of family politics was closely associated with the ethnogenesis of the Sarawak Malays and subsequent structural amnesia regarding their origin. According to the district report of 1908, all new residents of Lundu had Sambas origins (*SG*, June 1, 1908: 136), but within a few decades, people of Lundu were being labeled "Melayu Sarawak" (Sarawak Malay) instead of "Melayu Sambas" (Sambas Malay). Children and grandchildren of Sambas Malay immigrants who were born in Sarawak were classified under the new nomenclature. The birth of more and more people who identified themselves as "orang Sarawak" (Sarawakians) gradually resulted in a collective forgetting of the migratory past. Memory attached to a homeland across the border withered, and a new identity emerged. The government took advantage of people's structural oblivion for the sake of nation-making. While all identity is individual, there is no individual identity that is not historical or, in other words, constructed within a field of social values, norms of behavior, and collective symbols. Through the creation of a new ethnic nomenclature, the state succeeded in mapping the location of people's identity within the bounds of national territory.

A related concern of the Brooke government was the public health of the colony. Before the first government-conducted vaccination in the borderland area in 1895, the only way to prevent the spread of epidemics from Dutch Sambas to Sarawak was to close the border. Once an outbreak of small pox or cholera was reported, traffic between the two colonies was banned and inhabitants of the border area ordered to evacuate to safer places. Ports were of special concern and frequently the site of "[p]recautionary measures … against the epidemic being brought in through boats arriving from Sambas en route for Kuching…." (*SG*, September 2, 1895: 167). Fear of epidemics was intense enough to inscribe difference between the two colonial spaces, and this public health practice contributed to the realization and control of national space. It continued through the 1930s:

> On 24th the Orang Kaya Pasir reported that there was small pox in Kg. Arok on the Netherland India-Sarawak frontier. A dresser arrived on the 25th and vaccinated over 600 people, as yet there have been no cases discovered in Sarawak territory. All passes to Sambas have been stopped and nobody is allowed to enter from there (*SG*, August 1, 1932:142).

As the frontier became a homeland for the migrants from Dutch Sambas, a slow but steady process of naturalization — of both people and boundary — proceeded. People's affiliation in ideational as well as bodily form would have remained ambiguous without state intervention preventing the maintenance of dual nationality. The goal of the state was to impose its geographical grid upon mobile identities in order to substantiate the designated boundary and map "internal frontiers". As Fichte pointed out in his Addresses to the German Nation in 1808, "the *external frontiers* of the state have to become *internal frontiers* or — which amounts to the same thing — external frontiers have to be imagined constantly as a projection and protection of an internal collective personality, which each of us carries within ourselves and enables us to inhabit the space of the state as a place where we have always been — and always will be — *at home*" (Balibar 1991: 95).

The internalization of national territory as home required the relinquishment of an old identity and the production of a new one. In Sarawak, the collective memory attached to the place of origin, a kind of primordial identity, was gradually replaced by a new identity through the state's efforts to determine and preserve the national affiliation of individuals and families through the process of spatial encroachment.

Colonial Encroachment on Commodities

In addition to encroachments upon populations claimed as "Sarawak subjects", the imposition of duties on commodities moving in and out of the territory became a pivotal issue for the government. Before Sarawak territory was ceded to James Brooke by Sultan Omar Ali Saifuddin II of Brunei, a special department had collected tribute from subjects of the Brunei sultanate. Chiefs with the title *pengiran* were responsible for tribute collection in their respective provinces. *Pengiran*, in turn, paid annual tribute to the Brunei Sultan in goods.

Table 6 The Collected Tribute from Subjects of Brunei Sultanate

Item	*Number*	*Area*
war boats	2 from	Kalaka district
	1	Saribas
	1	Sebangan
	1	Sadong
	1	Sarawak
padi	800 pasau from	Kalaka
	800	Sadong
	800	Sarawak
	600	Sebuyow
	150	Sebangan
sago	2000 lajang 6 jengkal long from	Muka
	2000 lajang 6 jengkal long from	Patanak
cotton	3 bohara from	Batang Lupar
	1 bohara	Skrang
	12 yuta from other dependencies	
gold	paid by people of Oya and Rejang	

Source: Parnell 1911: 127–8.

Under the Brooke government, the traditional tributary system was replaced with import and export duties. This transformation required two distinct processes. The first was the commodification of goods. Whether jungle or cultivated produce, goods had to pass through the mechanism of market exchange to acquire a taxable value. Second, for taxes to be levied on the import and export of goods — the government's ultimate aim in promoting cash crop production — articles of merchandise had to move spatially between the territories of modern states. The inter-colonial border, an imaginary construct related to sovereignty to begin with, acquired real meaning in connection with the flows and movements of commodities.

During the initial period of Brooke colonization, timber and jungle produce were the focus of economic management. The commodification and taxation of natural resources only became possible with the formation of colonial governments on both sides of the Sarawak-Dutch Borneo border; and the national affiliation of things in Sarawak proceeded apace after all unoccupied land was declared a national possession.

Because jungle produce commanded high prices on the Singapore market, Sarawakians collected the products as far inland as Dutch Sambas. In 1876, in response to a complaint from the Sambas Sultan, Charles Brooke issued an order discouraging border crossing to gather jungle products. The order acknowledged "that the inhabitants of Sarawak are in the habit of working jungle produce in the country of H.H. the Sultan of Sambas without his permission" and henceforth required residents to present their passports in Sambas, "in order that permission may be obtained from H.H. The Sambas Sultan before any work of this kind is commenced". The order alerted Sarawak residents that the Sultan would demand "a payment of ten per cent on primitive produce ... before such produce can be taken out of his country." The order was issued in English, Malay, and Chinese (*SG*, June 5, 1876: 3). But even into the 1890s, when a monopoly on jungle produce collection in Sambas had been granted to a Mr. T.W. Kaat of Java, the exploitation of forest resources in Sambas by Sarawak subjects had not ceased, occasioning further complaint and notices of prohibition (*SG*, October 10, 1890: 125).

Natural resources within the territory of Sarawak were similarly attractive to outsiders and gave the state an opportunity to levy taxes. Because of its proximity to Singapore and such regional commercial centers in Dutch Borneo as Pontianak, Mempawah, and Sambas, the coastal area of Lundu District was frequented by non-Sarawakian *nakoda* traders, who came to cut timber and build boats (*sampan*). The Lundu authorities reported enforcing a regulation that "[n]o strangers are permitted to work timber without first obtaining a permit at the Court House", and in at least one case, "in lieu of taxation [collected] one boat out of ten...." (*SG*, February 1, 1893: 26). In other cases, government officials collected tax in cash:

> On the 7th, Tan Ahmat went up-river amongst the Sambas people who are working timber and sampans, the majority paying the 10% ad valorem on their labours, i.e., non-residents in this country. All was found in order (*SG*, April 2, 1894: 56).

> Towards the end of the month, a Singapore tonkang arrived at Simatan [Sematan] to cut and load peñaga wood along the coast, and payment of $75 was made in lieu of duty (*SG*, August 1, 1895: 144).

There is some evidence that government officials succeeded in instilling the mindset of territoriality, as when "Haji Matsalli, a Sambas Malay, asked and received permission to work tingar bark with 13 companies, and export the same to Java" (*SG*, August 1, 1895: 144).

As the timber market expanded in Singapore and Java in the latter half of the century, a substantial number of *nakoda* traders cut timber along the coast. These exploiters of forest resources were not regarded as foreign intruders, and were welcomed as long as they paid duties on the timber they exported. Charles Brooke ordered his officers in Lundu to open up forest in Sematan to facilitate timber work by anyone wishing to do it (*SG*, December 1, 1894: 208). Consequently, officials at the Lundu District Office were kept busy collecting export duties as the volume of exports from Lundu and the Sematan coast increased. They watched incoming and outgoing vessels to ensure the legal traffic of goods and devised ways to improve their surveillance:

> Hearing that a lighter was shortly expected to arrive to load timber at Lebak for shipment to Singapore, I dispatched a constable to warn the timber cutters against shipping any timber until it had been officially measured and also to give notice of the arrival of the lighter.
>
> The Hon'ble Divisional Resident has since directed that the export duties of the Rambunga River shall be collected from Lundu and to minimise the difficulty of gaining early information at Lundu of vessels entering the river for cargoes of mangrove bark and timber has authorized me to appoint a customs collector for the eastern part of the coast of the Lundu district who living at Sompa will be in a position to see vessels entering the river and to act accordingly (*SG*, September 1, 1900: 175).

Engkabang (illipe nut)[4] was another important export commodity whose sporadic fruiting attracted collectors from across the border.

---

[4] In Sarawak, *engkabang* refers to the oil-bearing nuts of the forest tree species Shorea spp., which belongs to the Dipterocarpaccae family. Owing to its high oil content (50 per cent of the nut's total weight), *engkabang* is normally in high demand in both local and foreign markets. The principal foreign markets

A Malay tree-owner in Lundu asked the Rajah to protect his interests in this procedure:

> He asked leave to go up-river himself to see that the engkabang trees were not being damaged and was given permission to do so. Tan Ahmat begged that persons from other districts should be forbidden to collect engkabang fruit in this district and the Court Writer at Simatan wrote in asking whether permission to collect this fruit might be refused to natives of Sambas and asking that a notice to that effect might be sent him (*SG*, February 1, 1912: 33).

Before the turn of the twentieth century, dutiable commodities were mostly uncultivated and non-manufactured produce; the exceptions were pepper, gambier, *belachan*,[5] *nipa* sugar,[6] and uncultivated *getah* (rubber) leaves, which required only simple processing. Import duties were first levied in 1893 on all articles entering Lundu with the exception of tobacco.[7] In 1895 taxation on imported and exported

Table 7 Import Duties, 1895

Item	
Brassware, etc.	$2,571.28
Chanangs and Tetawaks	95.06
Excise	2,450.45
Jars	1,184.38
Kerosene Oil	3,579.76
Guns and Muskets	96.40
Salt	8,729.45
Tobacco and Cigars	27,972.63
Total	$46,679.41

Source: *SG*, April 1, 1896: 80.

are Britain, Holland, and Japan's confectionery industries, especially chocolate manufacturing. In 1973, Sarawak exported a record crop of 28,061 tons of nuts for a total value of $20,158,938. In 1954 and 1959, its export exceeded that of round timber (*SG*, March 31, 1977: 45).

[5] Paste made of small shrimps which are salted, sundried, and allowed to ferment.

[6] Sugar made from *nipa* palm (Nipa fruticans).

[7] Import duties levied by the Dutch government also affected Malays in the border area. When the Dutch authority first levied import duties on *belachan*, it caused the decline of the local *belachan* industry at Sematan (*SG*, August 1, 1912: 172).

Table 8 Export Duties, 1895

Item	
Billian, Timber, etc.	$2,142.17
Bee's Wax	893.73
Birds' Nests	1,934.49
Camphor	258.90
Cutch	4.20
Fish, etc.	735.66
Guliga	0.20
Gutta P.L. and In. Rub.	13,849.28
Gambier	2,419.15
Pepper	3,216.54
Rattans and Canes	6,017.46
Sago Raw	895.08
Flour	16,641.20
Vegetable Tallow	630.71
Miscellaneous	610.69
Total	$50,249.46

Source: *SG*, April 1, 1896: 80.

Table 9 The State Revenue of Sarawak, 1895

Area	*Revenue*
Baram	$10,113.19
Bintulu	9,430.90
Muka	9,180.71
Oya	7,924.03
Trusan	4,174.72
Limbang	5,963.52
Lundu and Simatan	3,101.69
Sadong	7,460.93
Kalaka	6,407.45
Simanggang	12,364.97
Upper Sarawak	1,558.42
Saribas	3,289.47
Rejang	46,859.76
Kuching	325,970.48
Total	$453,800.24

Source: *SG*, April 1, 1896: 80.

Table 10 Export Duties on Commodities Shipped from Sarawak (1875–1908)

Notice	*Date*
Gambier and pepper	Dec. 8, 1875
Blachan [Belachan], prawns, and fish	May 19, 1882
Bird's nests	Nov. 27, 1885
Sea, jungle, and other produce transshipped from Sarawak	Feb. 27, 1886
Rattans and other canes	April 20, 1891
Gutta percha	Jan. 2, 1901
Rattans, pepper and damar	June 27, 1901
Gutta, jelutong and pepper	June 1, 1901
Pepper	Dec. 24, 1903
Salted fish	Jan. 1, 1903
Illipe nuts	May 1, 1903
Damar	Jan. 12, 1904
Jelutong, gutta & white pepper	Dec. 29, 1904
India rubber	April 29, 1908
Order	*Date*
Kulit tengar	Nov. 16, 1865
Jungle produce	May 30, 1896
Cultivated produce	June 24, 1896
Nipa sugar	Oct. 18, 1898
Working and collecting timber	June 22, 1899
Wild gutta and India rubber	Oct. 24, 1901

Source: *SG*, 1875–1908.

commodities generated $96,929, or 21.4 per cent of total revenues of $453,800.

The final decades of the nineteenth century were a transitional period in state taxation, as the main source of revenue shifted from uncultivated jungle produce to cultivated cash crops. As the colony's economy became more export-oriented with the growth of the Singapore market, increases in state revenue depended on customs duties levied on commodities. Table 10 shows government-imposed export duties collected on commodities shipped from Sarawak. It should be noted that among export commodities whose duty taxes were repeatedly revised, pepper and gambier were the important sources of state income. Accordingly, the Sarawak government raised export duties on these commodities as their value increased on the Singapore market.

They remained Sarawak's major export earners until the 1920s, when they were overtaken by cultivated rubber. In 1935, one year after the International Rubber Regulation Agreement (IRRA) was implemented, the value of rubber exports reached $7,692,851, which represented one third of total exports (Takumusho 1938: 146–8).

State, Society, and Resonant Circuit

A multitude of regulations and reports on border crossing and control issued to outstation officers were recorded in the pages of the *Sarawak Gazette* and the Lundu District Monthly Report during the reign of Charles Brooke. The issues reflect the will of the state to circumscribe its subjects and determine their affiliation to Sarawak; they also reflect the borderland community's responses to regulation. Several categories of regulation concerned the mobilization of agricultural labor for commodity production: passports, arrest of criminals from across the border, chase of runaway estate workers, prohibition of border-crossing during epidemic outbreaks, control of opium trade, prohibition of cross-border swidden cultivation, and registration of cultivated land. Another series of regulations — concerning naturalization, marriage registration, prohibition of bigamy, and spousal support and child rearing — supported the effort to make sedentary people on the move, their families, and their offspring.

Colonial Sarawak offers a very specific platform from which to view competition between state and society over their respective social spaces. The Sarawak government in the reign of the second white rajah exemplifies a case in which state-society relations are not explicable in binary opposition between society and the Weberian sense of state as political machinery with a legitimized right to exercise physical force. State-society relations at the margin embodied specific representations of the colonial world by state agencies, social organizations and networks in an incubatory stage.

In the Sarawak/Dutch Borneo borderland, policing by state agencies was minimal and where it existed was largely ineffective. Lundu District at the turn of the century covered an area of approximately 1,900 square kilometers with a population density of fewer than three persons per square kilometer. The borderland lacked physical signs of demarcation such as immigration posts or border gates. Only one European and one native Malay officer administered the district's 80-kilometer long border. Most areas of the district were covered by

Table 11 Government Notices, Orders, and Reports Related to the Border Incidents in Lundu District (1871–1917)

1871 5/12	Marriage Law: prohibition of bigamy by non-Sarawakians in the Sarawakian territory and obligation of family support
1874 5/11	Border demarcation between Sarawak and Dutch Sambas (Sarawak/Dutch Sambas Committee of Administration)
1874 5/11	Punishment of the Jagoi Dayaks engaged in swidden agriculture in Sarawakian and Dutch Sambas territory
1876 6/5	Prohibition of exploitation of forest produces in Sambas territory by Sarawakian subjects
1876 6/27	Order: prohibition of travel to Sambas territory without passport
1876 6/27	Order: obligation to obtain permit from Sambas Sultan for the exploitation of forest produce in the Sambas territory, to carry passport, and to pay 10 per cent tax on forest produce.
1878 8/31	Notification: export tax levied on natural rubber and sago flour
1879 3/4	Search for a criminal, Hj. Bakar who fled to Sarawak (Sarawak/Dutch Sambas Committee of Administration)
1879 3/4	Attack against Sarawak subjects in Dutch Sambas territory (Sarawak/Dutch Sambas Committee of Administration)
1883 9/27	Murder of a Sarawak subject in the Dutch Sambas territory (Sarawak/Dutch Sambas Committee of Administration)
1883 12/8	Notification of export tax levied on gambier and pepper
1884 8/1	Request of Sambas Sultan to levy poll tax on the Jagoi Dayaks in Sarawak/Dutch Sambas borderlands
1884 7/22	Border demarcation between Sarawak and Dutch Sambas (Sarawak/Dutch Sambas Committee of Administration)
1885 5/1	Report on the arrest of the Chinese merchants travelling in the Dutch Sambas territory without passport
1887 12/20	Agreement on the deportation of Sarawakian criminals from Dutch Sambas
1890 10/10	Prohibition of exploitation of jungle produce in Sambas territory by Sarawak subjects
1891 2/5	Procedure for the search for criminals who fled to Dutch Sambas territory from Sarawak
1891 3/2	Procedure for the search for criminals who fled to the Dutch Sambas territory from Sarawak

(Continued overleaf)

Table 11 Continued

1891 4/1	Report on the Chinese coolies arrested by Dutch Sambas authority
1891 12/31	Agreement between Sarawak and Dutch Sambas on the deportation of runaway criminals from Sarawak
1892 1/2	Agreement between Sarawak and Dutch Sambas on the deportation of runaway criminals from Sarawak
1892 3/3	Report on the evacuation of locals to Dutch Sambas territory due to the breakout of small-pox in the borderland of Sarawak
1892 3/17	Report on the deportation of runaway criminals from Sarawak
1893 1/3	Report on the Sambas immigrants who obtained Sambas Sultan's permission to settle in Sarawak
1893 2/1	Report on the migrants from the Serasan Islands settled in Telok Serabang
1893 2/1	Notification of tax levied on the logs shipped from Sarawak and taxation on ships built by Sambas subjects
1893 3/1	Arrest of Sambas Chinese at Samunsan, Sematan
1893 4/2	Notification of tax levied on the logs shipped from Sarawak and taxation on ships built by Sambas subjects
1893 6/1	Notification: compulsory registration of commercial schooners and captains (*nakoda*)
1893 9/1	Notification of tax levied on logs shipped from Sematan coast
1893 10/2	Report on the illicit sale and purchase of pepper at Lundu bazaar
1893 10/2	Notification of tax levied on logs shipped from Sematan
1893 10/2	Report on the fifty immigrant families from Semudun, Sambas that settled in Sematan
1893 12/1	Report on the arrest of a runaway coolie from Sarawak
1894 3/1	Notification of tax levied on the logs shipped from Sarawak and taxation on the ships built by Sambas subjects
1894 3/1	Report on the Sambas Dayaks harvesting birds nest at the caves near Cape Dato
1894 4/1	Report on the arrest of a Chinese merchant who conducted illicit sale and purchase of pepper at Lundu bazaar
1894 4/2	Report on the procedure for the surveillance of traffickers crossing Sarawak/Dutch Sambas border without passport
1894 5/1	Report on the arrest and three-month imprisonment of a Malay merchant who smuggled muskets

Table 11 Continued

1894 11/1	Report on the locals who returned from Dutch Sambas to Sarawakian territory after the outbreak of epidemics
1895 1/2	Report on the divorce granted to a Malay woman who had been left unsupported for 11 months by her husband who fled to Sambas territory
1895 9/20	Discussion on the arrest of runaway coolies (Sarawak/Dutch Sambas committee of Administration)
1895 8/1	Report on the measures used by the merchants in Lundu Bazaar
1895 8/1	Regulation on the smuggling of muskets from Dutch Sambas territory
1895 8/1	Permit granted to Sambas merchants who applied for the exploitation of timber in Sematan
1895 8/1	Report on the commencement of vaccination in Sematan
1895 9/2	Report on the outbreak of cholera in Sambas and subsequent prohibition of the anchorage of Sambas ships at Sematan
1895 10/1	Request of the Sub-Magistrate of Sambas District regarding the arrest of runaway Javanese coolies
1896 1/2	Report on the smuggling of muskets and arrest of a Sambas Malay merchant
1896 8/1	Report on the arrest of a Sambas Malay who committed a bigamy offense in the Sarawakian territory
1899 8/1	Repot on the outbreak of epidemics in the borderland between Belingsah and Telok Melano
1900 6/1	Notification: obligation of carrying passport by the travelers to Sambas territory
1900 8/1	Notification: naturalization procedure
1900 6/1	Report on the arrest of runaway Malays in Sambas territory and subsequent deportation to Sarawak
1900 8/1	Report on the measurement of exportable timber for duty inspection
1900 9/1	Report on the surveillance of commercial ships at the mouth of the Lundu River for taxation purpose
1912 2/1	Report on the *engkabang* nuts harvested by the Sambas subjects in the territory of Sarawak
1914 6/1	Report on the village boundary dispute between Dutch Sambas immigrants and local Dayaks
1917 9/1	Report on the bigamy offence by a Sambas Dayak in Lundu and by a Lundu Dayak in Sambas

Source: *SG*, 1871–1917.

dense primary forest, and the frontier region was inaccessible by sea during the half-year long monsoon season. Officers stationed at Lundu fort had to walk overland to inspect sparsely populated communities, a trip that usually took more than a week. It was simply impossible for borderland communities to be put under close surveillance.[8]

Society, for its part, was also deficient in social organization and collective actors — corporate descent groups, domestic business networks, rigid patron-client dyads, ethnically mobilized interest groups — capable of struggling for personal survival and power against the state. Sporadic and small-scale contraband activities were limited to the smuggling of outdated muskets and salt, escape by individually-motivated coolies, tax evasion by petty traders, and transnational bigamy by mobile locals, and these activities did not make the borderland of southwestern Sarawak a conflict-ridden environment for the colonial state. It was instead a kind of incubator in which state and society prepared for upcoming confrontations concerning state agencies, peasants, and merchants during the interwar period, when smuggling rubber across the border became the major industry of Lundu District. The colonial state of Sarawak and local society of Lundu were in a relationship of mutual engagement, constitution, and transformation during this five-decade long embryonic period (see Table 11).

Violation and enforcement of the same kinds of law took place repeatedly through the reign of the second Rajah. Measures implemented by the Brooke administration to counter recurrent problems were ad hoc and inconsistent. It was only after specific "border problems" had been reported that new regulations were written and notification made to administrative officers. Laws were rarely announced directly to inhabitants of the borderland; instead they were published in government gazettes and official reports. Even where prohibitions were announced, certain violations never ceased — agricultural laborers fleeing estates, border crossing without passport, and cross-border swidden cultivation, for example. Such cases were reported to the capital, which led to the issuing of identical regulations or orders, as the cat-and-mouse game between administrators and unsubmissive locals continued.

[8] Wadley (2001) examines the differences between the Dutch and Brookes in their colonial attitudes toward the territorial boundary in West Borneo borderland. Based on archival research, he points out a more relaxed attitude toward boundary demarcation on the side of the Sarawak government, which was less concerned with territoriality but more with people as the subject of control.

State-society relations at the periphery of Sarawak were contentious — albeit at a low intensity — and also complementary. Cases of offence and punishment returned as local people maneuvered for personal profit and state authority attempted to enclose a national space. State and society formed a resonant circuit in which a dialectical process between state policing and the adaptive strategies of local society contributed to the genesis of a national space. What is observed at the periphery of this colony, however, leads neither to the counterpoising of state and society nor to assertions of "strong" society and "weak" state or "weak" society and "strong" state (Migdal 1988).

Theory generated from the state-society relationship in this setting necessarily differs from that based on the hydraulic societies of mainland Southeast Asia or densely populated Java, and the governing apparatus established by colonial governments then. This chapter, adding to the few studies of political ecology of the "outer islands" of maritime Southeast Asia (Tagliacozzo 2005, Warren 1981), seeks a new way of locating society and state outside of conventional conceptual models of state-society juxtaposition as well as societal inclusion of state (Migdal 1988, 2001, 2004).

Rather than discussing state and society as two separate entities, I consider synergy and resonance between the state policy implementation and cross-border flows of people and things, an approach that allows better theorization of peripheral state-society relations. The following chapter further looks into the intensification of policy implementation and social response in the twentieth century, as rubber booms, the Great Depression, and imperial intervention in the production and circulation of rubber precipitated total (yet undeclared) confrontation between the state as territorial entity and a local economy based on cross-border commodity smuggling.

The discussions in previous chapters have dealt with the emergence of state territory and national space with the units of analysis exclusively confined within the colony of Sarawak. The next chapter will examine the dynamics of boundary making at the interface between local marketplaces and imperial commodity chains by looking at the introduction of rubber into the hinterland of the British and Dutch Empires.

CHAPTER THREE

Contraband and *Konfrontasi*

The introduction of such cash crops as pepper, gambier, and coconut under Charles Brooke contributed to the formation of an ethnically segmented migrant society in the late nineteenth-century Sarawak (Chapter 1). This was the period when the colonial space of Sarawak was gradually taking shape, as a series of policies on land registration, migration, marriage law, and taxation attempted to establish the national affiliation of land, people, and commodities (Chapter 2).

In the twentieth century, the Sarawak/Sambas borderland was again transformed by the introduction and tremendous success of rubber. This new export commodity made the region significant within global commodity chains and intensified the tension between the state's efforts to control its economic space and borderland society's habitual traversing of the national boundary. In 1934 the International Rubber Regulation Agreement (IRRA) was invoked by rubber-producing colonies in the tropics to support rubber prices in the face of the Great Depression. The regulation on cultivation and export necessitated tighter control of the cross-border movement of dutiable rubber, which resulted in rampant rubber smuggling from Dutch West Borneo to Sarawak.

This chapter analyzes how Malay and Dayak rubber cultivators and Chinese merchants resisted a European imperial regime that tried to contain their activity in favor of the colonial plantation system. The development of a smuggling economy coincided with a larger social process in which a colonial state with a porous boundary transformed itself into a single territorial geo-body with its own customs regulations and domestic market networks. Through their participation in transnational contraband trade, the borderland residents attempted to maximize profit, which led to the state policing for boundary maintenance. This chapter juxtaposes two seemingly contradictory social dynamics at the boundary — the construction of a national space and the simultaneous deconstruction of a state boundary through parochial, illicit transnationalism — as general features at the interstice of territorial state.

Sarawak and Rubber Booms

Rubber came to Southeast Asia from Brazil, where it was tapped and traded by the local population. It was known and used in Europe but did not become an important commercial crop until after 1841, when a process called vulcanization was developed that prevented rubber from degenerating into a soft and sticky mass. In 1876, rubber seeds were smuggled out of Brazil and germinated at Britain's Kew Gardens. About 2,000 seedlings were sent to Ceylon and India, some of which were then sent on to Singapore. These seedlings were the progenitors of practically all rubber grown in Malaya and Borneo (Rawlins 1969: 219).

Bishop Hose brought three rubber seeds from Singapore to Sarawak in 1881 and planted them in the mission compound in Kuching (Rawlins 1969: 219). However, the Sarawak government did not become interested in rubber production until the turn of the century. In 1902, the government-funded Borneo Company acquired a land concession in Bau, the First Division, as this later became the Dahan Rubber Estate. The Sarawak government, later established experimental Para Rubber Plantations in Sigu and Satap and by 1908, according to the *Sarawak Gazette*, "about 650 trees [were] fit to tap ... from seven to ten years old, and about the same number more will in a short time be of sufficient size"; another "3,000 young trees some two years old are doing extremely well at Sigu and 4,000 more were to be planted at each site" (*SG*, October 1, 1908: 247). The government sent rubber samples obtained from these estates to Singapore for the evaluation of their commercial value. One sample was found to be of an unusual color, and others were of "nice quality" and "fair quality", but not properly processed (*SG*, December 1, 1908: 297).

The government's diligence in developing rubber for commercial cultivation would be rewarded. As the automobile industry developed in the 1900s and 1910s, it created a huge demand for rubber tires, generating a rubber frenzy among planters and peasants alike in British Malaya and other tropical countries. From exports of virtually zero in

1900, rubber had become by the 1930s the most important export from the British and Dutch colonies. In the first four decades of the twentieth century, Southeast Asia was the source of 90 per cent or more of the world's rubber, and Malaya and Netherlands East India together consistently accounted for at least 75 per cent of the total (Steinberg and Chandler 1988: 230). Colonial governments favored plantation agriculture, but smallholders actively pursued rubber profits as well, and by 1921, smallholders accounted for one third of the 1.6 million ha of planted rubber in Southeast Asia (de Jong 2002: 84).

Nevertheless, Sarawak was a relative latecomer to the rubber boom. At the time its government was planting a few thousand trees on a trial basis, other European colonies had already established large-scale plantations with European capital. The delayed inception of a plantation economy in Sarawak was a reflection of Charles Brooke's anti-European sentiment. He was highly skeptical of plantation-based rubber production and steadfastly refused all applicants who aspired to start European-financed rubber enterprises in Sarawak, including his youngest son, Harry, who applied in 1910 on behalf of a British consortium. He wrote to Harry: "[N]ot believing in the performance of the Rubber Boom, I don't wish Sarawak to be a great producer of this article — except [that] it can be planted by natives who could afford to sell it a 20th part less than European Companies…." Brooke suspected that rubber, "now turned to account in making the fortunes of many", would one day "be the means of depriving the poor and ignorant shareholders of their hard-earned savings" (cited in Reece 1988: 28).

Brooke's views became policy later that year, when the government prohibited "native inhabitants of Sarawak, and settlers of Chinese, Indian, Eurasian or any Eastern nationality" from selling their rubber gardens to any European firm or individual. The notice explained:

> The object of the Sarawak Government is to develop the cultivation of the land for the good of the inhabitants in order that they may have the profits and benefits in the possession of such gardens as an inheritance or pesaka to their descendants — and this object would not be achieved or realised unless the plantations were protected and strictly prohibited from falling into the hands of the richer and more speculative class of the white races. The above policy may be criticised and objected to as not being very loyal to the white man's interests but on the other hand it may be said that by selling wholesale the land of the dark races to foreigners and speculators an injustice is done to the inhabitants of these Eastern countries (*SG*, November 1, 1910: 227).

Although he refused foreign capital and large-scale rubber plantations, Brooke encouraged rubber smallholding by distributing seeds to his subjects.[1] The slow response to rubber on the part of pepper, gambier, and coconuts cultivators meant that Sarawak continued to slumber peacefully under the eccentric despotism of the while Rajahs, leaving it outside of the rubber frenzy that covered much of the soil of the tropical zone under European colonization with para rubber trees.

The International Rubber Market and Colonial Symbiosis

The Versailles Treaty of 1919 set the tone for colonial symbiosis in postwar international relations, but it was not until the 1930s that the coordinated effort for maintaining rubber's market price was pursued by the British and Dutch empire in Southeast Asia. In the 1920s the British first tried to inhibit the growth of native rubber smallholders in favor of plantation system, implementing a series of policies on rubber production and trade in the colonies. One of such regulations was the Stevenson Restriction Scheme (1922–28). In accordance with the strict export quota, the British colony banned new rubber planting, controlled harvesting, and regulated the number of rubber sheets circulating through domestic trade networks. It is important to note that it was not the case in the Dutch territory where there was no such policy. The high price of rubber in the international market in 1922 and 1923 was a factor promoting cultivation and production of rubber in the Dutch territory. Because of the increase of Sumatran rubber production, the Stevenson Scheme closed down Malaysian production to some extent.

The Great Depression, however, brought a deep slump to the rubber industry. The production of automobile tires declined drastically, and with it the price of rubber went from $4.17 per kg in 1925 to $0.13 per kg in 1932. By this time, the total area planted with rubber in Sarawak had reached an estimated 86,000 ha, with 90 per cent of this planted by smallholders. Of an estimated 75,000 gardens, about 80 per cent belonged to natives (Cramb 1988: 114). Thus the Great Depression was felt even in remote areas of Sarawak, located at the periphery of the modern world system. The market price of rubber

---

[1] In Lundu District he personally inspected local rubber gardens and promised to send free seeds from Kuching (*SG*, July 15, 1910: 151).

dropped so low that a substantial number of smallholders abandoned their rubber gardens:

> All the farmers are now busy, and all the hill land has been cleared and burnt — in many cases far more than the actual farms have been burnt, including numbers of rubber gardens (*SG*, October 1, 1930: 254).

Given that it takes six years or more for a rubber tree to produce latex, it was an unfortunate irony that the maturity of many rubber plantings coincided precisely with the 1930s plunge in the market. When the price rose slightly in 1933, many smallholders started tapping their trees again, first clearing neglected "gardens which very much resembled jungle" (*SG*, July 1, 1933: 90).

In 1934, Sarawak reluctantly joined the International Rubber Regulation Agreement (IRRA) under pressure from the British Colonial Office. The British and Dutch governments mediated among rubber-producing exporters such as British Malaya, Netherlands East India, Ceylon, India, French Indochina, Thailand, British North Borneo, and Sarawak, forcing them to participate in a scheme for comprehensive control of rubber production to prevent further price declines. Under the terms of the IRRA, all new planting was forbidden and state-wide "Tapping Holidays" were declared every fourth month.

The governments first controlled the amount of raw rubber exported through quotas and issued "Rubber Occupation Tickets" to regulate the number of producers. Sarawak's quota was set at 30,000 tons per year, and the amount exported each month was strictly calculated (Pringle 1970: 334). The Tapping Holiday system, though, proved ineffective. In 1937, a far more complicated "Coupon System" was introduced in Sarawak. This arrangement regulated the number of rubber trees planted and the quantities of rubber sheet sold to local dealers. Both rubber producers and dealers were issued government coupons, which authorized them to market an approved quantity of rubber. The next section examines how the people of the borderland of western Borneo, at the margin of the British and Dutch empires, responded to the restrictions of the IRRA.

Smallholders, Merchants, and the Colonial Regime

For many years the people of Lundu were reluctant to engage in rubber cultivation. A colonial officer stationed there in 1913 reported that "government rubber plantation trees had grown well ... but the ground around trees was in many cases getting rather overgrown with lalang [weed], and required attention (*SG*, September 1, 1913: 213). In contrast, coconut and pepper gardens were abundant and flourishing (*SG*, July 15, 1910: 151). A 1916 inspection of all coconut gardens on the coast "as far as Tg. [Cape] Datu [Dato]" found the largest one "belonging to a Malay woman at Lubok Gadong, who has planted out 6,000, and as a catch crop hundreds of bananas" (*SG*, May 16, 1916: 100).

That same year "the recent rise of the price of rubber" was reported by the *Sarawak Gazette* (February 1, 1916) to have "taken practically everybody by surprise". But more than a year later, rising prices had hardly dented local adherence to pepper production:

> There is not much rubber planting to be noticed. Only one garden has been registered this year, one in 1916 and five in 1915. Several of the Government rubber trees are ready for tapping but they might be left till a large proportion reach the tapping stage.
>
> The number of new pepper gardens registered this year is 19 and the number of new vines 6,000, whereas in 1916 50 new gardens were registered with roughly 17,000 new vines. The existing gardens appeared in good condition.... About 200 gardens paid vine tax this year (*SG*, September 1, 1917: 223).

Throughout the 1910s, pepper and coconut remained the major cash crops of Lundu, but by the mid-1920s rubber production was finally gaining on these older crops. Developments following the short price slump of 1920–22 seem to have been the turning point. The British government, whose colonies then produced 72 per cent of world rubber output, implemented the Stevenson Restriction Scheme (1922–28).[2] By reducing the amount of rubber traded on the international market, the scheme led to a price recovery, which peaked in 1925 before diminishing toward the end of the decade. The beginning of rubber cultivation in Lundu District was apparently a response to the 1924–25 price peaks. In January 1925, there was a rush of applications by Chinese *taukay* merchants for permits to plant rubber; in August of that year, fourteen permits were issued for rubber and only one for pepper (*SG*, January 2, 1925: 10; August 3, 1925: 193).

---

[2] According to Pringle (1970: 334), Sarawak participated in the scheme, but the policies implemented by its government are unknown.

When new rubber planting was banned and its production and circulation in the market controlled under the IRRA, some Lundu planters returned to cultivating coconuts and pepper. "Applications for coconut land on the coast are on the increase", the *Sarawak Gazette* reported in 1936, noting that "[t]he embargo on rubber planting [was] probably partly responsible, but the success of other coconut gardens on the coast which have been under the supervision of the Senior Agricultural Officer [was] probably the main reason for this demand" (October 1, 1936: 242).

Other peasants turned to smuggling, locally called *smokel*, probably derived from the Dutch word *smokkelen*. It referred to the illegal trafficking in commodities from Dutch Borneo and their sale to Chinese shops in Sarawak. The first accounts of small-scale smuggling in Lundu District appeared in the 1890s, with dutiable imports like muskets and salt constituting the first contraband-items (see Table 7).

By the 1930s, when Lundu District as a whole had been incorporated into the state-led commodity production system, a parallel set of transnational networks was swiftly established to evade tightened border controls. In making the smuggling of rubber and other dutiable commodities between Dutch West Borneo and Sarawak, peasants and merchants were responding to the limitations and opportunities presented by production quotas.

The limitations of the rubber restriction schemes were felt disproportionately by smallholders throughout rubber-producing Southeast Asia. Before the schemes were implemented, rubber land in British Malaya had reached three million acres (about three times the area planted of rice, the next largest crop), and rubber exports amounted to 446,000 tons in 1929 (Steinberg and Chandler 1988: 228). European-run plantations in Malaya followed shortly by plantations in Sumatra had led the way, but smallholders in those two colonies caught up after 1910. Rubber was widely and rapidly adopted by the peasants of Southeast Asia for three main reasons.

Ecologically, the rubber tree was very well suited to the poor soils and fierce botanical competition of Southeast Asian forests. It required little effort to plant seedlings on an already cleared and previously used swidden plot before moving on in the swidden cycle, or to plant an acre or two on permanently cultivated land (de Jong 2002: 85–9). Once planted, rubber trees grew just like other secondary forest and required little tending. Smallholders often regarded as unnecessary the practice insisted upon by European planters of keeping the ground between trees clear. Simple tapping and processing techniques were easily learned.

Rubber was also ideal in economic terms. While waiting for seedlings to mature or when rubber prices were low, peasants could live as before on subsistence activity, which meant swidden agriculture in the case of the western Borneo borderlands. When rubber prices were high, a few acres of trees provided quick income. Middlemen were needed to move the rubber to market, and Chinese traders filled that role. Finally, rubber was ideal in social terms for peasants venturing into a cash economy. Nearly all smallholders of the 1930s grew a few acres of rubber, in addition to cultivating rice or other crops, and could enjoy the advantages of a prime cash crop without incurring risk or leaving the village community (Steinberg and Chandler 1988: 229–30).

By 1929, a million or so smallholders in Sumatra, Malaya, and Borneo were producing almost 40 per cent of the world's supply of rubber. A decade later, smallholders held more than four million acres of mature trees and were capable of satisfying most of world demand at prices few European plantations could meet.[3]

The coupon system introduced under the IRRA was the primary trigger of large-scale smuggling of raw and smoked rubber sheet. In order to implement the system in Sarawak, officials from British Malaya helped local officers count and survey more than 90,000 smallholdings. Each owner received coupons entitling him/her to market a specified amount of rubber in accordance with the size of the holding. Coupons were to be attached by the cultivator to the rubber sheets when they were sold to Chinese dealers. Local farmers in Lundu District quickly grasped the limits imposed by the system but also recognized the potential it offered for evasion of the rules.

> During the month the specimen coupons were received and intensive propaganda work has been carried out with their assistance. They are really of immense value in enabling the propagandist to convey the essentials of the system to his audience....
>
> Malays have been particularly quick to understand the principles involved and on the whole the response of the Dayaks is most gratifying. The word "coupon" seems to be preferred to ticket jual

[3] It could be possibly argued that only gross discrimination under the 1930s commodity control programs prevented them from dominating production of one of the world's most important export products (cf. Steinberg and Chandler 1988: 229).

> getah [sell rubber], and if this is the experience of other districts, perhaps the official terminology will have to be altered accordingly (*SG*, December 1, 1937: 252).

A market for coupons developed rapidly, even though it was illegal to buy and sell them. Some rubber smallholders sold coupons to dealers without rubber sheets, and others sold more rubber sheets than they were allowed. The separate marketing of coupons and rubber sheets allowed flexibility in the illicit trade.

Dutch Borneo's abundant rubber supply was another prime factor in the emergence of smuggling in Lundu District. According to the *Handboek voor de Residentie Westerafdeeling van Borneo*, rubber cultivation in Dutch West Borneo started earlier than in Sarawak, and the output was considerably higher (Uljee 1925). Rubber export was first from Pontianak in 1911 and skyrocketed in the 1920s. In the late 1930s, when rubber smuggling into Sarawak was at its peak, Dutch West Borneo accounted for as much as 15 per cent of the Netherland East Indies' total rubber acreage excluding Java (Aikawa 1944: 188). In the Sambas region of Dutch Borneo, rubber production was carried out mainly by Malay peasants along the major rivers (the Sambas, Duri, and Paloh) and by interior Dayaks who lived near the border.

Table 12 The Amount of Rubber Exported from Dutch West Borneo

Year	*Amount (ton)*
1911	128
1912	132
1913	96
1914	147
1915	412
1916	876
1917	1,325
1918	2,671
1919	2,571
1920	2,087
1921	2,079
1922	4,675
1923	9,056
1924	1,524

Source: Uljee 1925: 75–6.

In Sarawak, the scale of cultivation was smaller and rubber trees were just beginning to be productive, when new planting was prohibited under the IRRA. The result was a price difference between the Dutch and Sarawak markets and a flow of Dutch rubber into Sarawak, which had the higher prices.[4] The peripheral location of the Sambas peasantry in relation to the political geography of western Borneo also supported the logic of smuggling. Pontianak was the center of western Borneo's economic network due to its close connection with the thriving Singapore market. But the Sarawak market was much closer and more accessible for rubber cultivators in Sambas, and they shared common interests with Chinese taukays in Sarawak.

Smuggling was conducted both overland and by sea. When rubber sheet was brought to Kuching by sea, smugglers' boats usually came around Cape Dato. Two Malay villages located near the cape, Telok Melano and Telok Serabang, functioned as transit points (see Fig. 9). Others carried the bulky rubber sheets across the border on foot, entering Sarawak through Bidayuh (Land Dayak) villages such as Biawak, Kandai, Stass, and Serikin (see Fig. 8). By land or by sea, local peasants at the margin of the state brought their rubber sheets to the transit points, and Chinese merchants shipped them to Kuching and Singapore, supplementing their legitimately bought rubber. Traffickers from Dutch Borneo, mostly Sambas Malay peasants, carried rubber by boat to the relay points, where larger and well-equipped Chinese vessels were waiting.

Smuggling was of course contrary to the government's economic policies of cash crop production and taxation. Smugglers neither produced crops in Sarawak nor paid custom duties to its treasury. Their profit represented a loss in government revenue. In Lundu District from the mid-1930s, it became an important task for officers to arrest and punish those engaged in the illegal transaction of rubber and coupons:

> There is little doubt that a considerable amount of rubber smuggling is going on in upper Sarawak, Chinese and Land Dayaks being concerned. While on a border patrol Corporal Ali succeeded in arresting two Chinese and 16 Dutch Dayaks, who had some seven pikuls of rubber bearing Sarawak stencil numbers which clearly could not have been produced by the stencil holders. One of the Chinese had

---

[4] Smuggling activities from Sambas to Sarawak also took place in the 1950s. According to a Sambas Malay villager, rubber fetched a higher price in Sarawak (Rp. 20/kg) compared to local market prices (Rp. 6/kg).

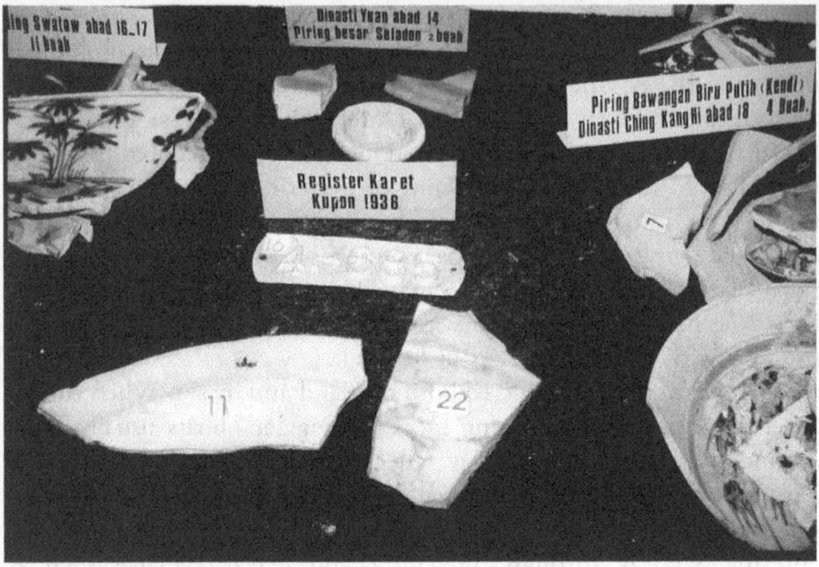

Illus. 4 A rubber registration plate (1936) (courtesy of the Sultan Sambas Museum, Sambas, West Kalimantan)

> a letter in his possession signed by the Kapitan China, Ong Tebang, warning him to be careful, as the police were rather inquisitive! (*SG*, April 1, 1936: 86).
>
> On March 3rd, a Malay named Talip bin Abas was fined $500 at Lundu for smuggling rubber into Sarawak (*SG*, May 1, 1936: 107).

The rubber smuggling, which continued as the main industry of Lundu District up to the early 1960s, developed as part of an emerging national and supra-national order. In fact, it can be argued that what made the Sarawak colony a full-fledged state was its incorporation into the world-wide rubber production system and especially the rubber restriction schemes. Its participation in rubber restriction gave Sarawak internationally recognized status as an independent economic unit charged with controlling the production and distribution of an important commodity within its territory.

Living on Contraband: Postwar Western Borneo

During the reign of the third and last white Rajah, Charles Vyner Brooke (1917–46), Sarawak underwent a series of complex political and economic changes. During his reign, the British Colonial Office in London gradually asserted greater control, and after Japan surrendered in 1945, the British government insisted that Sarawak be ceded to the British Crown. In July 1946, a new colonial government took over in Kuching, and Sarawak became a British Crown Colony.

After the Japanese military occupation, when shortages of food and commodities severely plagued the area, the informal economy in the Lundu hinterland revived. Transnational smuggling brought a variety of goods — clothes, food, tobacco, livestock — from West Kalimantan into Sarawak through the transnational networks established in the 1930s. Colonial officers of the British Crown Colony and their Indonesian counterparts had occasional success in the continuing cat-and-mouse struggle with traders handling contraband:

> There have been reports of increased activity by Indonesian police patrols on the border, and the Kandai route into Sarawak is now used very little due to the difficulties the smugglers experience avoiding these patrols (*SG*, June 30, 1952: 135).

But the remoteness of the borderland continued to be a source of difficulty in apprehending smugglers. "The areas which need watching and in which most of the smuggling activities take place are inaccessible by land", officials complained in the early 1950s: "a sea going launch is required" (*LDQR* 3rd Quarter: July–September 1951). Near the end of the decade, nothing had changed:

> Compared with the land border there is even less control over coastal trade round Tanjong [Cape] Dato. It is ... big enough to justify the continual hiring of a Chinese vessel plying between Telok Serabang and the capital. The nearest custom point is in Sematan, which is avoided on the direct run to Kuching, and the possibilities for duty evasion are consequently limitless. This is an isolated area, expensive to patrol at any time, and almost impossible over which to exercise control during the long season of monsoon from a station which is still without a launch (*LDR* 2nd Half Year 1959).

In 1959, the value of smuggled goods "reached almost a million dollars"; the smuggling industry had become so dominant that "[f]luctuations in border trade alter the whole economy of the District and affect almost every aspect of Government" (*LDR* 2nd Half Year 1959). Sometimes fluctuations were caused by successful policing, as when "energetic patrols" stopped goods from entering, causing a "fall in quick profits" (*SG*, July 31, 1959: 164).

> Several leading merchants told me how difficult it is for the local traders to carry on when dutiable goods are seized, and smugglers punished; after all, they say, Lundu exists on smugglers, and if the latter are all to go to prison when caught, Lundu Bazaar will be put out of business (*LDQR* 3rd Quarter 1954).

But border patrols alone could not hope to shut down the illicit trade, and this became even less effective in the early 1960s: "[F]inancial chaos over the border and a decrease in patrolling by the Indonesian police livened conditions in Lundu's second economy and helped to maintain the newly-awakened air of confidence in Lundu bazaar" (*SG*, March 31, 1960: 59).

Smuggling followed patterns established in the 1930s. Interior Land Dayaks and Sambas Malays from Indonesian Kalimantan traveled up swollen rivers during *landas* (monsoon) season or carried rubber sheet by foot. In Sarawak, Chinese merchants waited for them at designated spots. After the Indonesians received cash for their rubber, they purchased goods to sell back home for "double profit" (*dua kali untung*). Besides pre-ordered goods needed by fellow villagers, popular items were Chinese medicines and nylon clothes.

The profits to be made from smuggling justified the effort. The following is the statement of a rubber smuggler, reconstructed from memory by a Sambas Malay journalist who entered Sarawak in 1962 with a guide who smuggled rubber sheets across the border (see Fig. 8).

> From his village in Sanggau Ledo, we reached Seluas first. The guide bought in 31 kilograms of rubber sheets, carrying them to Jagoi Babang. He further added 18 kilograms there and 5 kilograms at Serikin, and 17 kilograms at Borring. In total he carried more than 70 kilograms of rubber sheets, walked over the border, and sold them at a Chinese shop across the border. We cooked rice in the jungle and walked on animal trails. The trip took us a good two days.
>
> In case wealthy Chinese smugglers were arrested in Sarawak, severe punishment by the police and custom officers waited for them. Many Chinese smugglers who took a sea route were caught off Cape Dato. Individual, small-scale Malay smugglers, who entered Sarawak overland, were often condoned by the authority.

In accordance with the greater risk, much greater rewards accrued to those at the top of the chain:

> The trade is highly organised and competitive. Big business from Kuching is represented, and agents on this side of the border are equipped with portable radios to keep them in touch with the latest Singapore prices (*SG*, March 31, 1960: 59).

Over the course of the 1950s and early 1960s, the economy of Lundu became dependent on the smuggling industry. With the Kuching-based distribution network far away, bazaars in the frontier district obtained Indonesian goods from smugglers and distributed them to the local merchandizing network. Many peasant communities adjacent to the border gave up planting commercial crops in favor of the more profitable smuggling business:

> Farms are deserted for the more lucrative work of portering; labour grows scare and expensive; and it becomes impossibly difficult to demonstrate that attendance in school is a worthwhile occupation in areas where a child can earn dollars in a day (*LDR* 2nd Half Year 1959).
>
> Profits from dealing in smuggled goods are high enough to make threats of prosecution for illegal trading small deterrent. Colonies of bamboo trading huts mushroom overnight, and fines imposed seem to be accepted as an unfortunate kind of tax (*LDR* 2nd Half Year 1959).

The interior of Lundu District retained its dual character as a stateless, isolated enclave and an economic hub between two countries. The smuggling of rubber and other dutiable commodities from West Kalimantan to Lundu continued apace until military confrontation between Malaysia and Indonesia violently demarcated the boundary between the two nations in 1963.

The Informal Economy and the Territorial State

The development of the informal economy in the Lundu hinterland, which was the basis of peasant maneuvering against the macro-structural forces of global colonialism, can be divided into three phases. After the traditional trading activities of the Malay/Bugis *nakoda* merchants — illegally marketing muskets, salt, and other daily necessities — the second phase of an organized cross-border economy began with trafficking in rubber sheets from Sambas. Activated by the production and distribution controls of the IRRA, this phase lasted from 1934 until the Japanese military occupation began in 1941. After the war, cross-border smuggling revived, invigorated by the economic and political instability of the newly established Republic of Indonesia and the British crown colony. The informal economy now expanded to include the transnational movement of such commodities as tobacco, textile products, pigs, coconuts, and gold. The Kalimantan side also became dependent on Sarawak's commercial network, as a substantial quantity of Indonesian goods were regularly carried into Sarawak and sold to Chinese dealers.

The incorporation of Sarawak and Dutch Borneo into the global market economy through the export of rubber had a marked effect on the peasantry of the borderland. But capitalist penetration did not transform rubber cultivators on the Sarawakian border into a passive peripheral element in the modern world system. Paradoxically, it led to their detachment and dissociation from the sphere of agricultural production. The economic marginalization of the borderland peasantry — interior Dayaks and coastal Malays — consisted in their breaking away from the state-led system of commodity production/distribution and engagement with the informal transnational economy as porters and operators of smuggling transshipment points. With the decline of pepper and coconut cultivation, a substantial number of peasants became heavily dependent on traditional swidden rice cultivation and did not participate in rubber cultivation even during boom periods.

The emergence of a cross-border economy complete with an illicit market coincided with the creation of numerous local communities forming a long, permeable economic membrane along the national boundary. The local economy operated according to its own internal logic: marketable commodities moved from Indonesia to Sarawak, and the network expanded and shrank with fluctuations in commodity prices and currency exchange rates.

When the state tried to become a closed economic unit — an independent, income-generating machine based on its own customs regulations — the borderland communities of western Borneo responded quickly. State policies making the national border more definite encouraged cross-border smuggling rather than suppressing it; emergent transnationalism made the border more permeable, not less so. It is crucial to emphasize that two levels of location work were involved in the realization of space in the borderland, one by the state and one by local communities. Clarifying how these two intersected offers a way to understand how two seemingly contradictory social movements — the construction of national space and the simultaneous deconstruction of a state boundary through parochial transnationalism — can be general features of a borderland where two geo-bodies join.[5]

The Emergence of a Politicized Frontier

The hinterland of Lundu District adjacent to the border remained in isolation at the periphery of national space during the heyday of the smuggling industry, even though it was part of a dense socio-economic interface that facilitated the flows of people and goods. However, this transnational link abruptly collapsed in 1963, when the Republic of Indonesia and the newly independent Malaysia began to engage in geo-political conflict. The borderland of western Borneo now became a politically charged frontier where a series of violent events with direct relevance to the Cold War politics would take place, including military confrontation and guerilla activities by communist cells. In the end, the wave of politicization emanating from Jakarta and Kuala Lumpur would deepen the isolation of this economic frontier.

Political development heading toward Sarawak's independence from British colonial rule had been slow during the first post-war decade. Peninsular Malaya achieved independence in 1957, and in December 1961, Prime Minister Tunku Abdul Rahman proposed the establishment of a federation bringing together the Federation of Brunei, Malaya, Singapore, British North Borneo (Sabah), and Sarawak. Local sentiment in Sarawak favored a smaller Borneo federation as an alternative to, or an intermediate step toward, a wider federation with Singapore and Malaya, but the proposal to create a large union won out, and Sarawak became part of Malaysia, which was officially established in September 1963.

The new federation was not born without trouble. In Borneo, there were those who opposed its formation on the grounds that

[5] Tagliacozzo (2005) looks into how illegal trafficking in the form of smuggling and contraband activities led to the formation of an international border between the British and Dutch colonial regimes in maritime Southeast Asia from 1865 to 1915. Also see Tagliacozzo (2001) for the examination of border permeability in Southeast Asia from the regional perspective.

a "Malaysia" was premature; they argued that Sarawak and Sabah should gain their independence first and consider joining a federation afterwards. In December 1962, a revolt led by Inche Azahari broke out in neighboring Brunei, a sovereign Malay sultanate under British protection. Azahari hoped to find enough support in Brunei, Sarawak, and Sabah to overthrow all three governments and unite the territories under one government with the Sultan of Brunei as head of state. In Sarawak, he found support in some areas of the Fourth and Fifth Divisions. The rebels seized Limbang and the area around Niah and Subuti, and British troops intervened to quash the rebellion. The incident caused unrest, and a secret communist organization which had been working in Sarawak for some years became more active as a result. Indonesia also encouraged Azahari's supporters.

President Sukarno of Indonesia criticized the proposed federation as being a neocolonial creation, claiming that Malaysia would be greatly influenced by Britain and would rely heavily on British finance and military bases. He also accused pro-federation politicians of failing to consult the people of Sarawak and Sabah, and demanded a referendum in both countries. The government of the Philippines joined the opposition, and a top-level meeting was held in Manila in August 1963. Tunku Abdul Rahman, Sukarno, and Philippine president Diosdado Macapagal asked the United Nations to dispatch a team of officials to Sarawak and Sabah to ensure that their people favored joining Malaysia.

On August 16, 1963, a UN working party arrived in Borneo; in mid-September it submitted a report confirming the support of the people of Sarawak and Sabah for joining the Federation of Malaysia. On September 16, the last British governor of Sarawak, Sir Alexander Waddell, left Kuching, and Malaysia Day was officially celebrated throughout Malaya, Singapore, Sarawak, and Sabah.[6]

But the governments of Indonesia and the Philippines continued their opposition after the establishment of Malaysia. The Philippine government refused to recognize the new federation and claimed part of Sabah as its territory, although it never attempted to enforce the claim through military measures. Talks were held between the two countries in Bangkok in July 1963, but no agreement was reached.

---

[6] For political developments in independent period, see Leigh (1974), Mackie (1974), Ongkili (1967), Rawlins (1969) and Sanib Said (1985).

Opposition from Indonesia was more intense, reflecting the strong sentiments of President Sukarno. Although the UN working party had been sent to Borneo at his request, Sukarno did not accept its verdict. He insisted that the Brunei Rebellion of 1962 indicated a lack of support for a federated Malaysia and called for freeing Southeast Asia from neocolonialism under British hegemony. Early in 1963, under a policy of *Konfrontasi* (confrontation), he started sending armed groups of volunteers, and later trained soldiers, across the border to attack communities in Sarawak. Other Indonesians crossed the porous border and had some success persuading locals to oppose the Malaysian government. In the main, however, support from Sarawak was meager, with the exception of Chinese communist elements that the government later labeled the Clandestine Communist Organization (CCO).[7]

In Indonesia, the large and powerful Parti Komunis Indonesia (Indonesian Communist Party, PKI) was legally recognized and politically active. Thousands of Chinese youth therefore left Sarawak to undergo training in the jungles of Indonesia in preparation for liberating their homeland in line with communist ideology. During this Konfrontasi period, which lasted more than three years, between 10,000 and 15,000 British troops were stationed in Sarawak, and Australia and New Zealand sent troops to protect East Malaysia, as did West Malaysia.[8]

Konfrontasi ended with dramatic and devastating political change in Indonesia. On October 1, 1965, a group of soldiers attacked and murdered several generals and high-ranking officers of the Indonesian armed forces. Suharto replaced Sukarno, who began negotiations to bring military confrontation to an end, and a peace agreement was finally signed on August 11, 1966.

Konfrontasi and the Communist Insurgency

The hinterland of Lundu District experienced political turmoil in the postcolonial period. Located on the border between newly independent nation-states, the region became a political frontier and the frontline

[7] For political developments from Konfrontasi to communist insurgency in West Kalimantan, see Davidson and Kammen (2002) and Davidson (2008).

[8] For a historical description and analysis of the Indonesia-Malaysia Confrontation, see Mackie (1974) and Dickens (1991).

of strife. In the two decades following independence from British colonial rule, Konfrontasi and the communist insurgency intensified the economic, ethnic, and national displacement of borderland communities in Lundu.

During Konfrontasi, fighting between Malaysian allied forces and Indonesian soldiers took place in areas on the Malaysia-Indonesia border. More than a dozen battles of military confrontation were officially recorded in Lundu District (Dickens 1991). There were numerous routine encounters with soldiers, and more than a dozen peasant communities in Malaysia were guarded by British Gurkha soldiers from Nepal and soldiers from the Malay Peninsula, and there was a strict curfew.

Peace returned with the 1966 pact, and following the restoration of diplomatic relations, on May 26, 1967, the two nations concluded a new agreement governing relations between border communities. The agreement specified the basic procedure for border crossing by Malaysian and Indonesian nationals residing in what was called the Border Area, stipulating that anyone who wished to cross the national boundary had to present a Border Pass for endorsement at border control posts. Sarawak posts were established at Biawak, Kandai, Stass, Serikin, Gumbang, Sapit, Tepoi, Pang Amo, Pelaman Mapu, Bunan Gega, Telagus, Padawan, Batu Lintang, Lubuk Antu, and Ba Kelalan. Those wishing to obtain a border pass had to provide their name, sex, identity card number, date and place of birth, height, hair color, visible distinguishing marks, address, occupation, photograph, and signature or right thumbprint (Bala 2002).

The tranquility of the 1966 peace was short-lived. From the early 1970s to the late 1980s, communist insurgents were active in this remote border area. Guerrillas took refuge in the ideal dense forest of the borderland. The very last surrender of communists to the authorities in Sematan sub-district occurred in 1988.

Konfrontasi and communist activity in the area's primary jungle furthered the separation of the borderland communities from the newly inscribed national terrain in two related ways. One was the disassociation of peasant society from the state's project of economic integration. Military confrontation and communist insurgency not only stopped cross-border trade, but also paralyzed the socio-economic network connecting Lundu's regional bazaars with the state capital of Kuching. The consequent exclusion of the Lundu hinterland from the nation-wide commodity network caused economic stagnation. Instead of being connected to newly emergent national and international markets, many farmers became dependent on shifting rice cultivation for subsistence, even if they had earlier been engaged in commodity production. The military zone became a new frontier, and subsequent communist activities along the border made the implementation of state development programs difficult throughout the 1970s and into the early 1980s.

Further dislocation took place in the realm of social affiliation, where newly demarcated nationalities clashed with existing ethnic symbiosis across the national boundary. This involved two distinct social processes. First, military confrontation swiftly and violently drew an absolute political boundary between Malaysia and Indonesia, resulting in the sudden formation of the social categories "Malaysian" and "Indonesian". Unlike the porous colonial boundary between the Sambas District of Dutch West Borneo and the Lundu District of the Brookes' Sarawak, the border demarcation between the independent nation-states was concretized by the presence of military and border posts. Indonesian and Malaysian soldiers were stationed face to face, and as enemy Malaysians, locals became subject to Indonesian military attack. Dayaks, Malays, and Chinese who shared ethnic nomenclature and cultural elements with communities across the border became divided between warring geo-polities. Yet this transnational socio-economic symbiosis was resilient all along the frontier where Sarawak meets Indonesia.

From an Economic to a Political Frontier

The advent of rubber cultivation in western Borneo marked a new era for the borderland, tying the periphery of the European colonial empire directly to the international commodity market. The 1920s was a turning point, as the focus of commodity production shifted from pepper, gambier, and coconut to rubber. Market demand for rubber rose as the supply was restricted through the Stevenson Restriction Scheme (1922–28), and there was a temporary price recovery that peaked in 1925 before declining toward the end of the decade. Thereafter, the Great Depression resulted in a prolonged slump of the market and further intervention by the government in rubber production and export. The International Rubber Regulation Agreement (IRRA) of 1934 was invoked by rubber-producing colonies in the tropics as a way of sustaining prices when the Great Depression began to ease.

The regulation of cultivation and export through a national quota system resulted in tighter control of the cross-border movement of dutiable rubber sheets. When a series of regulations banned new rubber planting and controlled harvesting, some peasants in the hinterland abandoned rubber and reverted to planting coconut trees and pepper vines. Some also resorted to other measures, and the transnational smuggling of rubber from Dutch West Borneo to Sarawak flourished. The interwar years became a special period in the history of the borderland, as rubber cultivators and merchants waged undeclared war against a European regime that tried to inhibit the activity of rubber smallholders in favor of the colonial plantation system.

The development of a large-scale smuggling economy in the borderland coincided with the economic process in which a colonial (and then a national) state with a porous boundary gradually transformed itself into a single economic unit. When the state tried to implement an income-generating taxation system, the borderland residents of western Borneo responded by engaging in cross-border smuggling, making the borderline ever more permeable.

The border trade also reflected the economic positioning of neighboring countries. During the five decades of the rubber economy up to the 1960s, rubber sheets were smuggled in one direction, from Dutch Borneo/West Kalimantan to Sarawak. The economic chaos of post-independence Indonesia also led to illicit commodity flows in goods ranging from *batik* cloth to logs. The magnitude of such activities made contraband trade "the second economy of Lundu District" (*SG*, March 31, 1960: 59).

The hinterland of Lundu District adjacent to the border remained in curious isolation at the periphery of the colonial space during the heyday of smuggling. In responding to imperial networking within and beyond state territory, local communities on both sides of the border had established socio-economic symbiosis through the transnational flows of people and goods. However, these transnational chains were suddenly broken, when the Republic of Indonesia and the newly-formed Malaysia engaged in geo-political rivalry starting in 1963. The borderland was then transformed into a politically charged new frontier where a series of violent events directly related to international politics occurred — first, military confrontation between Indonesia and Malaysia, known as Konfrontasi, and then guerilla activities by communist cells in the jungle adjacent to the border.

This chapter has argued that ethnic symbiosis as well as tension generated along the social interface of the national border has its origin in boundary inscription during trans-border *smokel* era, Konfrontasi, and communist insurgency. The divergence between a newly imposed nationality distinguishing "enemies" from "us" and the local identity and economic interests transnationally shared by border residents generated two opposing social vectors: hegemonic separation on the nation-state level and local-level symbiosis based on daily interaction between communities on both sides of the boundary. Nationality inscribed on the locals divided them, yet cross-border interaction in the peripheralized border zone has remained strong and was essential for the survival of local communities, particularly when out-of-the-way communities in close proximity were excluded from the socio-economic networks of their respective territorial states.

A Prelude to Part II

While Part I of this study has examined the historical trajectories of the colonial borderland up to the independence of Sarawak in 1963, Part II is an ethnography of a community at the northern extremity of Lundu District. With the extension of temporal frame up to the present and the focus down to a critical point of state territory, Part II links the everyday lifeworld of borderland residents to the larger histories told in previous chapters. Part I and Part II thus form a set of nested structures that provide viewpoints on various scales.

Telok Melano is a Muslim community whose boundary coincides with an international border. This hinterland village of the Sarawak Malays was strategically chosen as an alternative to the conceptually closed functional whole that ethnographers conventionally examine. Described by the residents as *hujung Malaysia* (the edge of Malaysia), the village is located at the margin of the state, where a local but transnational symbiosis has clashed with the postcolonial project of nation-state making.

Although the following chapters are in essence a village ethnography, the frame of reference goes well beyond the conventional units of analysis. As an ethnographic locale, it eludes the analytical limits of "community" and even "state". Dealing with a settlement connected to the other side of national space, my analysis is intended to be relational in order to illuminate the transnational nature of a community whose history, culture, and ethnicity are at odds with the national order of things.

The emergence of a center-periphery relationship in the making of the geo-body of the territorial state has been a crucial factor for the uneven expansion of national life. My examination, on the one hand, shows the artificiality and transience of social classifications, categories and boundaries, molded by a continuous exclusivist-inclusivist struggle for the making of national space, and on the other hand, it reveals the creativity and innovativeness of social actors as well as their consciousness and competency in coping with the complex everyday existence in order to eke out a living on the border. While the discussion is grounded in a particular example from the corner of Borneo, the issue is general, and my argument is intended to raise questions of border identity.

PART II

Inscribing a Village and a Nation on the Border

CHAPTER FOUR

On the Periphery

Encounter with a Malay Community

I caught my first glimpse of Cape Dato from the beach near Pueh village. It was my first visit to Sematan, a sub-district of Lundu, a trip made in order to select a coastal community for fieldwork, and a Sarawak Malay anthropologist kindly brought me there on the back seat of his 125 cc motorcycle. After a four-hour ride from Kuching on a dusty, bumpy mountain road, I was more than relieved when we finally reached a Dayak longhouse near the port of Sematan. After greeting the headman and people in the village, we walked down to the beach to stretch our aching backs. The setting was picturesque, a broad stretch of white sand and casuarina trees. After pointing out Mount Pueh and other local spots of interest, my fellow anthropologist pointed across the sea to a promontory that marked the border of Indonesia and Malaysia. On Cape Dato, Malays lived in complete seclusion planting hill rice by swidden cultivation.

Cape Dato was barely visible in the distance. What first intrigued me was its remoteness, the absolute isolation of these villagers living there from other Malaysian communities. Indonesian territory is much closer to Cape Dato than is Sematan, the nearest Malaysian town. Nor is there any road or path through the long stretch of abandoned coconut plantations and full-grown secondary forest between the cape and Sematan. The villagers come to Sematan by boat to buy market goods, and the journey takes several hours. The exact time of the trip depends on the size of the boat's engine and the weight of the passengers and cargo. During the northeast monsoon season (October to March), strong currents and extremely high waves make it impossible to travel along the coast by boat. Then residents have to walk eight hours along the beach at low tide to reach Sematan (see Fig. 9).

The people of Cape Dato are the only Malays practicing swidden agriculture. In the delta near Kuching, where Malay communities are concentrated, economic activities are very much oriented toward the sea, and include fishing and planting coconut trees along the coast. My understanding of Sarawak Malays at the time did not go beyond the essentialist definitions of ethnographic and historical writings, which underline the coastal/riverine economic niche that most Malays occupy in Sarawak. In orthodox ethnographies, Malays have typically been depicted as coastal fishermen, coconut/rubber planters, and petty traders, but never as subsistence farmers in the tropical forest (Abang Yusuf Puteh 1996, Harrison 1970, Leach 1950, Sanib Said 1985, Zainal Kling 1973).

Sitting at a coffee shop at Sematan bazaar, I was told, "If you check the Identification Cards of the people here, you would see that many of them are Indonesians, or former Indonesians who have applied to become Malaysian." I observed the port traffic and noticed several ships with the Indonesian flag ferrying goods to and from Indonesia. Tanned, thin, yet strongly built Indonesian sailors carrying fuel tanks and other daily necessities onto wooden boats were a common sight. Sematan is essentially a frontier port, where the Indonesian accent is part of daily life.

The hinterland Malay community I first glimpsed during my trip to Sematan was Telok Melano, situated at the heart of the Indonesian and Malaysian borderland, an area geo-politically once divided between two ancient sultanates, and later by colonial and postcolonial states. The village was a tiny historical enclave in the middle of nowhere.

It did not take me long to decide that Telok Melano was a promising place to conduct fieldwork. The village is located at the most peripheral part of Lundu District, on which I had been collecting information through the intensive reading of the *Sarawak Gazette* and travelogues written by British colonial officers. I thought it was the most critical point in the borderland of Lundu, a place that would provide a microcosm of a border society. My primordial desire as a fieldworker to observe and think about borderlands by placing myself right on the border also attracted me to this out-of-the-way village. In addition, I have an interest in people who are not "ethnographically correct", and this is the reason I did not choose a prototypical "Sarawak Malay" village. It was the early 1990s, and anthropologists were starting to question "essentialism" in their ethnographic endeavors, and to avoid creating a single image of a culture, an ethnic group, or a tradition. Rather than carving out a representative anthropological discourse on the Malays in Sarawak by conducting research in the cultural heartland of the Sarawak River Delta and Kuching, I wanted to place and to investigate the Sarawak Malays in a dislocated social field created by nation and state, specifically, in a cultural, political, and economic border zone.

When I returned to Kuching, I told local scholars and government officials that I was interested in conducting fieldwork in Telok Melano. When I explained that the villagers were not fishermen but farmers, and that their subsistence depended largely on cultivation of hill rice with minimal involvement in cash crop production, the official who originally suggested a pilot study trip to Sematan seemed apprehensive about a foreigner conducting research in a community not offering an "ethnographically correct" picture of Malays. Others implicitly suggested that I choose another field site because I would not find any "Sarawak Malay culture" among these Malay folks in the border region, and some staff members at the Sarawak Museum let me know in a roundabout way that people on the coast used to be smugglers.

Some of my Malay friends in Kuching, on hearing that the community was near the international border and the people practiced swidden agriculture, were also dubious about the ethnicity of Telok Melano, and asked, "Are they really Muslims?" By then it was clear to me that the villagers did not represent typical "Sarawak Malays". In this part of Borneo, slash and burn agriculture in the forest is a distinctive cultural trait of inland Dayaks, whose religion, whether pagan or Christian, distinguishes them from Muslim Malays. The geo-political isolation of the Malays from the state capital, and their close proximity to Indonesia, has much to do with their peripheral social standing as Sarawak Malays.

As my wife and I were busy with shopping and packing before leaving for Telok Melano, our Malay neighbors in Kuching, who knew the borderland warned us, "Just be careful dealing with village folks there. They are already mixed with Indonesians as well as local Dayaks and their *ilmu* [magical power] is quite strong." They kindly prepared a Muslim charm, an amulet to fend off misfortunes caused by "*ilmu hitam*" (black magic, a term often used for sorcery). We put several shallots in our bags on the advice of the neighbors, who said that they offered protection against sorcery.

We headed for Telok Melano with the amulet and shallots hidden in our bags. We did not want to offend people by bringing them to the village, but could not leave them behind. It was already October and the beginning of *landas*, the northeastern monsoon season. Our journey by sea was extremely rough. Right after we left the port of Sematan, it started pouring, and the waves grew larger the further we went. Then the Yamaha engine in our chartered boat broke down. After the boatman struggled with a small paddle for what seemed an eternity, we finally landed on the shore not far from the port where we began our journey. The boatman hurried back to borrow another engine. When we finally reached Telok Melano, it was late at night. The Islamic Jawi script on both sides of the amulet, exposed to sea water for so long, had become unreadable red stains, but we still kept it, grateful that it helped fend off the danger posed by the South China Sea. Thus began our fieldwork in Telok Melano.

Ethnography as Time-Space Extension

The ethnography of Part II is more concerned with the part of "nation" in a hyphenated "nation-state". In contrast to Part I, where the main focus is on the state apparatus for territorialization and structural determinants affecting the nature of national space, the following chapters are intended to approach agency of people on the ground. Two kinds of ethnographic extension will be added to the regional history.

The first extension is spatial. Tightening the ethnographic lens from an administrative district to a village, Part II presents the microscopic dynamics of the borderland. A regional history of Lundu District and a village history at the margin of the state complement each other, forming a nested structure of description and explanation. Introducing actual faces and voices of people of Telok Melano village, located at a critical point of the state dominion, gives body and substance to the larger story told in previous chapters.

The second extension is temporal. Carefully piling up the local micro-history of Telok Melano on the colonial history, the border history will extend itself up to the year of 2006. The historical documents, which often took a form of inaccessible confidential reports prepared during Konfrontasi and communist guerrilla insurgency, will be supplemented by the local microhistory of a border zone.

The two extensions, both spatial and temporal, are important, enabling me to work on transnational ethnography and to connect histories from above and below. Let me explain first the spatial extension and its implications to the following ethnography.

Conducting long-term anthropological participant observation in a community where the village border coincides with the national boundary enabled me to bring transnationalism "down-to-earth". Working on transnationalism through field research has been an important agenda for anthropologists for years, but methodologically it has been also difficult. Talking about transnationalism by conceptually connecting social phenomena across national boundaries under the structural forces of socio-economic networking and coercion is one thing. But examining everyday transnational flows and movements at eye level through conventionally anthropological "fixed-point" observation is another. It is easier said than done. The following ethnography is an attempt of transnational ethnography, but without complicated epistemology. Simply locating myself in the socio-economic interface between two nation-states, I conducted fieldwork in a quite conventional sense, examining everyday transactions between a Malaysian and an Indonesian community sharing an international boundary.

The second extension, in time, produced an unexpected byproduct — the encounter with Haji Taha, Nakoda Hitam, and other Malay traders recorded in the *Sarawak Gazette* in the vivid memories of villagers as founders of communities and ancestors. Telok Melano village served as a connecting point between colonial history and local memory. Let me briefly explain the long journey we took from the colonial documents at a corner of the Sarawak Museum Library to the realm of local memories.

In order to reconstruct regional history of Lundu District, after the acquisition of a research permit from the Sarawak State Planning Unit, my wife and I started reading the *Sarawak Gazette*, and particularly the "Monthly Lundu District Report" prepared by colonial officers. Everyday from 8:15 am to 4:00 pm (with time out for lunch), we took notes on everything related to Lundu District and its borderland. The *Sarawak Gazette* was deteriorating because it was printed on acidic paper, and we could not make photocopies of articles. It took us a good half of a year to cover the years 1871 to 1963, the point when we decided to end our archival exploration of Lundu District. After the independence of Sarawak and its incorporation into Malaysia, the section containing district-based reports disappeared owing to a change in format. The activities of "Clandestine Communist Organization" (CCO) in border zones also affected the nature of administrative reports because national security-related issues became confidential.

The *Sarawak Gazette* is a unique resource, featuring detailed reports made by officers stationed in outstations. With their command of Sarawak Malay dialect, a basic requirement for Sarawak colonial officers, and possibly because they had ample time to kill in rural postings, they sent detailed monthly reports on the matters of their districts. These reports, filled with lively descriptions of local events, provide a first-class social history of colonial Sarawak. From an account of how many punctures a Jagoi Dayak boy received on his head when hit by a falling durian, to how Sambas Malay family members died of food poisoning after eating mangrove crabs, that included circumstantial descriptions of decaying conditions and the order of death, to fights among Chinese coolies in opium dens and drinking places and numbers of coolies who hanged themselves out of depression, to detailed statistical data on the number of newly opened coconut plantations, the district reports are an incomparable source of colonial microhistories on Sarawak.

We were extremely fortunate to see the convergence of such colonial record with the oral history collected in Telok Melano. Before departing for the village for fieldwork, we had already become familiar with the substantial numbers of names of people and places recorded by the colonial officers stationed at the Lundu Fort. With the 11 volumes of archival fieldnotes, we became strange local ethnographers, since we had never visited the area.

After starting our fieldwork, whenever villagers mentioned the names of people and places we had been acquainted with, with great excitement, we hurriedly went back to the pages of our notes to find them. Retrospectively locating old friends and familiar places in the notebooks, now we connect the colonial records and local memories. This temporal convergence enabled us not only to explore the micro-macro nexus in time and space but also to grasp the nature of people acting as agents within structural historical forces.

The Landscape of Telok Melano

Telok Melano is a Malay village administratively located in Sematan Sub-District, Lundu District, Kuching Division (former First Division) of Sarawak, Malaysia. Sematan Sub-District has 23 administrative villages in approximately 390 square kilometers, comprised of three major ethnic groups, i.e., Malay, Selako Dayak, and Chinese, respectively occupying coastal area, inland, and town bazaar area, with the exception of Pueh longhouses of the Selako Dayaks on the Sematan coast.

Table 13 The Population of Sematan Sub-District (1991)

Ethnic group	*Population*	*Household Numbers*
Malay	2,553	436
Selako	2,581	343
Chinese	686	103
Total	6,102	882

Source: Sematan Sub-District Office, 1991.

Telok Melano is the most southwestward village in Sarawak, and the closest to Indonesian Kalimantan. Between Sematan and Cape Dato, there are no settlements except Telok Melano and Telok Serabang. There were Malay communities along the 40-kilometer coast until Indonesian military aggression in 1963, and one can still find a series of plantation sites with old, unproductive coconut trees and dense secondary forest. At the river mouths of Bekuching, Belingsa, and Samunsan, there are the heavy concentrations of coconut tress, a reminder of Malay *nakoda* entrepreneurship (see Fig. 9 and Illus. 2).

Proceeding by boat from Sematan, travelers see a set of turtle-shaped islands, namely Talang Talang Kecil and Talang Talang Besar

Illus. 5 Overlooking Telok Melano Bay

on the right. The islands are egg-laying sites of sea turtles and under the management of the Turtle Board of the Sarawak Museum. On the left, a low mountain range separates Sarawak and West Kalimantan, eventually converging on a 30 square centimeter official concrete panel that makes the international boundary at Cape Dato (see Illus. 20).

Telok Melano village is located on the coast between Samunsan wildlife sanctuary and the Cape Dato National Park, surrounded by old secondary forest. As already stated, during the northeast monsoon season, rough currents and high waves prevent villagers from using boats, and they simply walk eight hours along the beach at low tide to reach Sematan. At such times, visiting Indonesia on foot is much safer and easier for many Telok Melano people in need of daily goods.

Entering shallow Melano Bay, one sees a very typical Malay *kampung* (village) with wooden houses on stilts surrounded by coconut tress. The village once won a contest and was declared the most beautiful *kampung* in Sarawak. There are several traditional houses whose roof and walls are all made from palm leaves. The total number of households in 1994, when I first visited the village, was 41 with a total population of 211 (male 108, female 103). The population is all Muslim with an exception of a Chinese man. There are six Indonesians married to the villagers, all in the process of naturalization.

Twenty houses are lined up along a small village path and 17 others are located elsewhere in the compound. There are also four houses scattered in the jungle and a weed-infested plain adjacent to the Indonesian border. The Chinese house is situated at the edge of the village compound. A Chinese man in his 50s, a second generation immigrant from Leizhou, Guangdong Province, earns his living by hunting wild boars in the jungle. Wild boars are not hunted by Muslim villagers, and they are abundant. He hunts them with a sharpened bamboo, and sells salted meat to Chinese merchants in Lundu. Villagers sometimes call him "anak komunis" (a child of communists) but their overall relationship with him is good, and some of them have fictive kin relations with him. There are also two Dayak teachers living at school compound at the edge of village, along with three Malay teachers from Kuching and West Malaysia. Teachers stationed in remote villages such as Telok Melano receive priority if they seek transfers to more congenial places.

The village has no permanent supply of electricity. From 7:00 to 11:00 pm, a village-owned generator is supposed to provide electricity every night, for which residents pay M$11 every month. However,

Illus. 6 Telok Melano village

Illus. 7 The arrival from Sematan to Telok Melano

they experience many nights of darkness owing to shortages of oil and mechanical breakdowns of the generator. Piped water reaches individual households from the neighboring river. Propane gas tanks purchased in Sematan are used for daily cooking, but many households still use older hearths for coconut oil making and smoking fish.

There are many dogs walking around and chasing each other in the village compound. This is an astonishing sight to Muslim visitors from Kuching and other towns. Not to mention, they are not treated as pets, but tolerated because they chase away wild boars from coconut plantations. Those who raise chickens inland to avoid the spread of infectious diseases keep dogs for their protection, and sometimes give them names and take them hunting.

Houses are located inside of coconut plantations. Along a path houses are lined up, facing each other. From childhood, the lesson not to stand under coconut trees is internalized. Falling coconuts fronds and seeds and ocean waves are part of the soundscape of Telok Melano. In the back of the village compound is secondary forest used for swidden agriculture over many generations. In addition to two

Illus. 8 The traditional and modern houses on stilts

main paths connecting Telok Melano to an Indonesian migrant village of Temajuk and to a neighboring Malaysian village of Telok Serabang, there are several paths leading to *padi*, cacao, pepper, and rubber fields. The cultivation of cash crops such as pepper and cacao is pursued minimally. Many of the pepper fields, for instance, just have *belian* (ironwood) poles standing idle in fields covered in weeds (see Appendix, Agriculture in Telok Melano).

While swidden cultivation of hill *padi* has been intensively carried out for generations, marine resource utilization has been minimal in Telok Melano. For many of the villagers, boats are a means of transportation and not used for fishing. Housewives and their children often come out to the sea side to "hunt" small fish in tidal pools, paralyzing them with the juice of *akar tuba* (a poisonous plant root), and then striking them with *parang* (a machete-like knife). Small oyster shells are also collected by women and brought to Sematan for sale. Other than these seashore gatherings, fishing is a minor activity in the village.

The international border between Malaysia and Indonesia is approximately three kilometers from the village compound of Telok Melano. A small and winding path takes you to the border, where

Illus. 9 A village elder making up a traditional prescription

Illus. 10 The children of Telok Melano

Illus. 11 A border gate separating Telok Melano (Malaysia) and Temajuk (Indonesia)

you go through a wooden gate bearing the words "Selamat Datang di Indonesia" (Welcome to Indonesia). The gate was constructed and has been maintained by the Indonesian hamlet of Tekam Patah, one of five hamlets that make up Temajuk village, whose population now amounts to 1,300.

Telok Melano people have been dependent on swidden agriculture for their survival since the maritime networks of *nakoda* traders were cut up by the boundary-making activities of colonial governments. Its history is closely linked to the long process through which Sarawak Kingdom, the British Crown colony, and then Malaysia have emerged as territorially independent sovereign states. To comprehend the historical experience of the village on the national border requires careful examination of how people have lived in and dealt with political, economic, and cultural interfaces between two nation-states.

Pirate Bay: The Creation of a Maritime Frontier

The earliest account of Cape Dato was written by an Italian botanist who visited the area to collect samples in 1864. There were no villages there at the time:

> We came to anchor near the westernmost extremity of Borneo, in a small cove, which my Malays called Telok Saruban, or Serban [Serabang]. Here we found a spring of excellent water, and used it at once to cook our rice. After our very frugal breakfast, I started to climb the small mountain which rose at our backs. Naturally, in such out-of-the-way and uninhabited places, there were no paths. The place, and, indeed, the whole coast as far as Santubong, had a bad name for being the habitual resort, during the fair season, of the prahus [boats] of the Lanuns and Balangini, the boldest and most dreaded pirates of the whole archipelago, and Telok Serban was their favorite anchorage (Beccari 1904: 225).

Cape Dato and neighboring inlets, collectively known as "Pirate Bay" by Brooke-era colonial officers, were frequented by pirates from the southern Philippines seeking fresh water and firewood as well as refuge from storms. According to Hugh Low the west coast of Borneo was:

> annually infested by the fleets from the Soolu Archipelago, which, leaving their own islands, situated on the N.E. of Borneo, about the middle of the N.E. monsoon, sail round the island with a fair wind, stretching across to the coasts of Java, Banca, Singapore, and the peninsula, and visiting all the islands in the way, attacking all the trading boats they meet, and carrying their crews into slavery, frequently landing and capturing the whole of the inhabitants of small villages (Low 1848: 129).

According to Low, Serabang Bay, located next to the present Telok Melano village, attracted many pirates:

> Teluk Serban, a bay inside of Tanjong Dattu, and opposite to the islands Telang Telang, was a station occupied during the S.W. monsoon by the pirates of Soolu and Magandanau. Here their principal fleet lay anchored, while small and fast cruisers in the offing constantly communicated to them the appearance of a sail: a force deemed sufficient was immediately sent out to capture it, when, if it proved to be from a distance, the slaves or goods were sent into Sarawak or Sadong rivers to the sereibs, who then governed this part of the coast, in exchange for provisions and other necessaries, of which their long absence from home had exhausted their stock; the prisoners captured in the neighborhood were handcuffed and bound until their captors were ready, on the approach of the boisterous monsoon, to return to their island homes (Low 1848: 128–9).

Like other Europeans in the nineteenth-century Southeast Asia, the first white Rajah, James Brooke, was inclined to label all of his numerous and varied local opponents "pirates". He used this word partly because he believed that his enemies were willful, lawless adversaries of free trade and good government, and partly because he hoped that public opinion in maritime England would be disposed to support "anti-piracy" campaigns (Pringle 1970: 66–7). James Brooke left a vivid description of his encounter with pirates at Talang Talang Island and Siru near Sematan in 1842:

> In the evening the Tumangong came over with certain news that the pirate Budrudeen was at Siru with eight followers; his band ashore, and he living in a house in the village. Abu Bakar, with a crew of fifteen men, chiefly Illanuns, I found living ashore at Talang Talang, with a small boat, and a huge long six-pounder in her, which, fired twice, must have separated her planks. I learned, also, that six Balinini boats had been to Talang Talang, and had had a friendly conference with Sheriff Abu Bakar....
>
> Arrived at Siru, I found the patingi waiting till the pangeran and the Illanun panglima came to the beach; and to prevent suspicion, my party kept close in the boat, whence I could observe what was passing without. The pangeran and Illanun walked down, both well armed, and the latter dressed out with a variety of charms. Once on the beach, retreat was impossible, for our people surrounded them, though without committing any hostile act. The suspicion of the two was, however, raised, and it was curious to observe their different demeanour. The Borneo pangeran remained quiet, silent, and motionless; a child might have taken him; the Magindinao Illanun lashed himself to desperation, flourishing his spear in one hand, and the other on the handle of his sword, he defied those collected about him: he danced his war-dance on the sand: his face became deadly pale: his wild eyes glared: he was ready to amok, to die, but not to die alone. His time was come, for he was dangerous, and to catch him was impossible; and accordingly, Patingi Ali, walking past, leaped forward, and struck a spear through his back, far between his shoulders, half a foot out his breast. I had no idea that after such a thrust, a man could, even for a few instants, exert himself; but the panglima, after receiving his mortal wound, rushed forward with his spear, and thrust it at the breast of another man; but strength and life failed, and the weapon did not enter. This was a work of a few seconds (Mundy 1848: 307–9).

As examined in Chapter 1, numerous Malay communities were established in the area by Sambas Malays migrating from Dutch territory in the 1880s and 1890s, but before that time the Sematan-Lundu coast was sparsely populated, with just a small number of Malay communities consisting of local Dayak converts and migrants. When James Brooke first visited Lundu from Singapore in 1839, he asked a Lundu Dayak man how many of them had converted to Islam, and he was told "a good many" (Mundy 1848: 24). Brooke himself also left an early description of Sematan in 1842:

> Siru and Samatan [Sematan] are both fishing stations. At the former place is a colony of Kadyans from Borneo — originally, only six or seven men, now amounting to thirty families, from having intermarried with the Dyaks and Malays. These Kadyans are Islamites, and form the rural population of Borneo, where they are numerous (Mundy 1848: 310).

At that time, the Malay population in Sematan included immigrants from Brunei and from Trengganu, the Malay Peninsula, as well as local Dayak converts to Islam. Their communities were widely scattered on the coast and inland and coexisted side-by-side with those of Selako Dayaks. Even in 1894, there were only 34 Malay houses in the Sematan area — nine at Sematan; nine at Sabahat, "where sub-Magistrate of Sematan, Lebi Maludin resides"; eight at S'Larat, "near the westerly slopes of Lundu mountain"; six at Poi, "about six miles along the coast"; and two at "S'bako pangkalan" (*SG*, January 2, 1894: 10).

Alienating Origins

The historical process of formation of the Malay communities in the Cape Dato area in a sense excluded them from national space right from the start. Telok Serabang, the older of the two villages in the vicinity of Cape Dato, was established mostly by migrants from Dutch Borneo territory; subsequent migration extended to Telok Melano. Rajah Charles Brooke himself, allowed no Sarawak subjects, but only outsiders to settle this frontier region of his colony. The following account by a village elder in Telok Serabang offers some clues to understanding how Telok Serabang and Telok Melano took shape:

> Until lately this place was not inhabited, except by a party of pirates originating from Kepayang, Manila, and stationed at Tanjong [Cape]

Pirate which is known as Tanjong Keramat by the local people now. The chief of the pirates was Batin Begentar. This pirate caused great trouble to vessels sailing between Sarawak, Java, Sumatra, Brunei, Malaya, etc. During the reign of the First Rajah this news came to him. He not long after equipped his steamer with fighting armed men, headed by Panglima Seman; they sailed for Tanjong Pirates, to attack the pirates there.

On sighting a steamer approaching the land, the pirates thought she was a merchant's ship and went out to sea in full strength to attack her. When the two parties clashed, a fierce fight ensued. During the fighting, Batin Begentar met Penglima Seman; and after a long fight, Penglima Seman was able to defeat him by catching him alive.

The Rajah noticed, during the fighting, that Batin Begentar was a very strong man. No weapon could pierce his body. When the pirate was defeated, the Rajah ordered those arrested to be bought to Kuching, but Batin Begentar to be killed on the spot, by tying a piece of iron to his body and throwing him into the sea, then towing him with the steamer. This was done. But it did not cause him any harm. The next order was to throw him into the steamer's boiler. This caused him no harm, too. Then he was placed in the funnel of the steamer, head downward, until killed by choking of smoke. The body was buried at an unknown spot.

On arrival at Kuching, the Rajah ordered his men to select each of the remaining pirates to be taken as servants. Some of the good-looking ones were selected. Those who appeared to be fierce and bad were ordered to be slain. When this was over, the Rajah ordered that Telok Serabang was not to be inhabited by Sarawak people, but open to any person or family from outside Sarawak. The reason was that Sarawak people naturally did not know the characters of outside people, but the outsiders surely knew the habits of their own.

As soon as this order was made known, people from Sambas and the Natuna Islands removed here and made this place their home, to start gardening, farming and fishing.

During the reign of the Second Rajah, approximately fifty families, headed by Penghulu Taha from Kampong Melano, Mempawah (West Borneo), obtained permission to reside here. As the place was fully occupied, these people then were given permission to make a new settlement at Telok Melano, which was named according to their original homeland. The name Telok Melano remains as it is now (Harrisson n.d.: 418–9).

From the viewpoint of administrators in Sarawak, these frontier communities settled by non-Sarawakians were marginal to the colonial establishment, but served a crucial function as a buffer between Sarawak and Dutch Borneo territory. The formation of frontier Malay communities corresponds to the first two decades of the Second Rajah's reign, the critical period of state formation and territorial encroachment by the colonial administration.

Immigrants from across the border continued to form Malay communities along the Cape Dato coast. The region was no longer infested with lawless pirates, but instead fell under the influence of the state's social engineering. As examined in Chapters 1 and 2, plantation communities were formed with the intention of developing an export-oriented peasant economy.

In the 1890s, *nakoda* traders began to develop Telok Serabang and Telok Melano. As stated in the village elder's account cited above, one of the pioneers was Haji (Penghulu) Taha from Mempawah in Dutch West Borneo, whose name is still remembered in Telok Melano as one of the founders of the village. Haji Taha's activities are well recorded by the colonial office:

> On the 16th a man named Pengeran Seman reported that he had come over from Sambas directed by one Haji Taha to look at the land at Simunsan, as the later wished to come over with a following of 30 families. I advised P. Sean to look at the land and coffee in this neighborhood adding that during the N. E. monsoon the people would find themselves a good deal shut in at Simunsum. He reports that there is likely to be a movement after the harvest (*SG*, February 1, 1894: 24).
>
> On the 28th I [the Assistant Resident] left Simunsam arriving there next morning. Hj. Taha, the chief, has planted 600 cocoanuts which are looking well; he is clearing land for more. A number of small clearings have lately been made along the coast by Sambas people who are said to be going to settle here (*SG*, October 1, 1896: 202).
>
> The plantations made by Hj. Taha and his followers at Telok Serabang and Telok Melano are doing exceedingly well and are expected to fruit a little in another two years. More people are coming to join Hj. Taha this year and will settle at Telok Serabang or near Kuala Samunsam where Hj. Taha has now made a second plantation (*SG*, August 1, 1899: 261).

Opening a new coconut plantation on the uninhabited coast required hard labor to clear the virgin forest. All phases of copra production, from planting seeds, to weeding, harvesting, husking and drying seeds, also involved substantial labor. *Nakoda* entrepreneurs thus brought Malay peasants from the Dutch territory to supply labor to their plantations. The scale of labor migration was relatively large. Several dozen families moved together to the new frontier under the direction of *nakoda* entrepreneurs. The sailing could have been dangerous because of rapid currents and high waves off Cape Dato. Even today, a number of motor-equipped Indonesian ships are wrecked each year in the area.

> On the 13th I visited Simatan and on the 15th I proceeded to Telok Serabang where I met Haji Taha of Mempawa, who arrived at the same time with a number of his people. He reported that seven boats, with seventy men, women and children, left Mempawa on the 6th instant. Unfortunately one boat, the day before (14th), struck a rock off the mouth of S. Temajok during a squall, the occupants — four men — escaping with their property with the exception of 100 gantangs of padi. Two boats had arrived; two were with the people who came to grief, and two, for some reason or other, had been delayed en route. The Haji reported that one Merali, a Sambas Tuah, intends coming over with fifteen families to settle in Telok Serabang (*SG*, October 1, 1895: 185).
>
> The Acting Resident directed me to pay a sum of $20 to the Mempawa people who were wrecked on their passage to Serabang last August (*SG*, January 2, 1896: 12).

According to local stories collected in Telok Melano, Haji Taha brought along his children, grandchildren, a traditional medicine man, a midwife, and carpenters on migrating to Telok Melano from Semudun village near Mempawah in Dutch Borneo. Descendants of these pioneers in Telok Melano without exception still claim their place of origin as Semudun village, and it seems likely that many migrants also left Telok Melano, either to return home or to move elsewhere.[1]

[1] In 1895, a Chinese rebellion was reported in the Sambas region, and Mempawah, where Semudun village is located, was under threat of Chinese attack: "Rumours have come round from Sambas to the effect that the Chinese at Mandore were about to attack Dayaks of Mampawah and that the Dutch would side with the latter" (*SG*, July 1, 1895: 125–6). However, the relationship, if any, between Malay migration from Mempawah and political turmoil in the region remains unclear due to the lack of further information.

The pioneer settlers of Telok Melano and other communities on the Sematan-Cape Dato coast were mobile peasants seeking a better future despite the high risk involved. Newly developed communities were often surrounded by thick virgin forest, and there was a great deal of illness among the residents. The hazardous environment was also a factor keeping the peasants on the move:

> Foolish superstitions about this part of the coast led these people to believe they had built their houses on paths used by spirits causing sickness amongst them. It has been explained that settling on newly felled virgin forest generally causes sickness at first (*SG*, November 1, 1895: 20).
>
> A good many people have gone away on account of sickness, about a dozen deaths having occurred last year among the small community scattered between Blinsah and Telok Milano (*SG*, August 1, 1899: 261).
>
> At Sematan, Johari, the Sub-Magistrate, reported that three more families, out of the number who left sometime ago on account of the scare [of sickness], had returned from Paloh, Sambas (*SG*, November 1, 1894: 189).

In today's Telok Melano, Haji Taḥa is remembered as simply as a pioneering settler rather than an entrepreneur who brought people to the village with the intention of opening new plantations. None of the families presently residing in Telok Melano is known to be a direct descendant from Haji Taha. The commercial activities of *nakoda* traders like Haji Taha, which contributed to the formation of Malay communities in the region, have vanished from the villagers' collective memory.

It seems that the village organization took shape gradually from loosely structured aggregates of people living on several coconut plantations. The Malay merchants usually developed more than one site. For instance, Haji Taha opened coconut plantations not only in Telok Serabang and Telok Melano but also in Samunsan further to the south. He submitted an application for land use for his plantations in Sematan and functioned as a broker linking local peasants and the Brooke government's administrative staff in the Lundu Fort (*SG*, July 1, 1895: 126). The Brooke administration recognized him as a *penghulu* (chief/superintendent).

Nakoda went back and forth between Dutch Sambas and Sarawak to bring more people for their plantations. They also brought trading goods to Sarawak, and shipped timber from the Sematan coast to Singapore and Java. A *nakoda* named Haji Usop, who developed a coconut plantation with 600 trees in S'apong, near Lundu, was involved in logging activities on the coast of Samunsam:

> Tek Him, a billian worker, who has a number of coolies in his employ, asked and received permission to work timber in the Simunsam river. This is the first application that has been made to work timber in this river with the exception of Haji Usop, who, having received Your Highness's permission, gave out that he had the monopoly of the river (*SG*, August 1, 1895: 144).
>
> Haji Usop has asked to have the monopoly of working timber and jungle produce in the head of the Stunggang river for the term of five years, he estimates it would cost him about $300 in making paths and damming the stream (*SG*, November 2, 1896: 225).

The expansion of coconut plantations started from the very edge of Sarawak's territory, mainly from Cape Dato area where unexploited forest was still abundant. Subsequent development expanded to Sematan and the Lundu coast:

> The Malays and Chinese still continue to apply for permits to open cocoanut plantations. The registry shows that there are over 300 of these gardens now in this district. In about five years time the coast between Rambungan and Simatan [Sematan] will be one long line of plantations. Seedlings are fetching $5.00 to $6.00 per hundred (*SG*, July 1, 1908: 169).

It is very likely that the development of coconut plantations in the border zone was closely related to timber exploitation in the coastal virgin forest. Cutting timber required government approval, as did opening plantations. Instead of applying for each concession separately, the *nakoda* traders simply applied to open new plantations, achieving two purposes at once: the extraction of timber and the cultivation of coconut for copra production. Coconut plantations were concentrated at the mouths of rivers, such as at Samunsam, Bedaun, Belinsah, where there was good forest access to upriver.

By 1898, as reported "the whole coast from S. Blinsah to Telok Milano has now been practically taken up for cocoanut planting" (*SG*, July 1, 1898: 142). The development of Sarawak coast by Sambas *nakoda* traders that started from the border area adjacent to Cape Dato, was not a peripheral activity, but rather a central element in Sarawak's economic development, although only open to "outsiders" (Harrisson n.d.: 418–9).

Peripheral Peasantry

The participation of *nakoda* traders in plantation management in Lundu District was part of a strategy to cope with the government's economic policy, which tried to diminish their position in maritime trade. From the outset of colonial rule, the government supported trading activities by Chinese and attempted to reduce the supremacy of the Malay merchant class, and as Chinese merchants began to dominate regional commerce, the *nakoda* lost their dominance in trade.[2] Their success was acknowledged when The *Sarawak Gazette* claimed that "the last Malay trader" died in 1886:

> All will receive with regret the news of the death of Haji Bani bin Haji Bijak, who died on the 6th Ultimo, aged 46 years. The deceased was an energetic and hard working trader, the owner of two or three vessels, and was a very popular man both with natives and Europeans. His death will be a loss to the country, he being about the last Malay trader of any standing and credit (*SG*, May 1, 1886: 72).

According to Robert Pringle, "it is safe to say that in every area of Sarawak, the advent of Brooke rule and the consequent influx of Chinese traders reduced the Malay element to a position of marginal importance in commercial life" (Pringle 1970: 287).

In Lundu District, the *nakoda* began participating in agricultural production in the 1890s, which brought them into the government-led agricultural production system. However, these Malay entrepreneurs maintained a rather non-capitalistic labor organization under the charismatic leadership of the *nakoda*. Some of the *nakoda* remained along the Sarawak frontier to operate their plantations, but most of the coconut estates were left in the hands of caretakers while the *nakoda* absentee landlords, who were not sedentary by nature, engaged in trading and shipping. A later account of coconut plantations in

[2] According to Morris, "When the Brooke regime first brought peaceful conditions to the Oya River, the purchasing and further refining and export of sago was in the hands of Malay traders. Today this is, for practical purposes, entirely in the hands of Chinese dealers" (Morris 1953: 44).

Santubong, near Kuching, may shed light on the Malay mode of managing estates:

> It should also be mentioned here that where absentee landlords let others collect for them on a share basis, as is usual, quite frequently serious disputes arise and charges of cheating. This has tended to decrease since 1947, as young people have learned to "keep accounts" which the older folks seem in general to find more assuring (Harrisson 1970: 463–4, fn. I).

Labor relations between the *nakoda* plantation owner and local villagers were loosely structured. Those who worked for the plantations were not indentured laborers in terms of their relationship with their employer-cum-village headman, and there was no labor contract between the *nakoda* and the villagers. The stereotype of colonial plantations, with workers strictly supervised by either owners or on-site managers, did not apply to *nakoda*-led coconut estates on the Sematan coast. Labor relations were very much embedded in the local belief system in which cultural, religious elements were more relevant than capitalistic contractual relations.

I was told by a descendant of Nakoda Hitam ("The Black Nakoda"), a female *nakoda* captain who developed a coconut plantation at Labuan Gadong near Telok Melano, that "there was no *gaji* [wage] paid. The *ilmu* of Nakoda Hitam was so strong that people were simply happy working under her protection and followed her anywhere she went."[3] Many stories about the charismatic Nakoda Hitam survive in the village. She is still remembered by a Puan Siti Mariam, whose deceased husband was a son of Nakoda Hitam's sister:

> Nakoda Hitam was a successful, brave nakoda. She was good at piloting various types of sailing vessels of the time, such as *kapal, motor* and *perahu*, and often reached as far as Singapore and Java. Not only could she read the wind, but she could control it in her favor and reached her destinations safely. Her crew members were all men. When Nakoda Hitam opened her mouth, everybody listened. Nobody dared to speak against her, for they were all scared of her.

---

[3] R.J. Wilkinson's *A Malay-English Dictionary* defines *ilmu* as "Knowledge; solid learning; science; magic; any branch of knowledge or magic .... In popular speech ilmu is used with a special suggestion of magic; cf. i. panas (black magic); membuat i. (to use sorcery). Branches of this ilmu are very numerous" (Wilkinson 1959: 421).

Illus. 12 Puan Siti Mariam (Nenek Ayong)

> Nakoda Hitam was a tall and strongly-built woman who usually wore trousers. She married seven times; six earlier marriages ended in divorce. Nakoda Hitam simply *ambil dan buang laki* [took in and then dumped her husbands]. Only with her seventh and the last husband, Jamal, did she stay married until her death. Jamal was said to be of Minangkabau origin. Unlike his outgoing wife, Jamal usually stayed home and did not seek to become a nakoda. They had no children.
>
> Nakoda Hitam was capable of changing her looks in any way she wished. She could look evil. She could look pretty and innocent. One day she looked fifteen years old, and the next day she had a look of seventy years old. She sometimes borrowed the look of somebody she was acquainted with and had it as her own for one whole day (M. Ishikawa 2005: 252–3).

When absentee landlords, who did not have any contractual relationship with their plantation workers, gave up their estates, the settlements left behind became "natural villages". Collective memories of the formation of each community, to which migrants had come as labor for coconut plantations, were lost within a few generations.

The withdrawal of the *nakoda* can be attributed to the low profitability of copra production, the difficulty of maintaining estates, and the disappearance of the high quality timber which they sought. Damage to young coconut trees by wild boars was also a major hazard faced by planters and often reported by district officers:

> Haji Sleman, Tuah of Samunsam reported that several plantations at Kuala Samunsam had been destroyed by pigs. The plantations belonged to Haji Usin and other Sambas men. When I was last at Samunsam, Haji Usin had a plantation containing some 1,500 cocoanuts but had not fenced it in, though it would have been easy to do as he and his companions had planted on a narrow piece of land with the Samunsam running behind it (*SG*, May 1, 1899: 118).

> A number of plantations made two years ago at Kuala Samunsam and which last year appeared to be flourishing have been abandoned on account of the attacks of wild pigs though they might easily have been fenced in (*SG* , August 1, 1899: 261).

Telok Melano, at the turn of this century, no longer had the character of a coconut plantation village. The migration from Sambas and the Natuna Islands continued, but the village was no longer under the management of Haji Taha and other *nakoda* entrepreneurs. This hinterland community seems to have experienced both sharp increases and declines in population due to the highly mobile nature of peasants migrating into and out of the village. Pak Mundung, aged 95, whose family migrated to Telok Melano in 1910, recalled that the village had only five households in the 1910s, all of them are ancestors of present-day villagers. They resided inland rather than on the coast, where the coconut palms were planted. These five families lived separately in the forest. They had no choice but to live in the vicinity of their swidden *padi* fields to protect them from the constant intrusion of wild boars. Swidden *padi* cultivation, sporadic small-scale copra production and sale, and fishing for home consumption were the basic economic features of Telok Melano. A sailing trip by boat to Lundu or Sematan to sell copra took an entire day, or more.

In the late 1910s, a Hong Kong-based logging company started operations around the Serabang Bay. Chinese capital changed the economy of the hinterland. By then, *nakoda* traders had ceased operating plantations in the area, and they simply gave way to the Chinese entrepreneurs. Nenek Ayong, aged 96, whose father opened Telok Serabang and lived there from the age of twenty-one, recalls that:

> Before the company came, the village was small. There were only two Chinese, Ah Chong, Serion, and four Malays, Mariam, Tarif, Pak Mentua and my father, Pak Baharuddin. Gradually people moved from Sematan, Kuching and other places. One person came, two came and finally the village became crowded. Chinese, Malays, Dayaks entered the forest and worked timber. The forest used to be so thick that it was difficult to walk even on the coast. A ship from Hong Kong came to the village every 3–4 months to ship timber. There was a Chinese manager named Sin Jang and his clerk, Ah Chong. They built twenty houses for workers to stay. I sold home-made cake to these workers and I made good money, hundreds of dollars! These coolies quarreled often. A Chinese was killed in a fight and was buried at Telok Serabang. The timber was exhausted within five years.

Some Telok Melano villagers went to Serabang to work as coolies. A villager recalled conditions in Telok Serabang and Telok Melano in the 1920s:

> A long time ago, the life of Telok Serabang was very difficult. When I was small, there was no shop. We just looked for food, caught fish. Cultivating fields was also difficult. There were wild boars everywhere. They were many, just like the dogs running around our village now.
>
> Telok Serabang villagers used to say "Telok Melano is like a village of Dayaks." At that time there was neither pepper nor cacao planted in Telok Melano. Villagers went to the forest in search of rattan canes. They just lived from hand to mouth everyday. They sold these canes in Sematan and purchased rice, kerosene lamp oil, sugar and then went to the forest again, working timber. Life was hard.
>
> A logging company started operation in Telok Serabang. A Chinese named Hon Sin Jang opened the company. A ship from Hong Kong collected the timber. Telok Serabang became crowded with coolies. All the Telok Melano villagers who knew the logging at Serabang then have passed away, except Pak Piee. Telok Melano villagers usually went down to Serabang and worked as coolies.
>
> Telok Melano people cleared the forest for *padi* cultivation. That's all. From grandparents to parents to children to grandchildren, they cultivated hill *padi* only. No rubber, no clove ... planting padi and catching fish only.

After the plantation economy ceased to function, Telok Melano's economy became subsistence oriented; villagers planted hill rice, exploited forest produce such as rattan, fished for their own consumption, and cultivated coconut. Copra production was carried out on a small scale, but did not generate a steady income.

As discussed in Chapter 3, when the regional rubber boom finally reached Lundu and Sematan in the late 1920s, coastal Malay communities failed to take advantage of it. After a short-lived boom, the government restricted the scale of production in order to comply with the International Rubber Regulation Agreement signed in 1934. According to Pak Mundung, colonial officials strictly prohibited new cultivation of rubber even in hinterland communities such as Telok Melano and Telok Serabang:

> There were village people who planted rubber before the Japanese occupation. But only in Sematan, not in Telok Melano. We could get rubber seedlings from Sematan, but could not plant them. The Brooke government prohibited the cultivation of new rubber. If we planted rubber, we were punished. There were a few villagers who planted rubber in Telok Serabang, but all of their plants were immediately cut down by government officials.

Besides the IRRA, practical calculations kept villagers from shifting from hill rice cultivation to rubber planting. Pak Mundung gave an account of villagers' decision not to plant rubber in its heyday in the 1930s:

> We chose to continue planting rice despite the rubber frenzy at that time. We did know that rubber sheets fetched a good market price. But we also knew that rubber took a long time to mature. If we cleared the secondary jungle for rubber, where could we plant rice for next year's harvest? We could not afford to risk the labor involved in opening extra virgin forest.

Telok Melano villagers thus continued their conventional life style during and after the rubber boom, cultivating *padi* inland, fishing, and selling copra to Sematan Chinese *taukay* to get a small amount of cash for the purchase of daily necessities. A village elder, who spent his adolescence in neighboring Telok Serabang in the 1930s, recalls that:

> Telok Melano used to be just like a Dayak village in the jungle. Villagers often went into the woods to seek rattan and timber. They came down to Sematan to sell the jungle produce in exchange with such goods as sugar and kerosene. It took their small boat with a mast

Illus. 13 Telok Melano before Konfrontasi (a photo taken on February 5, 1962, courtesy of the Sarawak Museum)

> a whole day to reach Sematan. The villagers brought uncooked rice, a rice cooking pan, and a portable oven (*dapur masak*). They cook rice on the boat in case they get stuck in a windless weather.

After the Sarawak government, along with other rubber producing colonies, began to implement a series of restriction schemes, smuggling in the Lundu District became endemic, as discussed in Chapter 3. The smuggling of raw rubber sheets and other commodities from Dutch Borneo remained the main industry in the border area until Konfrontasi in 1963.

Telok Melano was no exception. At the height of the smuggling boom, two Chinese moved to the village to receive smuggled goods. Situated right on the border, the village functioned as an entrepot between the rubber-producing region of Dutch Borneo and the underground commodity market in Sarawak:

> Before Konfrontasi it was quite crowded here in Telok Melano. There were boats equipped with 25 cc, 50 cc and even 100 cc engines. There were two Chinese shops here. Smugglers' shops! The shop owners received smuggled things from Indonesia. A lot of motor-equipped ships came here every day. Rubber sheets from Indonesia

> were brought straight to Telok Melano. I do not remember how many tons of rubber.... Before Konfrontasi, from the 1950s to the 60s, 1961, '62, or '63, Telok Serabang and Telok Melano were really crowded. Those who worked as boat drivers and helped to smuggle rubber could earn 150 ringgit per night. Rubber sheets and other commodities were shipped to Kuching by bigger ships. Chinese *taukay* waited for goods and bought them, then shipped them to Kuching. Rubber, pigs, rifles, things were smuggled into Sarawak from Tanah Hitam, Sambas, Pemangkat, and even Java.
>
> I already had a child then. Sahat was not yet married. We stole gasoline from smugglers' boats. Sahat went to the seashore. If a nightwatch was on duty, he just returned. Every night we stole a bit of gasoline from boats. Since we only used a small boat, we did not have to buy gasoline.
>
> At high tide, they started to load their ships. There were soldiers on alert on the coast, looking for smugglers. Smugglers just waited when soldiers were nearby. There were two Chinese *taukay* here. Ni Hon and Cimi Kei. In Serabang, Ban Jo Hong. Rich Chinese. Look at my brother now residing in Serabang. He worked as a driver for these *taukay*. His engine was 30 cc. He got 150 ringgit per night, dropping off and picking up people. His gold ring was this big! Most villagers were not brave enough to work with them. Sometimes they were shot by soldiers. (Interview with Pak Daud)

> At that time smuggled rubber sheets fetched the price of 18 cents per kati, 18 ringgit per pikul. A pack of cigarette was 5 cents. One kati of sugar was 8 cents. If you had 90 cents, you could buy 1 gantang of rice. (Interview with Pak Mundung)

> There were no governments, so that smuggling across the border flourished. It was before Malaysia and Indonesia came into existence. There was no cooperation between governments across the border. Nowadays, such a thing [smuggling] can no longer take place. People on this side of the border can telephone immediately. People on the other side of the border can call back immediately. No more today. Do not think of even trying it. The relationship between the Malaysian and Indonesian army is already back to normal. (Interview with Pak Daud)

It was like the old days, when "pirates" from the Sulu zone attacked trading vessels sailing between Sarawak and Dutch territory, Cape Dato area was again home to smugglers transgressing state boundaries. This time they brought goods by sea across the border without paying export and import duties to governments on either side. Authorities were well aware of the fact that from the 1930s to the early 1960s Telok Melano and Telok Serabang functioned as major smuggling points, but they could do little about it:

> At Telok Serabang it was reported that rumours had been received from Dutch Borneo to the effect that smugglers were now afraid to use the sea as means of importing rubber and tobacco (*SG*, August 1, 1936: 188).
>
> It is almost impossible to carry out customs work really efficiently in the District owing to lack of transport. The areas which need watching and in which most of the smuggling activities take place are inaccessible by land; a sea going launch is required (*LDQR* 3rd Quarter: July–September 1951).
>
> Trade in the district relied mainly on goods imported from Indonesia, the major part of which was rubber which came through several smuggling points such as Kandaie, Biawak, Pueh, Telok Melano and Telok Serabang (*SG*, April 30, 1963: 78).

Commodity smuggling bought profit to some in Telok Melano, but the beneficiaries were limited to those who risked working as boat drivers or coolies for the Chinese merchants. However, the long term effect of the smuggling economy on Telok Melano's agriculture was profound. Witnessing the tons of rubber smuggled from the other side of Cape Dato, people lost interest in planting rubber themselves. Even during the rubber boom of the 1950s, which was boosted by the war on the Korean Peninsula, the villagers' response was minimal. A few planted rubber in Telok Melano, but today only abandoned rubber gardens remain in the vicinity, and their scale is much smaller than those of the inland Dayaks, who actively engaged in rubber cultivation in the 1950s.

According to land use data for Telok Melano in that decade, obtained through a survey conducted by the Sarawak Museum (Harrisson 1970: 464), thirteen of the fifteen households in Telok Melano had an average holding of 1.92 acres of coconut garden, 2.2 acres of *padi* fields, and 1.15 acres of other crops. The two households without cultivated fields may have been those of the Chinese merchants engaged in smuggling, even though they were categorized as "Malays". The source does not specify what "other crops" were cultivated but they are likely to have been traditional plants commonly cultivated in the village, such as banana, corn, cassava, durian, rambutan, green vegetables, and other fruit trees. A small number of rubber trees might have been grown.

The history of Telok Melano reveals that the cultivation of coconut, the first cash crop introduced in the area, did not last. Before the military confrontation broke out in 1963, the agricultural landscape of Telok Melano was dominated by secondary forest that stretched to the national boundary. Harrisson's data shows that the acreage of slash-and-burn rice fields was greater than that of coconut gardens. And like coconuts, rubber was never significant for the village economy. Telok Melano villagers did not take advantage of high rubber prices in the international market not once but twice. During booms in the late 1930s and the early 1950s, peasants residing at the smuggling point linking the Sambas rubber region and the Kuching market were overwhelmed by the massive amount of rubber continuously coming across the border.

In rubber-producing countries throughout Southeast Asia, the rubber booms contributed greatly to the income generation of local peasants. Smallholders became directly connected to the international market through the cultivation of rubber. Although other Sarawakian cultivators increasingly specialized in rubber production in the two decades before the Japanese military invasion, this hinterland community increased its dependence on swidden hill rice on the jungle frontier.

International Politics and Swidden Cultivators

Telok Melano, although situated in a remote corner of Sarawak, has gone through periods of national as well as international political turmoil. Due to the remoteness of Telok Melano from the administrative center, the villagers had little day to day contact with colonial government officials. The weak, if not benign, sovereignty of the white Rajah regime was followed by struggle and hardship under the Japanese occupation from 1941 to 1945. Villagers experienced severe shortages of daily necessities. They were forced to give their rice to the authorities and had nothing but cassava and banana to eat. Selling rice at Sematan bazaar required permission from the Japanese military authority. Shortage of clothes forced them to make use of cloth made from tree bark. One village elder recalls the Japanese occupation as the most difficult period in his life.

A change in village settlement patterns took place during the Japanese occupation. Until that time, villagers had lived separately in the forest near their rice fields, but to minimize contact with Japanese soldiers, they gradually moved inland. About twenty houses were built deep in the forest adjacent to the present Indonesian-Malaysian border. They did not form a village cluster, and the occupants engaged individually in swidden agriculture.

After the war, Sarawak was ceded to Great Britain and became a crown colony. In Telok Melano, villagers continued to clear the jungle for hill rice cultivation. The British colonial administration, which ruled Sarawak from 1946 to 1963, enforced strict regulation of forest exploitation. Since villagers were not allowed to cut the virgin forest (*hutan tua*) at their disposal, they were forced to reuse secondary forest (*jerame*) repeatedly.

Independence from colonial rule in 1963 and the birth of the Federation of Malaysia were expected to bring better life to Telok Melano villagers. This expectation was soon called into question by Konfrontasi between Indonesia and Malaysia. Due to its proximity to the border, Telok Melano inevitably became entangled in the military activity. After two villagers were abducted and killed by the Indonesian army in early 1963, Malaysian authorities ordered all residents of Telok Melano and Telok Serabang to evacuate the area. Some fled to Indonesian territory, but the majority stayed on the Malaysian side. As they hurriedly escaped with a few belongings, they saw their houses being burnt to the ground by Indonesian soldiers. Most of the villagers moved to Sematan, Lundu, or Kuching.

The peace agreement signed on August 11, 1966 between Jakarta and Kuala Lumpur brought Konfrontasi to an end. In 1967, former inhabitants were first allowed to return to the villages in the daytime to collect coconuts under strict Malaysian military supervision. Two years after the peace agreement, the authorities finally allowed the villagers to resettle at Telok Melano and Telok Serabang. In Telok Melano, a headman and two others and their families were the first to return. Others gradually followed.

Before Konfrontasi, there had been twenty families in Telok Melano. Six families put down in their new locales and never returned to the village, and five persons died without seeing their former homes again. Village demography thus changed. According to the government census data taken in 1968, the population of Telok Melano numbered only 63 (Leigh 2002: 80). The five-year evacuation allowed swidden fields to regenerate to thick secondary forest. With decreased population pressure and regenerated forest resources, villagers were able to continue to exploit *jerame tua* (old secondary forest) for swidden agriculture.

Within a decade of the end of Konfrontasi, another tragedy struck Telok Melano when a village man was shot to death at his home by communist guerrillas who were hiding in the jungle near the border. After the shooting, the village was on immediate alert. Although villagers did not flee this time, they were ordered by the Kuching authorities to rebuild their homes close to one another on the coast, where previously only two houses stood. Communist activities continued until 1988, when the last guerrillas surrendered to the authorities.

Maritime History and Microhistory

Telok Melano village can be seen as a microcosm of the social configuration of Lundu District, but it presents a more extreme case of displacement and dissociation. Building on local historical experiences and local memories, which have not and will not become part of the official history of the state, my reconstruction of micro-social history from the 1890s reveals how villagers have coped with the web of larger, complex, and changing center-periphery relations under the colonial and postcolonial state.

The formation of Telok Melano as a peasant village in national territory was a product of the state's mobilization of labor. The village was initially designated by the Rajahs as an outsiders' village, where only non-Sarawakians were allowed to come to work the land. Under the economic policies implemented by the second Rajah, the formerly pirate-infested coast between Cape Dato and Sematan was developed as a coconut plantation belt, and Malay communities were established for estate management. Plantation development relied on foreign entrepreneurs, that is the *nakoda* merchants and Malay peasants both of whom were from Dutch Borneo.

The decline of the *nakoda* class at the turn of the twentieth century removed these Malay peasants from the sphere of commodity production. The rapid withdrawal of the *nakoda* from the plantation industry deprived plantation workers-cum-villagers of their livelihood, and they turned to subsistence cultivation of hill *padi*. As the state gradually succeeded in fixing its borders by controlling the movement of people and commodities, Telok Melano villagers were stranded on the utmost periphery of the state. Land registration policies bound the villagers to *kerangus* forest, an unproductive coastal ecological niche, and their mobility was curtailed by restrictions on immigration and naturalization.[4]

From the 1920s, with the rise of the rubber economy and subsequent implementation of international production restrictions, Sarawak was incorporated into the global system of commodity production led by the British and the Dutch governments. Due to its geographical location on the border between two states, the Cape Dato area escaped state border control and operated as a major transnational smuggling site for raw rubber. In the center-periphery structuring of the capitalistic world system, much of the Bornean hinterland was incorporated into a rubber production system governed by international price fluctuations, but the location of the borderland communities disallowed them from participation even at the periphery of the capitalist system. They remained an economic frontier between two states, where residents decisively chose not to participate in cash crop cultivation.

Telok Melano experienced periods of national or international political turmoil as part of its local history. Political conflicts not only took the lives of Telok Melano villagers but also fundamentally damaged local economic formations. The Japanese military occupation of 1941–45, post-independence Konfrontasi of 1963–66, and guerrilla activity of the Clandestine Communist Organization (CCO) from the 1970s through the late 1980s paralyzed both the commercial agriculture of Telok Melano and the regional market economy, and the villagers continued to survive through shifting cultivation on the jungle frontier.

The next chapter examines how Telok Melano villagers have been marginalized within the ethnic category of "Sarawak Malay" through the historical process of their land-based adaptation, specifically specialization in swidden agriculture at the margin of national space. Taking the locally specific experience of Telok Melano as a case in point, the discussion focuses on a general process in which economic peripheralization leads to cultural peripheralization.

[4] For the detailed description of *kerangas* forests in Sarawak, see Andriesse (1972).

CHAPTER FIVE

The Genesis of Ethnic Displacement

Culture and Economy

A social segment engaging in what elite segments of the Malay population view as non-authentic economic activity becomes culturally marginalized, disavowed, and pushed to the edge of the ethnic and national boundary or even beyond. To elucidate the processes and consequences of the uneven expansion of national space in a territorial state and the disproportionate allocation of cultural resources to various segments within an ethnic group, two contrasting group descents are compared in this chapter, one at the fringe of national space as represented by Telok Melano peasants and the other at the pinnacle of the Malay cultural construct, a space traditionally dominated by urban Malays in Kuching, Sarawak's capital city.

As Wilson and Hastings rightly point out, "while the use of 'borderland' as an image of the study of connections between cultures wherever these connections are found opened up new ground in social and cultural theory (see, for example, Rosaldo 1988, Gupta and Ferguson 1992, and Alvarez and Collier 1994), it has often done so at the expense of underplaying changes in political economy" (Wilson and Hastings 1998: 3). They add that attention to "a localised, particularistic and territorially focused notion of borders" (Wilson and Hastings 1998: 3) is necessary to investigate spatially and temporally specific social processes leading to what Eric Wolf called "the rise of heterogeneous social arrays" rather than "the development of homogeneous national or subnational totalities" (Wolf 1999: 12). The examination of the economic adaptation to the land of seafaring Malays in the borderland provides a clue to understanding a root cause of the ethnic peripheralization of Telok Melano villagers.

Narrow economism and neglect of the importance of culturally marked phenomena are often found in research into the political economy of specific geographical areas. In an attempt to comprehend the relationship between culturally encoded phenomena and the structural determinants of the economy, the following discussion focuses on culture in relation to separate but closely related social differentiation — internal-ethnic stratification and class among the Sarawak Malays. Such social stratification was initiated and accelerated by the workings of the state, both colonial and postcolonial, namely its territorial encroachment and incorporation of people into official ethnic categories.

Into the Jungle

The traditional economic activity of the Sarawak Malays is fishing, and their ecological niche is largely confined to coastal areas, swamp land, and mud banks (Harrisson 1970: 59). As Harrisson pointed out, among coastal Malay communities in southwestern Sarawak, Telok Melano differs in that the lives of the villagers largely depend on land-based agricultural activities rather than fishing or maritime/riverine trading (Harrisson 1970: 59, 79–80). At one time, Telok Melano's strong orientation toward the land was reflected in its residential patterns. The village is currently located near the seashore, giving the impression of a typical fishing village. With the exception of a few inland houses, the settlement is formed along a path connecting Telok Melano with Temajuk village in Indonesia. As the previous chapter depicted, this beachside location is rather new in the village history. Let me briefly sum up the locational and demographic changes.

Before Telok Melano assumed its present shape, villagers lived separately in the jungle and cultivated swidden rice fields, but the pioneer settlers of the 1890s are known to have lived quite close to the seashore. They came as foreign laborers and cultivated coconuts on the edge of the sea, cultivated padi adjacent to their coconut fields, and built their houses in the middle of the coconut gardens. The locations are still remembered because the sites have old durian trees planted by the pioneers. Some houses were located between the present village compounds of Telok Melano and Telok Serabang, less than one kilometer from the sea. As an elder villager recalls, "Our forefathers cultivated *padi bukit* (hill rice) and *nio* (coconut) together. They worked in the swidden fields looking down on the sea!" (See Illus. 13.)

After the initial clearing of the coastal fields, swidden farms gradually moved inland, opening primary forest exploitable for cultivation.

When *padi* fields expanded into forested areas and left unattended, the rice would be destroyed by wild boars. This led many villagers to build houses near their rice fields. The move inland progressed during the Japanese occupation, when villagers sought to minimize contact with Japanese soldiers. At that time there were about twenty houses scattered across the primary forest adjacent to the present Malaysia-Indonesia border, far from the sea. Even after the Japanese surrender in 1945, villagers continued to reside inland, engaging in hill rice cultivation. Under the British colonial government, the opening of primary forest for planting padi was forbidden, so villagers had to work the same secondary forest repeatedly. The legacy of this exploitation remains today; a vast area around the Indonesia-Malaysia border is treeless, barren-looking, and overgrown with *lalang* (Imperata cylindrica) and other weeds. This is the land the villagers' forefathers lived on and cultivated during the Japanese and British eras.

Then, during Konfrontasi, villagers were forced to leave their homes, settling in Sematan, Lundu, Santubong, and other places. When they returned after the five-year evacuation, they again chose to live separately. With the exception of a small cluster of houses near the graveyard not far from the sea, their houses were scattered along the coast and inland. The current village compound adjacent to seashore was just formed in 1977 following the government's order in response to a communist incident.

The sparse population allowed swidden agriculture to persist for more than a century. Though no statistical record of the village's past is available, it is possible to speculate about demographic change based on the recollections of village elders.[1] The earliest information on the village population came from Pak Mundung, aged ninety-five, who migrated to Telok Melano at the age of eight. When he first arrived with his father, there were only five households. By the time the Japanese came to Sarawak, the number had increased to approximately twenty. All households evacuated in 1963, and fifteen returned by the end of the 1960s.[2]

---

[1] Elders usually recall the number of households, rather than the population. Years are estimated based on crucial events in village life, such as the Japanese occupation and Konfrontasi.

[2] The destinations and number of evacuee households that later returned to Telok Melano were Santubong (1), Kuching (1), Pugu (4), Siru (Sg. Kilong) (6), and Setoh (1).

By November 1994, Telok Melano had 41 households (211 persons). The increase came through the formation of independent households by younger generations and immigration.[3] Although the population has increased over the years, it remains small for the area the village occupies, and the village compound is still surrounded by virgin forest and old secondary forest.[4]

Village elders often recall the old days when they had better harvests. The oldest of them, Pak Mundung, talks about pioneer days in Telok Melano: "We planted *padi* every year using only *hutan tua* (the primary forest). Planting 1 gantang (3 kg) yielded 3 or 4 *guni besar* (large gunny sacks) (300 or 400 kg) of rice." Such a yield is exceptionally and perhaps overly high, but other villagers remember planting several dozen *gantang* of rice each year and enjoying quite good harvests until the late 1970s:

> Planting half a *gantang* of padi could easily yield one *guni besar*. Before Konfrontasi, my house was full of large bags of stored rice which were piled up to the ceiling. (Interview with Pak Jaya)
>
> Villagers worked on padi and coconut. My father and his fellow villagers never bought rice. They opened *hutan tua* and planted 30 *gantang* every year. Only lazy people opened *jerame*. When my

---

[3] During my fieldwork, two families left the village. Due to the death of her husband, a widow and her children went back to her parents' home in Kuching. The other left to seek employment in Sematan.

[4] In addition to restrictions placed on forest exploitation by the colonial government and the evacuation and subsequent population decrease due to Konfrontasi, two socio-economic factors are responsible for the under-exploitation of the forest: the lack of mechanical agricultural tools such as chainsaws and weak cooperative ethics in local agricultural practice.

Inactive agricultural cooperation (*gotong royong*) is notable in Telok Melano. Except for firing fields and planting *padi* seeds, hill rice cultivation is carried out entirely by individual households. For instance, clearing the field, the most labor-intensive of all phases of hill rice cultivation, is usually conducted by a household head and his sons (if any), taking thirty days or more for one plot. According to villagers, before the Konfrontasi evacuation, *gotong royong* used to be practiced for almost all stages of swidden rice cultivation. The evacuation and subsequent demographic change brought an end to institutionalized work-sharing and other agricultural rituals.

In the past, Chinese *taukay* merchants tried to lend villagers chainsaws in the hope that they would bring sawn logs to market. Due to the cost and difficulty of obtaining fuel, this plan did not work out. During my stay in Telok Melano, chainsaws were seldom used for clearing swidden fields.

> husband was killed by communists (1977), he left 23 *guni besar* (2,300 kg) of padi. People usually planted 20–30 *gantang* of padi at that time. (Interview with Mak Umi)

Telok Melano villagers say that they traditionally lived inland and preferred to do so. This land-orientation is quite strong in their ethos. According to the village head, in the old days, those who were reluctant to cultivate land were regarded as lazy. Villagers who fished through the night and slept during the daytime were ridiculed. The land has been the source of livelihood in Telok Melano for generations.[5]

Economic Exclusion and Ethnic Dislocation

As detailed in the Appendix, "Agriculture in Telok Melano", traditional swidden *padi* cultivation has formed the backbone of agriculture in Telok Melano. Although the degree of self-sufficiency in rice has been declining over the years, people continue to clear forest and plant *padi.* Recent cash crop cultivation under government schemes and traditional swidden agriculture do not conflict with one another; rather, the land surplus economy of Telok Melano allows swidden agriculture and cash crop cultivation to exist side by side.[6] The area's ecology,

---

[5] If we examine the case of a specific household, the mobile character of this Malay community becomes apparent. Pak Moshidi, who is in his early 60s, has moved seven times since his boyhood:

1. near the beach of Melano Bay (early childhood)
2. inland (boyhood)
3. near the present international border (Japanese occupation period)
4. six-year evacuation to Sematan (Konfrontasi era)
5. near Melano River (after evacuation)
6. near village graveyard
7. present village location (communist era)
8. near the beach of Melano Bay (present)

Pak Moshidi has been quite mobile, although in many instances he was forced to move rather than chose to do so, and it should be noted that he and his family prefer not to live near the beach. Most villagers have relocated as many times as Pak Moshidi, if not more.

[6] The key characteristic of a surplus land economy is that the marginal product of land (cultivated and fallow) is zero, so that an increase in the ratio of total labor to total land does not lead to diminishing returns. This is because the additional labor can be combined with additional land in constant proportions (Cramb 1988: 20).

coupled with its small population and reserves of land contributes to stable and quick regeneration to secondary forest of both *padi* fields and abandoned cash crop fields. Under such conditions, Telok Melano still displays a tendency to revert from cash crops to slash-and-burn cultivation of hill rice.

Telok Melano's involvement in shifting cultivation in the borderlands is the result of a historical process of socio-economic exclusion of the borderlands since the 1880s. As the history of the Cape Dato-Lundu coast shows, the incorporation of hinterland Malays into commodity production via copra cultivation was gradually brought to an end by a number of changes, including the decline of Malay supremacy in maritime trade, the regional emergence of a rubber-dominated economy from which Malay peasants on the border were virtually excluded, hardships arising from the Japanese military occupation, a five-year evacuation from the village during the Indonesian-Malaysia Konfrontasi, communist guerrilla activities in the neighboring jungle that paralyzed the Lundu-Sematan market economy and threatened the lives of villagers, and, finally, the establishment of a Kuching-based, national market distribution system to which Telok Melano does not have easy access.

The transformation of Telok Melano's economy from commercial cultivation of coconuts to subsistence-oriented shifting cultivation of *padi* illustrates a structural differentiation between two groups of Sarawak Malays, the urban elite segment in Kuching and Malays at the margin of the state territory. The aristocratic Malay class and their descendants in the urban centers, on the one hand, and Malay peasants practicing shifting cultivation on the jungle frontier near Indonesian border, on the other, form two poles of national geography as well as social stratification of Sarawak Malays.

It is important to note that the location of social groups both within the national territory and in terms of social stratification is closely related to their position in the realm of constructed ethnicity. While the upper class segment occupies the pinnacle of cultural authenticity, the lower social segment is often underrepresented and pushed to the outer rim of the cultural category. The gradation of ethnic authenticity is often linked to geography, and the dissociation of the periphery from the ethnic core coincides with a social segment's downward mobility in a class structure. Thus comparing aristocrats and their descendants in the state capital to peasants in the borderlands — looking at ethnicity from below as well as from afar — helps us comprehend the ethnic formation of the Sarawak Malays in western Borneo.

Center versus Periphery

Social displacement on the border involved two processes of state intervention: labor mobilization and territorial enclosure. The first and second white Rajahs implemented migration and land policies to mobilize agricultural laborers for cash crop production in Sarawak. Under colonial land policies, all land became state-owned, and part of it was allocated to entrepreneurs, who brought foreign immigrants and workers to open plantations. As explained in Chapter 1, Chinese *taukay* and Malay *nakoda* were two leading agents of labor mobilization. The ethnic division of labor became clear in Lundu in the latter half of the nineteenth century. Coastal Malay peasants came from the Sambas region of Dutch Borneo to plant coconuts. Chinese coolies, who had migrated from Dutch West Borneo and southern China via Singapore, and a small number of Dayaks, grew gambier, pepper, and rubber. The development of an ethnically specific agricultural economy led to the formation of a "plural society", although not in the sense of Furnivall's conceptualization of coexisting ethnic groups under colonial rule (Furnivall 1939, 1944). Rather, the colonial labor process generated an uneven distribution of economic resources within an ethnically segmented labor market.

With the introduction of commodity production for export in colonial Sarawak, the downfall of the Malay economy became irreversible. While a small elite segment of Sarawak Malays enjoyed privileged political status as colonial officials under Brooke rule, the majority of commoners, who had been active in the riverine and coastal trade handling commodities such as forest produce, lost economic ground to the rising Chinese merchant class that controlled the market in gambier, pepper, and rubber. The participation of the Malay *nakoda* class in coconut cultivation in the frontier land of Sarawak was in a sense the last stand of the traditional Malay economy.

From the turn of the twentieth century, coastal Malays were gradually excluded from the mainstream of Sarawak's colonial economy. Brooke government land policies restricted the economic niche of maritime Malays to coastal areas. The process of enclosure forced coastal Malay peasants of southwestern Sarawak to engage in the declining coconut economy, as the sandy coastal soil was not suitable for the other crops. Unlike pepper and rubber, which became major export commodities, coconuts remained a low-profit commodity, and the market value declined with the introduction of chemical substitutes for copra in soap production.

In these circumstances, the coconut plantation belt which was made up of more than two dozen Malay coastal communities between Cape Dato and Sematan gradually disappeared, with the exception of Telok Melano and neighboring Telok Serabang. As the village history shows (Chapter 4), Telok Melano took to subsistence economy with the cultivation of hill *padi* after the withdrawal of *nakoda* entrepreneurs.

For the inland Dayak population, ethnic identity was at one time closely associated with the production of hill rice in swidden fields. Despite participation in commodity production under Brooke rule, swidden agriculture remained a positive ethnic feature for many upriver Dayaks. In contrast, Malays on the southwestern coast lacked an appropriate economic expression of their ethnic and historical consciousness. Their traditional economic activities, maritime and riverine trade by the *nakoda* commercial class and fishery by coastal commoners, lost salience as ethnic markers because of the dominance of migrant Chinese in both of these fields. Yet being a hill rice cultivator in the borderland is inconsistent with Malayness in the context of Sarawak.

The historical process by which a certain ethnic category is invented and given shape as an established social group involves two kinds of social vectors: inclusion and exclusion. A group within an ethnic category that succeeds in monopolizing cultural assets is likely to develop the representative expression of the ethnic group, while other sub-groups may gradually become disassociated from this core group and ethnically ambiguous.

In the Sarawak context, the aristocracy monopolized the cultural assets of the "Sarawak Malay". They formed a distinctive social group called *perabangan* and their social status was created and politically supported by the Brooke colonial government, which they served as elite local officials. Sarawak Malay society was subsequently drawn into a conical structure in which the ethnicity of non-*perabangan* Malays in the Sarawak colonial territory became blurred because their actual kinship ties to the core aristocrats were non-existent or lost (cf. Kirchhoff 1959).[7]

In the contemporary context, the ethnically asymmetrical relationship within Sarawak Malay society is most noticeable in the class

[7] Historically, slaves (*gundik*), war captives of Dayak descent, occupied the most peripheral and lowest rung of this social formation.

structure and spatial distribution of the community. Most offspring of *perabangan* aristocrats reside in the state capital of Kuching and are involved in government service or the urban sector, while numerous communities of Malay commoners in rural coastal and riverine regions engage in fishing and petty trade. In the geography of the nation-state, the Malays most culturally distant from the urban core are also those living at the geographic fringe of state territory. As cultivators of hill rice in the deep forest, the villagers of Telok Melano in the Malaysia-Indonesia borderland fall into this peripheral category in the spatial construct of the Sarawak Malay ethnicity. As Eric Wolf pointed out, geographical positioning in national space is related to group formation under the state system:

> The expansion of the national life was uneven. Nations were constructed segmentally and unequally.... Some people and groups were drawn or propelled into the central orbits of national existence; others were ignored, marginalized, or obliterated altogether. There were winners and also losers, unequally distributed over the national terrain and unequally represented in the symbolizations of the nation (Wolf 1999: 11).

Narratives and Ethnicity

When one ethnic category is differentiated from others, an ethnic name, history, culturally specific elements and a narrative are invented and become fixed. Numerous other sub-groups with their own local histories and cultural practices face denial and neglect because of the dominance of established hegemonic expression of ethnicity. If the sub-groups become invisible and pushed out to the periphery of the ethnic category to which they ostensibly belong, their cultural and historical variants can also be excluded from the dominant narrative of ethnicity.

The official narrative of an ethnic group is given historical continuity by politicians, administrators, religious leaders, museum displays, tourism, ethnic media, and academic writings. Meanwhile, narratives that are not considered "ethnographically correct" are put aside as exceptional or deviant. This process of ethnic peripheralization is always related to the uneven distribution of power, and it leads to stratification among ethnic groups within the state as well as internal class differentiation within an ethnic group.[8] The state is an exclusive

---

[8] For the discussion on the peripheral identity of the Bajaus (Sama-di-Laut) in the Malaysian context, see Nagatsu's ethnographic account (2001).

social arena in which ethnic and class stratification takes place. Therefore discussion of the formation of ethnic groups and class should not proceed without taking the state into consideration. Posing the question "Who are the Sarawak Malays?" in the context of state making illuminates the uneven distribution of cultural and historical resources in the geography of difference.

The territorial borders of the Sarawak state and Malay ethnicity evolved in parallel. The emergence of the Sarawak Malay as a distinctive ethnic category has its roots in the political transformation induced by external political forces. Sarawak society, in its century and a half history, underwent a series of political transformations from the Brooke colonization (1841–1941), through the Japanese military occupation (1941–45), the British colonization (1946–63), to incorporation into Malaysia (1963–present). The most powerful interventions in the formation of ethnic groups were the Brooke colonization in 1841 and the establishment of Malaysia in 1963.

The first Rajah Brooke used indirect rule to control Sarawak. Much of his power depended on the leaders of various ethnic communities, particularly local Malay chiefs (*datu*) who had fought against Brunei rule in pre-Brooke days. According to Craig Lockard, "Over time these *datus* and the English Rajah developed what might be termed a 'symbiotic' relationship; this relationship in turn had a strong influence on Malay social and political structure" (Lockard 1987: 20). To secure political cooperation from the *datu* class, Rajah James Brooke assigned local leaders to political office in his colonial administration and paid them regular salaries. The inclusion of traditional Malay leaders in the new power structure reaffirmed the legitimacy of the Malay class system, and helped maintain Malay social structure throughout the early years of Brooke rule.

Sarawak Malay society had historically been divided into four social classes: aristocracy, middle class, peasants, and slaves. The aristocrats were the rulers and religious leaders. Those of the highest rank were the *perabangan*, headed by the Datu Patinggi, Datu Bandar, and Datu Temenggong. All male members of this group bore the title *abang* and females *dayang*; all were descended from *datus*. Endogamy was a norm, adhered to more strictly by female members. Those who claimed descent from Brunei were called *pengiran* and ranked slightly below the *perabangan* group under the Brooke regime. They were followed by those who boasted Arab ancestry and had the title of *sherif* or *tuanku* (Lockard 1987: 20–1).

Illus. 14 Kuching Malays (date unknown, courtesy of the Sarawak Museum)

The middle class of traditional Sarawak Malay society was composed of two major groups in the early Brooke period, the *nakoda* and the *orang pereman*. The *nakodas'* international trade and monopoly of coastal and riverine shipping made them the wealthiest of Malay society. As seen in previous chapters, *nakoda* traders played a pivotal role in the development of frontier coastal Lundu District into a coconut plantation belt. These highly respected entrepreneurs were the most prestigious commoner group. Some observers considered them almost equal in real status to the *datus* and *abangs* (Lockard 1987: 21). Because of their travels, the *nakoda* were known for their knowledge of Islam and of world affairs, and they gradually emerged as the educated elite among the Malays. The second commoner group, *orang pereman* or free citizens, made up the majority of the Malay population. This diverse lower class group included peasants, fishermen, laborers, and retainers to the aristocratic families. Slaves (*gundik*) formed the lowest social stratum. They constituted only a small segment of Malay society in Sarawak. Their function was restricted to serving their aristocratic masters, for whom they performed every kind of domestic chore (Sanib 1985: 7–8).

The nomenclature "*Melayu Sarawak*" (in Malay) and "*Sarawak Malay*" (in English) is used to denote the Malay population of Sarawak. Any individual who calls himself and herself Malay is by definition

Muslim.[9] Although there is no definite answer as to the origin of the words "Malay" and "Sarawak Malay" in the Sarawakian context, Robert Pringle suggests that the establishment of the nomenclature "Malay" for the Muslim population in Sarawak coincides with the formation of the Brooke colony in Sarawak in 1841. He contends there was no ethnic category called "Sarawak Malay" before the coming of the Brooke family to Sarawak:

> The word "Malay" is widely used in Sarawak today only because in 1841 James Brooke brought it with him from Singapore, where it had been vaguely applied to all the coast-dwelling, seafaring Moslems of the Indonesian archipelago, particularly to those of Sumatra and the Malayan peninsula. What lends credence to this theory is the fact that in Sabah (formerly British North Borneo) there are no "Malay", but only a variety of Moslem sub-groups: Bajaus, Sulus, Bruneis and so on. This is apparently because the administrative vocabulary of the Chartered Company which governed Sabah differed from that of the Brooke regime. If a Sabah "Brunei" moved to Kuching today, he would instantly be called a "Malay" in Sarawak terminology (Pringle 1970: xix).[10]

The incorporation of Sarawak into the Federation of Malaysia in 1963 also brought a fundamental change to the location of Sarawak Malay ethnicity. Through the formation of a Malay-dominant government in the Malay Peninsula (West Malaysia) and the subsequent participation of Sarawak in Malaysia, two kinds of Muslim social groups with different historical backgrounds were categorized under the same ethnic name "Malay". The present political unit led by the politically dominant Malays in the peninsula traces the origin of "Malaysia" back to the city-state of Melaka, which rose around 1400 and was conquered by Portugal in 1511. The state history of Malaysia finds its hegemonic as well as ethnic roots in the sultanate of Melaka, which is quite different from the historical experience of Sarawak.

---

[9] The reverse is not true; not all Muslims are Malay. For instance, the people called Melanau consist of Muslims, pagans (animists), and converts to Christianity.

[10] The word "Malay" was also used by Dutch colonial administrators for the Muslim population on the west coast of Dutch Borneo adjacent to Sarawak. The possibility exists that the word Malay (Maleier, Maleische) has its origin in the Dutch colonization of the region.

In the present Malaysian Constitution, a Malay is defined as those who speak Bahasa Melayu (Malay language), have "faith in Islam", and follow *adat*, the customary codes of the Malay. It is noteworthy that the definition is based solely on language, religion, and custom, and makes no reference to historical descent. An ethnic group is "a type of descent group whose members validate their claim to shared descent by pointing to cultural attributes which they believe they hold in common" (Keyes 1976: 208). The collective affiliation to a social category by which people share specific cultural elements gives an ethnic category a historically specific continuity. In the case of the Sarawak Malays, the major cultural element shared in common and the most important ethnic marker in Sarawakian context is the commitment to Islam, which distinguishes them from the Dayak and the Chinese:

> The Sarawak Malays do not to any significant degree represent any kind of evolutionary group, or even relic, of a distinct "Malay" people who "came in from the west" within any memory, or before. Rather, they reflect the movements of a few authoritative, aristocratic or able (guru, trader, etc.) Moslems — not necessarily always from Malaya or elsewhere in Indonesia. These individuals or small groups converted or led local, indigenous populations, or parts thereof, to embrace Islam, become Moslem, and thus in latter-day terminology *masuk melayu*, become Malay (Harrisson 1970: 648).

For the Malays, "being a Muslim" is a crucial ethnic criterion. This marker differs from other cultural elements gradually acquired in the course of socialization, such as language, in that it can be obtained literally overnight through religious conversion. In these circumstances, where being Muslim is the same as being Malay, any person who wishes to be a Malay recites twice in front of two witnesses: "there is no God except Allah. Mohammed is a messenger for Allah." This conversion process is locally called *masuk Melayu*, literally "to enter the Malay". Precisely speaking, the conversion should be called *masuk* Islam, but the common local expression inadvertently combines "becoming Muslim" with "becoming Malay".

Religious conversion efforts, a driving force in the spread of Islam in Borneo, makes the formation process of "Malay" as a distinctive ethnic category more complicated than the Dayak and the Chinese. "Malay" as an ethnic category based on personal religious affiliation lacks the concept of "blood". This absence of an ethnically specific descent line is one of the characteristics of the Malays in Sarawak.

The majority of ancestors of Sarawak Malays were either Malayo-Muslim immigrants, with diverse cultural and historical backgrounds, or Dayak converts. The maintenance of the ethnic category requires a manipulative strategy to create authenticity of descent and historical continuity. The ethnic narratives of the Sarawak Malays lead to the marginalization, if not the oblivion, of the multiple descent lines of the current Muslim population.

The Emergence of the Kuching Malays

James Brooke and his nephew Charles Brooke governed Malays in Sarawak through indirect rule. There was no ambiguity in the Malay leadership structure, as the *datu* was clearly recognized by all as the ruling figure. During Charles Brooke's rule, there were four datuships and Kuching Malays filled all of them; thus the *datu* and the Kuching Malay elite overlapped. Some aristocrats outside of Kuching held *datu* rank, but none received titled datuships or had state-wide authority (Lockard 1987: 51).

The biggest change colonial intervention brought to Sarawak Malay society was that the Malays in Kuching emerged as a distinct social category, and this led to their cultural dominance. The Sarawak River basin had been a backwater by the standards of northwest Borneo and there were no important settlements located there before the Brooke colonization. A Dutch visitor in 1823, just prior to the establishment of Kuching as the new capital, recorded about one hundred Malays in the main settlement, mostly "pirates", along with three Chinese households (Blume 1843: 147–8, cited in Lockard 1987: 9).

Under Brooke rule, Kuching became not only the political center of a growing state but also the primary trading port for a growing hinterland. The initial years of colonization marked the beginning of new social, economic, and political developments that paved the way for the emergence of a larger, more heterogeneous urban society in which Malays, Chinese, Dayaks, Indians, and Europeans played major roles. Although Chinese and Indians were the most prominent immigrants, many Malayo-Muslims settled in Kuching between the mid-nineteenth and early twentieth centuries. Several thousand probably arrived from western Borneo, Brunei, and various parts of the archipelago, as well as other parts of Sarawakian territory (Lockard 1987: 15–34).

Far from weakening the basic local Malay social structure, the influx of Muslim immigrants in Kuching gradually led to a cohesive

Kuching Malay community. The ease with which Malays assimilated immigrants with a similar language and identical religion had been apparent in the pre-Brooke period, when newcomers from Dutch Borneo, Java, Sumatra, Brunei, and elsewhere joined Islamized Dayaks to form Malay settlements. This assimilation continued into the middle of the Brooke period, when the number of Muslim immigrants increased considerably. These immigrants merged rather imperceptibly into the Malay group within a few decades, normally within a generation (Lockard 1987: 58–9).

Putative shared cultural attributes stand in diagnostic relation to the claim of shared descent because the former claim must be marked by particular examples. Such claims are commonly based upon language, origin myths, and folk histories, and the historical continuity of the Sarawak Malays is affirmed through the story of the legendary Datu Merpati and his family. Datu Merpati is believed to have been a member of the royal family of Minangkabau and a grandson of Raja Jawa. Datu Merpati came to Cape Dato from Sumatra together with his wife, Datu Permaisuri, a daughter of Raja Jarom of Johor, and settled at Santubong in southwestern Sarawak. Their sons subsequently became rulers of the riverine settlements from the Sarawak River eastward to the Rejang River. Merpati's eldest son, Merpati Jepang, married Dayang Murdiah, daughter of Abang Adi of Santubong, and later moved to Lida Tanah near the convergence of the two branches of the Sarawak River (Mohammed Yusof Shibli 1950).

A repeated theme in the sojourn of the nobles is their foreign origin and their close relationship with the sultanates of the Malay Peninsula, Sambas, and Brunei. Although the "historical likelihood is that *nakoda* or merchant-captains with aristocratic connections came from Sumatra or Johor to Sarawak during the Srivijaya period and intermarried with Melanaus, Bidayuh and Sebuyau Dayaks living along the coast from Cape Dato to the mouth of the Rejang River" (Reece 1993: 1), the oral tradition conceals local elements, primarily the substantial number of Dayak converts in the genealogy.

This origin myth supports the historical continuity of the Malay aristocratic *perabangan* in Kuching, which has often claimed a direct genealogical linkage with Datu Merpati (Reece 1993: 1). For instance, a genealogy of elite Kuching Malays collected in 1940 claims a kinship tie to Datu Merpati along with various mythical and supernatural figures (Mohammed Yusof Shibli 1950: 264).

For some Malays, ostensible kinship ties with the apical ancestor legitimizes the claim to represent authentic Sarawak Malay culture and society. In other words, the *perabangan* are at the apex of Sarawak Malay culture and society, and provide a canonical definition of ethnic virtue. As their kinship ties to the *perabangan* core group become distant, other Malays are progressively marginalized ethnically.

Stratification and Marginalization

The uneven distribution of political and economic resources between ethnic groups in Sarawak tends to attract more attention than the nested hierarchies within ethnic groups. This is partly because the anthropological as well as historical discourse on ethnicity has centered on inter-ethnic power relations, with competition for scarce resources generally attributed to ethnic stratification. Hierarchy within a single ethnic entity is considered class analysis, a less popular subject of inquiry (cf. Williams 1989: 401).

As an ethnic category emerged with a specific ethnic nomenclature, a process of differentiation took place in the cultural geography of Sarawak. In the case of Sarawak Malays, *perabangan* aristocrats came to occupy the core of ethnic hegemony, while other sub-groups with varied geographical as well as genealogical locations were pushed to the periphery of the ethnic entity. This gradation occurred within the boundaries of the territorial state, and the dissociation of the periphery from the core takes place alongside with the process of class differentiation.

Demographically, the *perabangan* class is a minority, and the majority of Sarawak Malays are rural, typically coastal and riverine dwellers whose main subsistence activity is fishing. Inland agriculture is considered the traditional occupation of Dayaks. In the ethnic discourse molded over one and a half centuries of Sarawakian history, rural Malay agriculturalists have been peripheralized in relation to both the urban Malay aristocrats and the rural fishing communities of the Kuching Delta. Land-based Malay peasants do not fit comfortably with the authentic ethnic expression of the Sarawak Malay, though the villagers themselves never question their own ethnicity.

From the beginnings of Brooke rule to the present, accounts of the origin of the land-based Malay peasantry are scarce:

> In the 1860's and 1870's, the Kuching Malays were still largely a maritime or riverine people. Apart from a small number who worked for government, most pursued traditional livelihoods as fishermen and small traders. Unlike the Dayaks, they were not farmers and

> did not engage in the collection of jungle produce. At this rate, they would never have been able to compete with the Chinese who were successful farmers as well as traders (Reece 1993: 22).
>
> The greater part of the Malay population was the peasantry. Contrary to common belief, this class was not entirely made up of poor agriculturists and fishermen. In Sarawak the peasant class largely comprised petty riverine traders and to a lesser extent agriculturists. The petty traders were mainly involved in riverine trade with the Dayak of the interior. They bartered salt, beads and cloth for jungle products such as rattan, camphor, gambier and damar (Sanib 1985: 8).

Swidden agriculture as a cultural expression of economic activity has contributed to the ethnogenesis of the interior Dayaks:

> It is evident, therefore, that the Iban in up-river areas who seem to be clinging to a traditional subsistence economy are in a sense being compelled to do so. Surrounded by a predominantly cash economy, and themselves willy-nilly encroached upon by it, they are trapped in the impasse of an involuted subsistence economy. At the same time it is true that they are also consciously attached to traditional Iban subsistence ethics.
>
> One might even say that the up-river inhabitants in question are, in their consciousness, subsistence cultivators par excellence. And yet this form of consciousness is a reaction, a kind of anxiety reaction, to their own transformed and threatened existence. The meaning of subsistence economy, both subjectively and objectively, for these "traditionalized" cultivators is totally different from that of the genuinely traditional cultivators of former days (Uchibori 1984: 258).

The Malay peasantry that emerged under Western colonization and the newly independent state was largely invisible. The Malay *perabangan* class formed in Kuching during the early Brooke period, a quasi-descent group symbolically affiliated to a legendary founding father, established a canonical expression of the Sarawak Malay ethnicity that excluded peasant agriculture. Any indications of the existence of Malay peasantry were concealed by the members of the Kuching elite in order to differentiate themselves from non-Muslim others. While this Malay elite was emerging at the urban political center, Brooke economic policy was creating a rural Malay peasantry that was largely ignored in the Kuching-centered cultural discourse on the Sarawak Malay. Considered ethnically peripheral, this group's social history went unrecorded.[11] Although subsistence diversification within a single ethnic group is the result of ecological adaptation (cf. Barth 1969), and the coexistence of different subsistence modes is not particularly special (cf. Galaty 1982), the formation of a land-oriented Sarawak Malay peasantry shows the universal process of ethnic marginalization.

Under the construction of ethnic categories by the state, urban Sarawak Malays, specifically those in Kuching, have occupied the dominant political status, while borderland Malays have been placed at the fringe of the Malay ethnic category. Sarawak Malays have been typically depicted as traders and fishermen, and their way of life as either urban or maritime-riverine-based. The Malays in the state capital and surrounding area represent the core features of Sarawak Malay culture, and consider the villagers of Telok Melano, who practice shifting cultivation in the primary forest adjacent to the national border, as "quasi-Sarawak Malays", and closer to "Dayaks".[12] Telok Melano's adherence to swidden agriculture is irregular and strange even in the eyes of neighboring Dayaks in Pue (near Sematan), who shifted to irrigated wet rice cultivation decades ago. Presently, the Telok Melano and Telok Serabang people are the only swidden cultivators in the Kuching Division of Sarawak (possibly in Sarawak, East Malaysia).[13] Despite Telok Melano residents' self-identification as Malay, urban Malays have questioned whether they fit into the ethnic category of "Sarawak Malay" established ever since the emergence of the state and its territorial boundary.

The next chapter continues to look into the spatial construction of social groupings, contending how the neighborhood of Telok Melano was transformed into both a village compound and a national territory. To explore relationships among various social categories and how a sense of belonging was formulated, I will reconstruct the history of a moving boundary created by the sultanates, demarcated by the colonial powers, and militarized by postcolonial nation-states.

---

[11] For the discussion on "para-Malay", see Leach (1950) and Benjamin and Chou (2002). According to Benjamin, para-Malay "shares the same general background with the Orang Melayu, but lack one or more criteria (Islam, ethnic identity, language, the centralized state) of full Melayu-ness" (Benjamin 2002: 27). Ishikawa (2008) examines the cultural geography of the Sarawak Malays.

[12] For detailed descriptions of Telok Melano's swidden agriculture, see Appendix: Agriculture in Telok Melano.

[13] Personal communication with Logie Seman, the Forest Department of Sarawak, Malaysia.

CHAPTER SIX

Border Location Work

A Village in the Nation and the Nation in a Village

As the system of nation-states prevailed over the greater part of the globe, categorical differences in human groupings, immanent in social spaces designated as national territories, administrative villages, and culture areas, became critical frames of reference on locating individual *vis-à-vis* others. The territoriality of the nation is indispensable for the formation of nationality, as is a geographically specific cultural extent for the formation of ethnicity, while the community — be it a rural village or urban quarter — is a basic social arena for fixing an everyday sense of belonging. This chapter and the one that follows deal with the two kinds of identity formation — those grounded in the geo-body of the nation-state and the village compound. The first step will be to look at to what extent national territory and village space have been ethnicized within the culture framework designated and propagated by the contemporary nation-states of Malaysia and Indonesia.

To explore the manifold relationships among nationality, ethnicity, and community, all grounded in specific social spaces, I will make an enquiry into how a sense of belonging becomes associated with a social space, drawing on historical examples. In other words, my inquiry centers on the *location work* of villagers at the margin of the state, where the village boundary coincides with the national boundary (cf. Appadurai 1996). The location work of peripheral villagers offers an attempt to incorporate people's agency and everyday decision making into the matrix of larger politico-economic forces related to the emergence of social identity.

Benedict Anderson has written, "all communities larger than primordial villages of face-to-face contact (and perhaps even these) are imagined". Villages, culture-bearing groups, and the nation are all imagined communities and these "communities are to be distinguished, not by their falsity/genuineness, but by the style in which they are imagined" (Anderson 1991: 6). If both a village and a nation are imagined communities, is there any difference between the modes of imagining them? Is the basic style of imagining identical but for the size? Can national identity and ethnic identity be regarded as mere extensions of village communalism? If not, how do villagers differentiate them? These questions become crucial when considering modes of social grouping at the extremity of the state territory, where things local, national, and even international represent themselves in a dialectical, synchronic manner.

For the villagers, the siting of a village space in the national space and the siting of the national space in a village space is a two-way process. In order to understand spatially-specific identity formation, I will examine how borderland populations naturalized their locality in a plantation-cum-village that is geographically distant from the center of the state, historically isolated from waves of politico-ethnic mobilization, and beyond the reach of the national order.

Telok Melano's marking of locality has three characteristics: *duality*, *simultaneity*, and *plasticity*. First, in most places, nation and village are different social fields, but for Telok Melano, the production of locality requires the distinct but interrelated spatial recognition of village and nation under circumstances in which the village boundary and national boundary overlap. Secondly, the villagers of Telok Melano are required to define national space and village space simultaneously. As will be shown in detail, neither precedes the other; the genesis of village territoriality and nation territoriality is a quintessentially dialectical process.

The third point is the plasticity of the spatial boundary. The locality of nation and village is arbitrarily defined in the extreme borderland where no instant module for imagination is disseminated from the center. Official maps, border gates, and other means of promulgating boundary demarcation from the political center do not exist here. The officially designated boundary, which passes through the middle of a pepper field, not far from Telok Melano compound, is porous and extrinsic to the lifeworld of the locals. The social boundary exists only in the balancing act between Malaysian and Indonesian villagers. In this chapter, I try to delineate the way in which villagers create, use, and abuse the social categorization of "village" and "nation" (Sahlins 1988, 1989, 1990a, 1990b).

History of Border Demarcation at Cape Dato

From Telok Melano village, a walk of approximately thirty minutes along a small path through cultivated fields, secondary jungle, and barren grassland takes you to the border, straddled by pepper fields stretching out into both national territories. Locally, the international border between Indonesia and Malaysia is acknowledged as the border between the Indonesian hamlet of Tekam Patah and the Malaysian village of Telok Melano. A simple wooden gate is the only indication of the presence of an international boundary, as the border crossing lacks an immigration office and police checkpoint. Just one step, without showing a passport and receiving entry and exit stamps, takes you into Indonesia. Approximately ten meters from the gate are several houses in the Indonesian territory (see Illus. 11).

Despite the absence of visible signs and the ease of crossing the border, its demarcation at Cape Dato reflects the historical configurations of the borderland from the precolonial to postcolonial era. The first boundary was recognized by the sultans of Brunei and Sambas and was further changed by colonial and postcolonial governments. The following stories were collected from the Indonesian Sub-District head officer of Paloh, Sambas District, West Kalimantan, and a Malaysian police officer stationed at Telok Melano.

> A long time ago, the boundary was marked by the Brunei sultan and the Sambas sultan. The border was located at Cape Belat. During the Dutch and British era the boundary was the Naning River, and it remained there during the Indonesian and British colonial period. In 1974 a new boundary was determined by Indonesia and Malaysia, based on the natural watershed. Stakes can been found in Tekam Patah village. There exist three stakes which demarcate the boundary. (Interview with Sub-District officer of Paloh, Sambas District, West Kalimantan)
>
> The borderline between the Brunei sultanate and the Sambas sultanate was marked at Cape Belat at the mouth of the Paloh River. Because the Sambas territory was smaller than the territory claimed by the Brunei sultan, the Sambas sultan later asked for the alteration of the borderline to Tanjung [Cape] Limau Manis. This was before the Dutch and British colonization. Now Tanjung Limau Manis is called Tanjung Bendera. In the past, there were two cannons at the edge of forest, and there was one more set on the coast. The one on the seashore is now sunk into the sea. The other cannon at the edge of forest was seen in 1987 at the seashore (see Fig. 18).

> During the Dutch colonial time, the authority set a borderline close to the Camar Bulan River, yet this borderline was not used by Indonesia. A new borderline was fixed along the Naning River in the present Tekam Patah village by the Indonesian and British authority during 1945 and 1963.
>
> In 1974 another boundary was determined based on the natural watershed. The region of Torio was not officially incorporated in the agreement because a substantial area claimed by the Indonesian authority was inside Malaysian territory. The [claimed] Indonesian borderline extends about two kilometers into Telok Melano. About two hectares of the upper part of the Naning River in Malaysian territory is claimed by Indonesia (see Fig. 13).
>
> Following a report from the Department of Land and Survey, a survey was conducted in 1974, which took 3 months to measure the borderline between Cape Dato and Biawak (see Fig. 14). (Interview with a police officer in Telok Melano)

To summarize, under the sultanates, colonial administrations, and new nation-states, the triangle-shaped Cape Dato was divided first at Cape Belat, then Cape Limau Manis and the Naning River. The existing national boundary between Malaysia and Indonesia was finally determined in 1974. The stories above are almost identical apart from some chronological confusion. Interestingly, both refer to actual territorial demarcation between the two sultanates, the borders of which historians have long described as either "non-existant", "symbolic", or "fuzzy" (see Chapter 2). But as described above, the border was clearly demarcated with geographical markings and even cannon. The subsequent movement of the boundary was recognized locally, with no categorical difference between boundaries as determined by sultanates or colonial and postcolonial governments.

While these accounts clearly explain the history of the moving boundary on Cape Dato, the local version presents a rather different picture. The official inscription of border space by the colonial and post-colonial states required such natural markings as a cape, a river mouth, and a mountain divide. However, the further inland the dividing ridge proceeds, the more ambiguous the border demarcation becomes to local inhabitants. Cape Dato does not exhibit any visible divide inland, and no clear watershed comparable to the Hose Mountains, which divide East Kalimantan and North Sarawak, is found on its triangle-shaped headland.

According to Telok Melano locals, the national boundary was drawn for the first time in the 1920s when Penghulu Man (district head) was in charge of village affairs. Since then the border has been officially determined by authorities twice, but neither made much sense to the locals. As recorded in the *Sarawak Gazette* of 1926, even a government conservator of forests who visited Cape Dato, B.J.C. Spurway, could not find any "rentis" (*rintis*: path) dividing Sarawak from Dutch Borneo:

> North of the mouth of the Semunsam river to Tanjong Datu [Cape Dato] the hills are covered with excellent old jungle stretching in some cases to the seashore. The district is very thinly populated.... On making inquiries as to the existence of any artificial boundary between Sarawak and Dutch Borneo, I was informed that there was a "rentis" as far as was known. No one had ever seen it, which was extraordinary as this "rentis" can be not less than a mile and a half from the sea coast at this point. The Tua Kampong [village headman] was away and a Malay by name of Udin acting for him was absolutely useless as regards local information (*SG*, September 1, 1926: 219–20).

Even today, long after Indonesian and Malaysian officials made a detailed survey to determine the dividing line between the two countries, the spatial divide is still very porous. When I stayed in Telok Melano in 1993–94, the villagers had no working knowledge of the actual whereabouts of the national boundary designated by the authorities. They were told by parents and grandparents that there had been stones designating the international border. When I visited the border for the first time in 1993, my friends from Telok Melano tried their best to find these stones in weed-infested fields, but without success. Some villagers insisted these stones had been destroyed by someone with explosives, several years later I found them in the middle of a beautifully cultivated Indonesian-owned pepper field for harvest. These stones had been fixed at the time of the official bilateral border survey in 1974 (see Illus. 15).

Local people recall the frontier moving eastward from Cape Belat, Cape Limau Manis, and the Naning River, to its present location. Some claim that Indonesian territory encroached upon Malaysian territory. A Telok Melano villager explained the local view on the moving boundary:

> In the past there was a rumor that Malaysian land was absorbed by Indonesia. Temajuk absorbed Malaysian land. This was just a provocation and never became a serious problem. A matter outside of the two villages, Telok Melano and Temajuk. Border problems are

Illus. 15 A national border point in the midst of a pepper field

not local problems, but something for bureaucrats. Until now the relationship between the people of Temajuk and Telok Melano has been good, and there exists no problem.

During the initial period of its settlement at the turn of the twentieth century, the borderland between Dutch Sambas and Sarawak had no settlements other than Telok Melano.[1] The area adjacent to Cape Dato was regarded as the neighborhood of Telok Melano and was frequented by villagers for fishing and the cultivation of hill rice. Inside what is now present Indonesian territory, there are still many *durian*, *cenpadak*, and *engkabang* trees planted by the forefathers of

[1] "The caves at the Cape Dato are said to have been gutted by Sambas Dyaks, who live a short distance across the frontier, making their way down to the Simunsan River. Since that part of the coast has no population, these Dyaks were not detected" (*SG*, March 1, 1894: 41).

Telok Melano. These trees are valued as *pusaka* (inherited wealth) because of the commodity value of the fruits, but the descendants of the people who planted them have no claim to the trees.

Having no permanent settlement across the porous national boundary, Telok Melano villagers nevertheless cultivated hills as far as the present Indonesian hamlet of Temajuk Kecil. The village elders of Telok Melano recalled:

> From grandfathers to fathers and grandsons, we have just planted rice for generations. We cleared the forest and planted rice until weeds grew. Then we cleared another forest and planted rice until weeds grew. Look at the barren grassland near Temajuk. We have cleared the field as far as the Indonesian border. Unlike today, the land we cleared did not have to be measured and recorded by the Land Survey officials. We used to clear as much land as possible. If you have the guts to open the primary forest, just go ahead! It was like that.
>
> I still have many durian trees across the border. They were planted near the present Temajuk Kecil by my grandparents after they cultivated hill rice. They bore more than 400 fruits at once! Now the fruits are enjoyed by the Indonesian folks. Some of the trees were cut down and used as firewood.
>
> In the olden days, our father and grandfather cleared jungle for rice cultivation as far as the present light house at the tip of Cape Dato. The land now occupied by the villagers of Tekam Patah was also Telok Melano's land. The land was divided by the Malaysian and Indonesian authorities before the communists came. The old boundary at the Naning River was replaced by the present one. Fruit trees planted by our forefathers were supposed to be compensated. People from the Land Survey Department promised, but we have not received any compensation.

Telok Melano villagers utilized natural resources in their neighborhood and expanded their swidden fields without regard for the colonial border. Fig. 10, which is based on a 1960 aerial map of the swidden fields around Telok Melano and the adjacent Telok Serabang, shows patches of secondary forest utilized for hill rice production in the year of 1960. The limit of *padi* fields roughly coincides with the boundary between Sarawak (then a British Crown Colony) and the Republic of Indonesia, except for a portion of swidden field extending beyond the present border. It would be erroneous to conjecture, however, that the national boundary mattered much to Telok Melano villagers at that

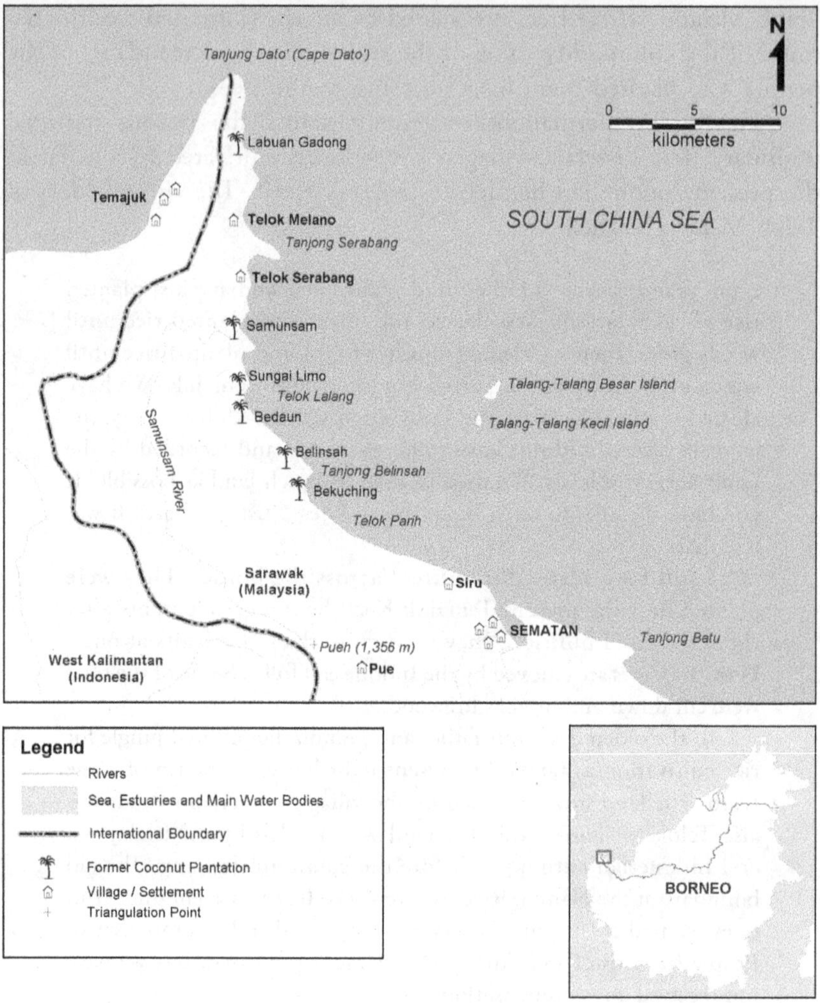

Fig. 9 Cape Dato–Sematan Coast

time. As will be shown, it was not until the boundary was violently drawn by military confrontation in 1963 that it became a feature of Telok Melano life. The fact that the cultivated field and the national territory very nearly coincided can be explained by ecological rather than political factors. Under extremely low population pressure — only 20 households resided in this vast tract of land — there would have been no ecological factors limiting the expansion of swidden field, if

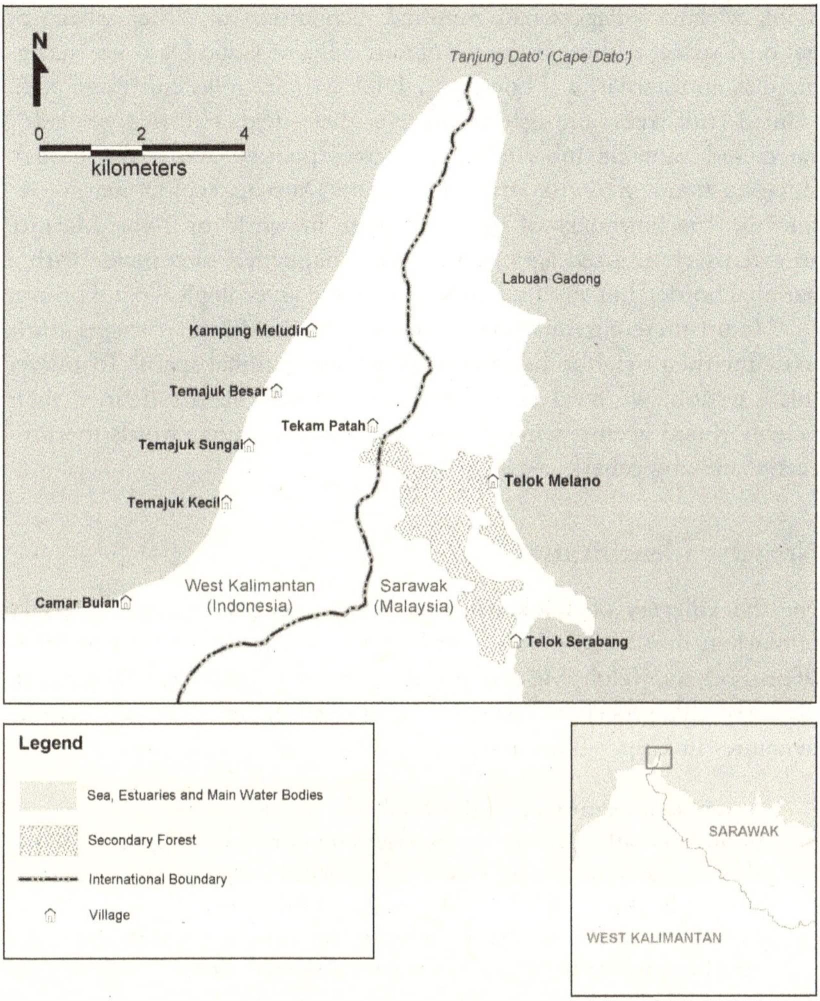

Fig. 10 The Secondary Forest at Cape Dato. An Aerial Map of Cape Dato (1960), the Map Division of the Sarawak Museum

Telok Melano were not a Muslim village. However, the constant threat of damage by wild boars, which Muslims cannot hunt, led villagers to cultivate fields only in the vicinity of their houses.

The recollections of the villagers on Telok Melano's exploitation of the borderland during the period preceding the formation of Malaysia in 1963 indicates the following points. In the absence of routine face-to-face relations with settlers in Dutch West Borneo/West Kalimantan,

Telok Melano villagers had minimal recognition of either village or national space. Although the mountain ridge of Cape Dato was recognized as an international boundary, Telok Melano folks cultivated padi, planted fruit trees, and fished wherever they liked. Hill rice was cultivated and valuable inheritable fruit trees planted across the border. Villagers frequented the coast near Cape Dato to exploit marine resources. The boundary of the immediate lifeworld of Telok Melano, an extensively utilized agricultural space, happened to coincide with a national border, but this probably represented an ecological equilibrium.

From these circumstances, how did Telok Melano villagers come to define their neighborhood as a village and national space? To answer this question, we need to see how borderland villagers defined their neighborhood against what it was not, this is in other words the process of making others.

Negative Identification

For the villagers of Telok Melano, group identity became necessary only when they faced others. Not by saying "who we are" but by identifying others, Telok Melano people defined their selves. E.R. Leach discussed this process of "negative identification" in his study of social dynamics in Upper Burma:

> It now seems clear that, in this whole region, the concept "tribe" is of quite negative utility from the viewpoint of social analysis. The significance of particular features of particular tribal organizations cannot be discovered by functional investigations of the more usual kind. It is rather that we measure these qualities against their antithesis in "Tribe B" (as in the gumsa-gumlao case). I reaffirm my opinion that, even at this late date, the extensive ethnographic literature of the Naga would repay study from such a dialectical "cross-tribal" point of view (Leach 1954: 15).

As Leach showed in the case of social oscillation between the *gumsa* and *gumlao* polities in Upper Burma, peoples define themselves in terms of differences between groups, rather than in accordance with a set of shared characteristics within a group. Particular features of particular groups are merely sociological fictions. Identity is only formulated against the antithesis in others. Negative identification offers a good starting point for analyzing the creation of spatial identity in the borderland of southwestern Sarawak, a place at the fringe of both the colonial and postcolonial state, where negative identity has for generations played a key role in giving meaning to others. The process of negative identity formation should be examined in a historically informed way (cf. Thongchai 1994: 5). When and under what conditions was negative identification formulated? What was the principal mode of seeing others before the emergence of negative identity? And how has the self-identification of Telok Melano villagers been altered by the presence of others?

The Production of Ritual Space

The locality of Telok Melano village as a collectively defined neighborhood was initially recognized as a ritual space, rather than a territorial or political space. Like other communal rituals whose participation is limited to the members of community, those of Telok Melano gave villagers a sense of exclusiveness *vis-à-vis* outsiders. Before Konfrontasi, Telok Melano villagers resided in a patch of primary and secondary forest near the present West Kalimantan/Sarawak border. Although they lived separately in order to take care of their own *padi* fields, they maintained a sense of neighborhood through their ritual participation in *sembahyang* (prayers) and *makan selamat* (communal feastings). Before a village prayer house was constructed by West Malaysian soldiers stationed in the village in the late 1970s, prayers were conducted at the village headman's house on Fridays. Villagers also occasionally attended communal feasts associated with the birth, illness, or death of family members, house building and housewarmings, and so on.

The *makan selamat tahun* (annual feast) had special meaning in Telok Melano's location work *vis-à-vis* others. The *makan selamat tahun* took place after the harvesting of hill rice, and for this reason was sometimes called the *selamat padi* or harvest welcome. To thank God for a good harvest, male villagers visit each others' houses to chant Islamic prayer (*doa selamat*) and enjoy rice cakes (*ketupat*) specially prepared for the occasion. As currently practiced, *makan selamat* is repeated on three consecutive Fridays. The rite is completed on the last of the *tiga Jumaat* ("three Fridays"), when villagers conduct *doa selamat* on the beach in front of the village.

Before the early 1960s, *makan selamat tahun* possessed a less Islamic character. The ritual was carried out over three consecutive days and was accompanied by a series of strict prohibitions and sanctions (*pantan*) centered on the quietude of daily life. The villagers tried

Illus. 16 *Makan Selamat Tahun* ritual performed on the Melano Bay seashore

their best to maintain tranquility and refrained from making any large noise, such as calling loudly, working in the field, felling trees, opening coconut shells, playing the radio, or even beating pillows drying in the sun. Village folks prepared all the firewood necessary for domestic chores before the commencement of *pantan* and spent three silent days eating only *ketupat* with a small number of side dishes.

During the period, entering and leaving Telok Melano was strictly prohibited, with village territoriality based on supernatural boundaries set for welcoming the guardian spirit from the South China Sea. At the edges of Melano Bay in front of the current site of the village, an altar (*ancak*) was built to notify outsiders that the village was ritually closed. The *ancak* was a tall bamboo pole affixed with a basket made of coconut leaves into which eggs, chicken hearts, and cooked rice were placed to welcome the *antu laut* (ghost from the sea). Villagers whistled three times on the beach to call upon the *antu laut* and made a wish for the welfare of the village and its residents. During *pantan* observance, Telok Melano became a ritually closed space that rejected outsiders and accommodated only the *antu laut*. During the arrival of the guardian spirit, intruders from the outside world were regarded as destroyers of the fragile relationship between the villagers and the *antu laut*. Before the early 1960s, *pantan* was rigorously observed in the borderland. Anyone entering the village while it was under *pantan* observance was required to contribute one hundred *ketupat* or pay the monetary equivalent.

The identity or collective consciousness of Telok Melano villagers emerged when they faced others who posed a possible threat to the lifeworld protected by the guardian spirit. *Makan selamat tahun* observed with *pantan* was ritualistic location work in which two kinds of boundary were set, one open to the *antu laut* and one closed to strangers. The boundary between the supernatural force and the community was a zone of danger requiring ritual maintenance. Following Arnold Van Gennep's periodization of rites of passage, the village under *pantan* was in a state of danger. The symbolic boundary was necessarily drawn for the exclusion of non-community members, who were potentially hazardous in their breaking of the fragile closedness.

Rituals such as this, which have been central to the inquiries carried out by anthropologists, need to be revisited and reread as context-generating practices for demarcating social boundaries. The ethnographic record can be reassessed as a record of "the multifarious modes for the production of locality" (Appadurai 1996: 181):

> ... Neighborhoods are inherently what they are because they are opposed to something else and derive from other, already produced neighborhoods [and] this something else is often conceptualized ecologically as forest or wasteland, ocean or desert, swamp or river. Such ecological signs often mark boundaries that simultaneously signal the beginnings of nonhuman forces and categories or recognizably human but barbarian or demonic forces (Appadurai 1996: 183).

Creation of a ritual space that differentiated village space from non-village space defined the neighborhood of Telok Melano in relation to a supernatural being and also to outsiders. The boundary marked by the communal ritual was set against outsiders who breached the *pantan* observance, regardless of where they came from. Not only Dayak and Chinese passersby, but also Malays from Sematan were required to pay a fine. In this ritualistic location work, national territoriality and the social affiliation of people had little meaning. However, after 1963 *antu laut* festivities gave way in the face of a new spirit of capitalism, and the tranquility of the village under *pantan* observance was replaced by the noise of the transnational smuggling economy.

Encountering Others

With the coming of smugglers to the village, the ritual space of Telok Melano quickly disappeared and residents became part of a new social field in which the politico-economic affiliation of people and commodities mattered. The first factor affecting Telok Melano's space making was the penetration of *smokel* (smuggling) activity, which became endemic in Lundu District. After the Japanese military occupation, the informal Lundu economy revived with the importation of various goods: agricultural commodities, precious metals, clothing, foods, tobacco, and livestock. Although the Indonesian republican government replaced the Dutch administration across the border, commodity smuggling from West Kalimantan continued unabated (Chapter 3).

On the Sarawak side, two Chinese merchants in Telok Melano received smuggled commodities brought by Malays and Dayaks from Indonesian territory via land and sea, respectively. Melano Bay was filled with incoming smugglers' boats and motorized vessels going out with transshipped goods. The border community suddenly became crowded with total strangers, and the bay visited annually by the *antu laut* became a busy transaction point. The ritual closedness necessary for *makan selamat tahun* vanished, along with the inscription of village space against outsiders (Chapter 4).

It is crucial to distinguish three levels of location work — the local, the national, and the international — and to clarify how these intersected in the new situation. After the implementation of the International Rubber Regulation Agreement, Sarawak and Dutch Borneo were designated as distinct economic units where the import and export of rubber sheets were strictly monitored. The national realization of economic territoriality and subsequent border policing by the states became a tangible part of daily life in the borderlands as commodity smuggling into Malaysian territory expanded to include a wider variety of goods and agricultural produce. Telok Melano became a relay point in the *smokel* business and witnessed the *in situ* deconstruction of the national boundary *before* the villagers had identified national space for themselves.

What was the reaction of Telok Melano villagers to the immersion of their community in the smuggling industry, which was essentially anti-national and anti-territorial in nature? How did they imagine, construct, and defend their space when their ritualistic location work suddenly disappeared and their communal space became transnational space? Their encounter with *smokel* led Telok Melano villagers to search for their locale in the social coordinates of criminality and state governmentality. For the first time in village history, state authority became real and constantly felt in daily life. Villagers became divided between those who had amicable relationships with the Sarawak Chinese merchants and Indonesian smugglers and those who disliked them. For the latter, the contrabandists were intruders in village space that was once under the protection of *antu laut* from the South China Sea. The divergence between pro-smugglers and anti-smugglers reflected the emergence of two opposing stances *vis-à-vis* the state, whose existence was now felt at its periphery in the form of chases, shootings, and arrests.[2]

The smuggling of rubber and other dutiable commodities from the Republic of Indonesia remained a major industry in the hinterland until 1963, when military confrontation between Malaysia and Indonesia and a subsequent communist insurgency set the stage for encounters with soldiers from Indonesia, West Malaysia, Britain, Australia, and Nepal, as well as armed Chinese communists. Between 1963 and 1966, Indonesia and Malaysia fought a small, undeclared war. The conflict resulted from the belief of Indonesian President Sukarno that the creation of Malaysia, which became official in September 1963, represented Britain's attempt to maintain colonial rule behind the cloak of independence granted to its former colonial possessions in Southeast Asia. Military activity increased along the Indonesian side of the Bornean border, early in 1963 when small parties of armed men began infiltrating Malaysian territory on propaganda and sabotage missions. These cross-border raids, carried out by Indonesian "volunteers", continued through 1963, but by 1964, Indonesian regular army units had become involved as well.

Owing to its proximity to the international boundary, Telok Melano inevitably became entangled in the confrontation. After two

[2] Van Schendel and Abraham (2005) focused on the contested boundary between the illegal and the illicit with detailed case studies of smuggling, migration, commodity chain, and borderland, allowing us to look into how criminality is produced by the space making and regulatory practices of the state.

villagers were abducted and killed by the Indonesian army in early 1963, Malaysian authorities ordered all residents of Telok Melano to evacuate the village, and they were forced to remain away from the village for more than five years. The forced evacuation became a critical moment for Telok Melano residents in defining their affiliation to one nation-state or the other. A number of villagers decided to go back to Sambas, while others hurriedly packed what they could carry and left for Sematan, after which their houses were set ablaze by Indonesian soldiers.

Konfrontasi ended in 1966, and Telok Melano villagers were allowed to go home in 1968. A decade after the end of Konfrontasi, another tragedy struck Telok Melano when a resident was shot and killed at his home by communist guerrillas hiding near the border. The presence of communists in the surrounding forest was known to villagers for a few years prior to the incident. Some villagers seem to have had a rather amicable relationship with them initially. A woman in her 30s recalled:

> Communists did not steal, but only bought foodstuff at a reasonable price. They were mostly Chinese, but some Dayaks and Malays of mixed blood were among them. There were women, too. They were well-educated. There was even a doctor and an accountant.

However, friction became inevitable as communist-hunting by Malaysian and Indonesian authorities intensified in the border area. The authorities ordered villagers to report immediately if they saw communists, and after incidents in which guerrillas were arrested in the Cape Dato area, the communists suspected the villagers had betrayed them. Local residents also became reluctant to contravene government orders by selling supplies to the guerrillas.

As suspicion mounted on both sides, tension grew and triggered the tragic killing. It happened one early evening in November 1977, in front of the victim's wife and infant son. After the shooting, the village was on immediate alert. Although residents were not evacuated, the government immediately took countermeasures. The border zone was manned by Indonesian and Malaysian soldiers, each building camps in the area, and Telok Melano became a frontline of defense against communist aggression. A volunteer village security force (RELA, Ikatan Relawan Rakyat Malaysia) was formed, each household secured a rifle, and a radio transmitter was installed at the village police station to contact the central authority in the case of an emergency.

During this era, villagers had frequent contacts with Malay soldiers from the Malay Peninsula. Although they shared the Islamic religion, this was the first time Telok Melano villagers met fellow countrymen from West Malaysia, who spoke a dialect of the Malay language that was substantially different in accent, tone, and pronunciation from their own. The villagers still remember trying to imitate how the soldiers spoke, an activity they deemed very amusing. It was also the first time they held their Friday prayers at a village mosque newly built by the soldiers. Moreover, a series of things related to the national order — firearms and military uniforms provided to the villagers, soldiers on alert, formal Islamic practice at the mosque, the new sound of Bahasa Melayu (Malay language) from the Peninsula — became part of daily life.

Identity becomes meaningful when people lose their own assurance in defining who they are and finally resort to a mirror image of themselves reflected in the eyes of others. The first and quite sudden encounter with social hybridity, criminality, and state authority during the *smokel* era and the introduction of a national order of things in successive periods of military crisis were prime elements in the process of identity formation in Telok Melano. Indonesians unlawfully importing rubber sheets every day, Chinese *taukay* merchants opening trading posts, armed government patrol boats on the sea, Javanese soldiers from across the border, clandestine Chinese *komunis* in hiding, and West Malaysian armed forces stationed in the newly established "village compound" — all these *others* added new dimensions to the location of Telok Melano villagers. "Who we are" was very much dependent on residents seeing themselves as the antitheses of these others. The negative identity process required neither their own identity nor a self-portrait; they defined themselves in terms of the differences among social groups rather than in accordance with shared characteristics common to Sarawak Malays or Malaysians.

A Political Exile and Telok Melano

Konfrontasi between Indonesia and Malaysia and communist guerrilla activities led to casualties, the destruction of homes, and evacuation. The belligerence of war and the liberation of Sarawak from British colonial rule clearly and violently inscribed a national boundary on the lives and thinking of borderland residents.

Much has been learned from the historical examination of these political events at the national and international level (cf. Mackie 1974,

Poulgrain 1998), but the ethnographic inquiry into their impacts on the daily life of the borderland has been largely neglected. A series of political incidents forcibly changed the positionality of the borderland villagers *vis-à-vis* the national order of things, their affiliation to the nation-state, and their identity formation.

The following section depicts a border scene in September 1963, seeking to locate points of articulation and disjuncture between international politics and local history. It is concerned with the location work of Telok Melano villagers who encountered political processes originating outside the realm of their lifeworld — the rivalry between newly independent Malaysia and Indonesia and the spread of communism to the Malay maritime world during the Cold War in Asia.

Two Village Elders and the Governor

From October to April each year, during the northeastern monsoon season, Telok Melano is isolated by bad weather and heavy seas. During this *landas* season, as it is locally called, my wife and I used to spend our days watching the rough sea through tattered banana leaves from a little wooden house on stilts. With the noise of rain spattering on the tin roof, we had to shout to hear one another. It was also a time to worry about diminishing food supplies and to check damp clothes that never seem to dry. In Sematan town, some 35 kilometers away, there is a regular bus service to the state capital of Kuching and wired electricity. Chinese shops in Sematan are lighted even in the morning hours, showing wrestling videos and martial arts movies to customers. But traveling to Sematan at this time of the year involves walking for eight hours along the coastline at low tide. The alternative is to venture onto the sea to face waves "as big as a coconut tree" for hours, and clinging to the steering so as not to "be cast away to Vietnam", as the villagers say.

The sound of rain, wind, swaying coconut leaves, and breaking waves became all too familiar, and any peculiar sound was a solace, as life grew monotonous during *landas* season. One day in February, we heard the sound of a helicopter approaching and thought a flying doctor was coming. We walked to the elementary school auditorium together with mothers with small children and a few older residents. Some Indonesians came from the other side of the border to ask for painkillers, a familiar sight after spending more than a year in the border village.

The sound of the propeller became deafening as a helicopter with the red, black, and yellow Sarawak state flag painted on its body landed in the school compound. Out came not a doctor, but Pak Daud, with his cowboy hat and leather shoes, an outfit reserved for his occasional visits to the city. He seemed to have visited Kuching, the state capital, from the way he looked. When I approached and greeted him, Pak Daud said it took him only half an hour to reach the village from Kuching (in contrast to up to two days by conventional means at that time of year), and that his VIP trip was arranged by the State Minister, an influential Malay statesman. In the capital, he had been interviewed about newly constructed "independence heroes' monuments" and particularly about those with whom he had personally been acquainted. After some exchange of news, he took his usual slow, steady strides back to his house at the foot of a hill, surrounded by pepper and cacao gardens and tall coconut and durian trees.

***

"Governor Ahmad Zaidi cannot come to Telok Melano due to his past," a number of villagers told me, usually in a low, contained voice, as if to share a secret. Tun Ahmad Zaidi's full name, including his title, was Yang Di-Pertua Negri Tun Datuk Patinggi Haji Ahmad Zaidi Adruce bin Muhammed Noor, and by then he had been governor of the state of Sarawak for fifteen years. As evidenced by his lengthy honorary titles, he is the most respected Malay statesman in Sarawak, the only person in this sultanless state to whom the prime minister must pay homage on official occasions. But people in Telok Melano say the governor is frightened of their village headman, Pak Jaya, a skinny but sturdy man in his 60s, about the same age as Pak Daud.

Pak Jaya's work as a village chief was limited by his inability to read official government documents. Nor was he skilled in dealing with officials. He thus let his son and Pak Daud's son deal with such affairs on most occasions. Instead, he used to issue somewhat bizarre orders to the villagers: "Do not fly kites. They invite ghosts." He also commanded people "not to wear footwear in the village compound and [to] walk barefoot", although no one but himself and the children playing on sandy soil adhered to such an order.

He was, frankly speaking, an other-worldly man. He was not, however, shunned nor held in contempt, as his strong *ilmu* (spiritual power) was known and revered by all villagers. Pak Daud, who belonged to the same generation, was a more pragmatic and quick-witted man open to the outside world. He understood the purpose and meaning of our research as soon as we settled in the village, and he shared many stories about the village's history, Sarawak's colonial past, swidden farming and government-assisted agricultural projects, the village's relationship with the Indonesian village across the border, and cultural overviews of southwestern Sarawak from the time of the kingdom of Majapahit. Pak Jaya's stories, on the other hand, ignored the historical or larger politico-economic factors surrounding village life. Yet Pak Jaya's stories were full of charm, and we came to look forward to his regular visits to our house on his way to the village mosque every Friday. He walked up the wooden stairs in front of our house, sat down, sipped lukewarm coffee, puffed a hand-rolled *rokok apong* (nipah palm cigarette), and started a story. "I used to go hunting. Even without searching, the number of deer I imagined before leaving home always showed up in front of me to be hunted." Or, "I know how to seal the village by creating a spiritual boundary and make offerings (*ancak*) to spirits from the sea in order to pray for peace and prosperity." Our favorite story was about a young but white-haired woman who crawled up onto his boat in the midst of the stormy ocean when he was still young and paddling home alone. She taught the frightened young man a spell to appease the rough waters and to make its surface like a mirror so he could walk on it even during a storm. "What a shame I forgot the spell," he lamented.

Pak Jaya sometimes embarrassed other villagers by raising the issue of his kinsmen's deaths with visiting government officials. I witnessed such an incident during a meeting to discuss arrangements for the annual "*Pesta Sempadan*" (Border Festival) at the primary school auditorium. With local government representatives present, he started pleading his case about his brother's abduction by Indonesians during Konfrontasi and his son's shooting death by communist guerrillas in the late 1970s. I later learned from other villagers that it was not the first time Pak Jaya had spoken about his family at meetings with officials. I felt a little pang imagining his feelings — how compelled he must have been to talk about the death of his loved ones even to inattentive officers.

Pak Daud and Pak Jaya lived on the north and the south ends of the village compound, respectively, rather isolated on the hills, as if to occupy the poles. The symbolic contrast went beyond the distance between their homes and extended to their personal relations with other villagers. I quickly realized that a subtle but definite line that divided the world to which the two elders belonged. The village consisted of more than 40 households with some 200 residents. People had close kinship ties that often overlapped. Cooperation was essential for swidden agriculture and rituals. Nevertheless, the two men remained rather independent of each other even on such occasions. Their spheres seemed to constitute a complementary set.

My wife and I lived with a middle-aged woman, the widow of Pak Jaya's son who had been shot to death by communist guerrillas. While she was Pak Jaya's daughter-in-law, her brother, who lived next door, was married to Pak Daud's daughter. So we had amicable relationships with both families. We were initially unaware of the fact, that village affairs were inexorably connected with the incidents of September 1963, with Governor Ahmad Zaidi, and with the murder of Pak Jaya's brother, and a series of events that took place against the backdrop of the larger politico-historical movements of nation-states and beyond in the early 1960s. It took me quite a few years to understand the complex interrelationships as well as disjunctures between international political events and the incidents as remembered by the villagers.

Tun Ahmad Zaidi and Malaysia

Tun Ahmad Zaidi was born in Sibu, a town at the mouth of the Rajang River, in 1924, during the reign of the third white rajah, Vyner Brooke. Soon after his birth, he was adopted by Wan Adruce bin Sharif Mashor, whose late father was a local Malay chief ruling the Rajan River basin. Sharif Mashor is known locally as the first nationalist because of his resistance to Brooke colonization. From his childhood, Ahmad Zaidi was seen as bright, and he studied in Kuching, Singapore, and Malaya. During the Japanese occupation, he went to the Javanese city of Bogor to study veterinary medicine. After Japan's defeat, 21-year-old Ahmad Zaidi joined the anti-Dutch movement and was involved for approximately three years in intelligence operations in Kalimantan as an information officer for the Indonesian Navy's Fourth Division.

After returning to his native Sarawak, he served in the Sarawak Education Department and worked in a teacher training school. In 1949, he went to England for further study. He earned an MA in

Political Economy at Edinburgh University and then went to the University of London to major in education, becoming the first Bornean *bumiputra* (non-Chinese native) to earn a degree from a Western university. After spending six years in England, he returned to work at the Sarawak Education Department and became increasingly involved in politics. In 1956, he was the acting president of the Sarawak Youth Front (BPS, Barisan Pemuda Sarawak) and he was then elected to the State Council and subsequently nominated to be vice president of the Kuching Municipal Council (Richie 2000, Sanib 1991).

The late 1950s, when Ahmad Zaidi gained prominence on the Sarawak political scene, coincided with the unfolding of the idea of establishing a Federation of Malaysia that would incorporate British Borneo and Singapore. Tunku Abdul Rahman, first prime minister of Malaya and a main actor behind this initiative, started discreet negotiations with local political leaders. In1958 he personally disclosed to Ahmad Zaidi and the Sultan of Brunei his plan for Sarawak to join the Federation, which had just achieved independence from the British (Richie 2000: 95). This proposed path to independence for Sarawak stirred heated political debate all over the territory.

During the period political movements were complex and driven by ethnic rivalries, and even supporters of Sarawak's inclusion in Malaysia were not united. Furthermore, two competing Muslim camps adhered to different objectives entirely, one supporting the establishment of and Sarawak's incorporation into Malaysia, the other seeking to unite with Brunei and North Borneo (the present Malaysian state of Sabah) to form the Federation of North Borneo. For Malays in Sarawak, the formation of a North Borneo federation meant the restoration of the traditional Malay world (*Alam Melayu*) with the Brunei Sultan as its political pillar. Sarawak Chinese, on the other hand, supported the concept because it offered political leverage against the "neo-colonialism" they claimed the formation of Malaysia would bring about by securing British interests in the region (Mackie 1974: 65). Opposition to the formation of Malaysia was therefore not unified either, but divided by two distinct political ideologies: one upholding the restoration of the Malay World and the other backing communism. Malays were cautious about embracing Chinese support. With communism widespread in Southeast Asia, particularly among the Chinese, they were wary of inviting the active involvement of a Chinese political party (SUPP, the Sarawak United People's Party), a step that might weaken the political stronghold thus far maintained by Malays.

The Brunei Rebellion of 1962 violently awakened both Muslims and Chinese to a deep rift between the two groups. The rebellion was led by Azahari, leader of a Malay political party (PRB, Parti Ra'ayat Brunei), who aimed to establish a Unitary State of North Kalimantan (NKKU, Negara Kesatuan Kalimantan Utara). Azahari's group occupied Limbang and Bekunu and almost seized Lawas in northern Sarawak, but was eventually suppressed by British military forces dispatched from Malaya and Singapore. The rebellion ended in failure after six months and resulted in the deaths of some 100 soldiers of the North Kalimantan National Army (TNKU, Tentra Nasional Kalimantan Utara) and the detention of a further 1,800. The British suspected Ahmad Zaidi's involvement in the insurgency since Azahari and Ahmad were close allies and had fought together in Indonesia's independence struggle (Sanib 1985: 94).

Ahmad Zaidi was detained and held under house arrest in Kuching. It is said that there was an offer from General Abdul Haris Nasution, Indonesia's defense minister, to "rescue" Ahmad Zaidi; in any event, he decided to flee to Indonesia in early September 1963 (Ritchie 2000: 97). In that same month, on 16 September, Malaysia was formally established. While military helicopters searched for the fugitive, Ahmad Zaidi hid in a fisherman's boat and reached Telok Melano by sea via Sematan.[3]

Telok Melano in September 1963

> Ahmad Zaidi hid himself in a Chinese temple near the port of Sematan. He remained underneath mangrove logs, as long as he was tall, spread on the floor of the temple and slept there to escape scrutiny by British soldiers stationed nearby. Five local Malays including the chairman of the BERJASA party's Sematan chapter, aided him. Ahmad Zaidi stayed there for three days before heading for Indonesia. On his way, he stopped by Telok Melano village where he stayed for one week in Pak Daud's house waiting for contacts from the Indonesian side. Three people eventually came across the border from Indonesia to meet him: Mani, Ibrahim, and another one from Bako. The entourage walked across the border near Cape Dato and fled.

[3] For a detailed description of Ahmad Zaidi's exile to Kalimantan, see Richie (2000: 97–105).

> There were two contending political parties in Sarawak at the time: BERJASA and NEGARA.[4] BERJASA was against the inclusion of Sarawak into Malaysia, while NEGARA represented conservative interests in the state. In Telok Melano, some joined BERJASA and others NEGARA, largely unaware of the ideological differences between the two but rather intrigued by the political movements of the time. Many in fact wore pins of both parties.
>
> Five sympathisers helped Ahmad Zaidi in the village: Pak Daud, Pak Ali, Pak Hitam, Pak Zaina, and another. Only Pak Daud was arrested by white men who came by helicopter after Ahmad Zaidi and his party fled to Indonesia. Not a small number of villagers were hostile to Ahmad Zaidi, and one secretly alerted the police about his escape. Pak Daud remained behind bars for six months in Lundu. Even after his release from prison, he had to report to the police station every week and was not allowed to go back to the village for a long time. (Interview with a Telok Melano villager)

After fleeing to Indonesian territory, Ahmad Zaidi reached Java via Pontianak, the state capital of West Kalimantan, and was appointed defense minister in a shadow cabinet of the Unitary State of North Kalimantan by Azahari, the prime minister-designate and mastermind of the Brunei Rebellion (Ritchie 2000: 113). Ahmad Zaidi remained in Indonesia and continued his political activities there until 1969.

During Konfrontasi, the borderlands between Indonesia and Malaysia became the stage for aggressive political activities including military incursions by the Indonesian armed forces, and NKKU guerrilla operations organized by Azahari's group. Indonesian soldiers were often spotted by local people in the hills and plains surrounding Telok Melano village. Pak Jaya claims he was "ready to shoot any Indonesians if they come too near my house", but others were too scared even to think of pointing a rifle at them. Looking back on those days, people laugh at being frightened enough to mistake cast-away logs for Indonesian soldiers in the dark and creeping flat on the ground to a neighbor's house.

One day in September 1963, when the camouflaged military attire of the enemy forces was no longer a novelty in Telok Melano, three

[4] BERJASA (Barisan Anak Jati Sarawak) was established in 1961 by Sibu Malays and Melanaus and led by Haji Tahir, who had been a prominent member of BPS led by Ahmad Zaidi. NEGARA (Parti Negara Sarawak) was a party based on the support of Kuching Malays. The Chinese-based SUPP also had a local chapter in Sematan backed by Teochew and Hakka merchants and peasants.

villagers were shot to death by NKKU guerrillas. A group of Indonesians attacked four houses, including two belonging to Pak Jaya's brothers, and abducted four men, taking them into Indonesian territory. They were all shot execution style with their hands tied behind them to wooden posts. Pak Saleh, younger brother of Pak Jaya, was the only survivor and told the story to villagers. Reputed to possess spiritual power as strong as his brother's, Pak Saleh "managed to escape when the rope tied to his wrists loosened. Guerrillas fired shots at him, but bullets mysteriously went out of the way." Others say he was fortunate to have a friend in the group and was pardoned. The other three men, presumed dead, were never found.

It was not the last tragedy to befall the village. One night shortly after rice harvest, seven out of the village's 21 houses were set on fire, including that of Pak Jaya. At that time of the year, all the houses were filled up with newly harvested hill rice. People not only lost the fruit of their labor but clothes, kitchenware, furniture, valuables, livestock, and everything else they possessed. As they escaped, they turned for a last look and still have painful memories of seeing black smoke pouring out of their thatched houses.

The authorities immediately ordered the village evacuated and blockaded. The borderland adjacent to Cape Dato became a military frontline where the British deployed the crack Special Air Service Regiment (Dickens 1991). As mentioned in earlier chapters, all residents were forced to relocate, and most settled into new lives in other towns and villages such as Sematan, Lundu, Kuching, or Santubong. Some were fortunate enough to lease small plots of land where they could grow tapioca to feed their family members. Others had to make ends meet through wage labor. In 1965 they were allowed to visit Telok Melano village in the daytime to collect coconut seeds and to fish. They had to cross a checkpoint manned by Gurkha soldiers from Nepal, "who ran faster in the jungle and had sharper eyes at night than local Ibans". Five long years passed before they were finally allowed to return to the village in 1968. Pak Jaya and Pak Daud returned first, and others gradually followed.

The whole experience — Ahmad Zaidi's move to Indonesia, Pak Daud's involvement and subsequent arrest, the abduction and murder of villagers, arson in the village, and the five-year forced evacuation — constituted, in the minds of local people, not separate incidents but a single series of events. It was clear to me from the beginning of my research that the political climate surrounding the village in 1963, which triggered Indonesian military incursions into Sarawak, was largely responsible for the murders. For a long time, however, I took the incident as one of many tragic consequences of such political instability. The death of three men, the Indonesian military action, and international politics were only vaguely interrelated in my mind. The three people were killed because of specific activities, but irrationally victimized as part of sporadic military violence as if struck by sudden lightening. People in the village did not talk much about the tragedy of 1963, and I did not press them about matters they were reluctant to share.

The longer I stayed in the village, however, the more the bits and pieces came to form a coherent story, one that was quite different from the original picture I had imagined. I came to perceive the death of the three villagers as something not inadvertent, deaths that had causality but had failed to take on meaning in the history of nation making. As I learned more about the actors in the politico-historical event staged in Telok Melano — the NKKU guerrilla fighters, Pak Daud, Pak Jaya, Ahmad Zaidi, and other villagers — I came to see the intricate web of relations in which local incidents are linked with national and supra-national political movements. The linkage between the everyday actors and the macro-level political movements is, however, never straightforward or unilinear. The following section illuminates the way a micro-level incident, in this case the killing of three men, finds both points of articulation and discontinuities with international politics.

How They Remember It

There was no media coverage of the incidents; those who perished were not revered as national heroes as were those enshrined in monuments in Kuching, and their fate is not recorded in histories of East Malaysia. Telok Melano villagers who lived to survive the era nevertheless remember the whole series of events and understand what happened from their own perspectives. When asked about the death of the three people and the seven houses set on fire, villagers offer two versions of causality.

The first version sees a vague link between the political acts of Ahmad Zaidi and Pak Daud in 1963 and the incidents. Many in the village believe that Ahmad Zaidi's move to Indonesia after he spent time in their village led to Indonesia's military aggression against Malaysia, NKKU guerrilla activities, and military operations in the border area.

Some claim that Ahmad Zaidi crossed the border into Indonesia seeking help, and that those who abducted people from the village were Indonesian soldiers who supported him. This may sound far-fetched, but these reasonings do not seem totally implausible to the villagers, considering that Ahmad Zaidi was later appointed shadow defense minister of the Unitary State of North Kalimantan and led military training in Indonesian Kalimantan (Ritchie 2000: 113).

This explains why the villagers say that Tun Ahmad Zaidi cannot come to Telok Melano to this day. He was implicated in political affairs allegedly related to the political events in 1963. It also explains the quiet but firm polarization between Pak Jaya and Pak Daud in the village. While pro-Indonesian villagers such as Pak Daud supported the ultimate objective of establishing a new and independent pan-Bornean state, the death of the three men antagonized most villagers, turning them against the Indonesian guerrillas and against Ahmad Zaidi's supporters in the village.

The second version of causality is personal and parochial, barely linked with the larger political picture. In part it reflects the unique positioning of Telok Melano village, where people sharing culture and religion divided by two geo-bodies meet and mingle every day:

> During Konfrontasi, three villagers were abducted by NKKU guerrillas and shot to death. The guerrillas responsible for the brutal killing in fact were Indonesian men who had lived in Telok Melano village prior to the Konfrontasi period. They worked on village farmland as wage laborers. The payment was meager for they were illegal workers on Sarawakian soil. In other words, they were taken advantage of by their employers. They had stayed and worked in the village for three years. After harvest, they asked for their wages. Instead of giving the payment due them, the employers threatened to make a report to the police and gave them less than the minimum wage of the time. They were, of course, angry and held a grudge against the abusers. During Konfrontasi, they simply retaliated. I used to tell people not to abuse Indonesians, but some just did not listen. During Konfrontasi, Indonesians attacked and set fire to 7 houses for revenge. (Interview with a Telok Melano villager)

This version does not depict the local incident as the micro-level manifestation of higher-level political dynamics involving Kuala Lumpur and Jakarta. We see instead people using and abusing the state's institutions and aggressions in pursuit of their own petty interests. Some in Telok Melano village are said to have exploited Indonesians, taking advantage of their nationality and illegal status, and Indonesians are believed to have pursued a personal vendetta through militarily organized violence in the name of political justice. Both stories perhaps have some truth in them and are not mutually exclusive. For the villagers of Telok Melano, believing in one does not preclude the other.

Pak Daud, though an eloquent speaker, never talked much about Ahmad Zaidi's sojourn and his own arrest. He eventually lost his voice to pharynx cancer late in life. I am certain that he acted with a firm belief in pursuing Sarawak's independence through the Malay nationalist movement and that is why he assisted Tun Ahmad Zaidi. Pak Daud told me stories about the greater maritime Malay world: "Sarawak used to be part of the Javanese kingdom of Majapahit. More than 5,000 Majapahit people lived in the Cape Dato area, not far from Telok Melano." He also taught us that the Sambas sultan in West Kalimantan was a cousin of the Brunei sultan and that the two sultanates have maintained close ties, and he described an ancient religious community or kingdom encompassing the whole region. He used the word *undang-undang* (laws/rules) to portray the series of political systems Sarawak had experienced since the demise of the sultanate, from the Brooke regime, Japanese occupation, and British colonial rule to the present-day Malaysian nation-state. He saw these passing *undang* quite objectively, but always hoped for the return of *tanah Melayu* (the land of the Malays), undivided by nation-states either colonial or post-colonial.

Pak Daud was born and raised in Santubong, the coastal village not far from Kuching, and spent his youth in the 1950s and 1960s involved in politics in the capital. Through his political activities in those days, he was acquainted with Ahmad Zaidi and other BPS members, as well as the important political figure who arranged his helicopter ride home to the village. "I am a peasant because I do not have school education. But look at him, he is the Minister now," he smiled.

Ahmad Zaidi was a Malay nationalist who advocated a pan-Malay movement calling for ethnic unity throughout the region. In contrast to that ideal, the antagonistic feelings held by Pak Jaya and some other villagers against Ahmad Zaidi, Indonesians in general, and Pak Daud to a certain extent, exemplify local, parochial sentiments towards outsiders, especially the neighbors across the border. Indonesia is only "one *kretek* (clove) cigarette away". In a place where the village border coincides with the international border, we may easily take village communalism, shared by kin and peer group members, as nationalism. However, it may be necessary to carefully distinguish the sense of belonging to specific spaces, i.e., village compound and national territory. The village communalism of Telok Melano and the national territory-bound structure of feeling we call nationalism seem akin, but are never the same. For borderland Malays, it was conservatism and primordial feelings against outsiders that turned them against Ahmad Zaidi, the Indonesian army, and the communist guerrillas.

Structures of Time

After a temporary respite following an operation, Pak Daud succumbed to cancer in 1997. In spring 2000, Pak Jaya died at home from a sudden illness. After returning to Sarawak in 1970 from Indonesia, Tun Ahmad Zaidi was elected to the State Assembly. He served in several state ministerial posts, and became governor of Sarawak in 1985, holding that position for 15 years. On December 5, 2000, he passed away in a hospital in Kuala Lumpur from kidney failure. His body was brought back to Sarawak the same day, and flags were flown at half-mast in all government institutions in the state.

These three deaths brought the saga of Ahmad Zaidi's exile to an end. There are two biographies of Ahmad Zaidi, both based on interviews with the governor (Richie 2000, Sanib 1991). In these authorized accounts, Ahmad Zaidi, speaking as a nationalist, talks about seven years in exile in Indonesia, and defends the propriety of his political stance at the time.

The governor's youth and his sojourn in Indonesia — a country then hostile to Malaysia — had been a blank in the political history of modern Sarawak until the appearance of these semi-autobiographies. The governor's trip to Telok Melano has become local memory in the borderland. Such memory, however, is not part of the national history and fades away as older generations disappear.

Historians have always been concerned with such sets of relations in space and time. While some take an inductive approach to infer structure from specific incidents, others employ an anti-structural position and focus on the events themselves. Ranging from long-term *géohistoire* (Braudel 1966) to *micro-histoire* (Levi 1991), various scales of time have been used to identify the different natures of history. In order to capture the meaning of the series of events and larger structures surrounding Telok Melano in 1963, one must be attentive to two scales of time, one charting the nationalist movement encompassing Borneo, the Malay peninsula, and Java, the other marking everyday life in an out-of-the-way village. The two blocks of time reflect the Cold War politics and official national history, on the one hand, the feeling and memories of local people, on the other.

An event that took place in Telok Melano at the time of national independence offers some insights into people's agency as expressed in the location work of Telok Melano villagers. My aim is to trace the chains of inter-personal and inter-group relationships surrounding Ahmad Zaidi's time in the borderland between Malaysia and Indonesia and to recount people's memories in depth, as an alternative to the elitist history of nationalism and nation building. The episode of Telok Melano in 1963 seems too trivial even for social historians engaged in micro-narratives, but such marginal narratives provide an understanding of the disjunctures and discrepancies surrounding nationality, ethnicity, and parochial communalism at the historical moment of nation-making.

The discussion of this chapter has centered on how the neighborhood of Telok Melano was spatially transformed into a village compound as well as a national territory. By looking into the history of a moving boundary and location work of the villagers at the margin of the state where locals on both side of border share basic culture and the same ancestry, it attempted to explore the way in which everyday spatial recognition relates to the emergence of social and political identities. The locality of nation and village is arbitrarily defined in the extreme borderland where no instant module for imagination is disseminated from the center. Nationality divides locals, yet transnational interaction remains strong and even indispensable for the survival of border communities. Malaysia and the Republic of Indonesia do not impose the national identities that have emerged on either sides of the border. Rather, the local communities construct, and sometimes strategically use the boundary of national territory. In the following chapter, I will explore economic location work of people with special focus on the transnational flows of commodity and labor between Telok Melano and Temajuk, an Indonesian migrant village, to look into how national economic difference structures everyday life on the border.

CHAPTER SEVEN

Osmotic Pressure of the Nation-State

Culture Area and National Territory

Over the course of Telok Melano's history, ethnicity has been a minor frame of reference for the villagers in differentiating themselves from others. Village-based communal identity, or the structures of feeling attached to specific spaces formulated through the realization of *kampung* compound and national territoriality, have been far more relevant. Although the Malay cultural complex in western Borneo has long been the subject of arbitrary division by both colonial and post-colonial states, cultural continuity and unity — based on commonalities of religion, ritual practice, and lifeways — have been a source of primordial identity as *orang Melayu* (Malays) on both sides of the border. One commonly hears from borderland Indonesian and Malaysian villagers alike: "We belong to one ethnic group, *bangsa Melayu*, although we have long been separated by *undang-undang* (state laws)." *Melayu Sambas* (Sambas Malay) and *Melayu Sarawak* (Sarawak Malay) are official nomenclatures given by their respective states, but these labels are never used by local residents to distinguish themselves. The only criterion presently separating Bornean Malays in the borderland is nationality. To Telok Melano villagers, fellow Malays from the other side of the border are *Indon*, and to Indonesian villagers the Malays of Telok Melano are *orang Malaysia* (Malaysians).

As the spatial distribution of various Malay *kampung* in western Borneo shows, Telok Melano is located on the northwestern tip of the Sambas Malay culture area (see Fig. 12). Many Telok Melano elders still recall their ancestral homelands by name, such as Semudun, Arun Medong, Hasbi — places all along the Kunyit River near Mempawah. The coastal arc of the Sambas Malay culture area in western Borneo,

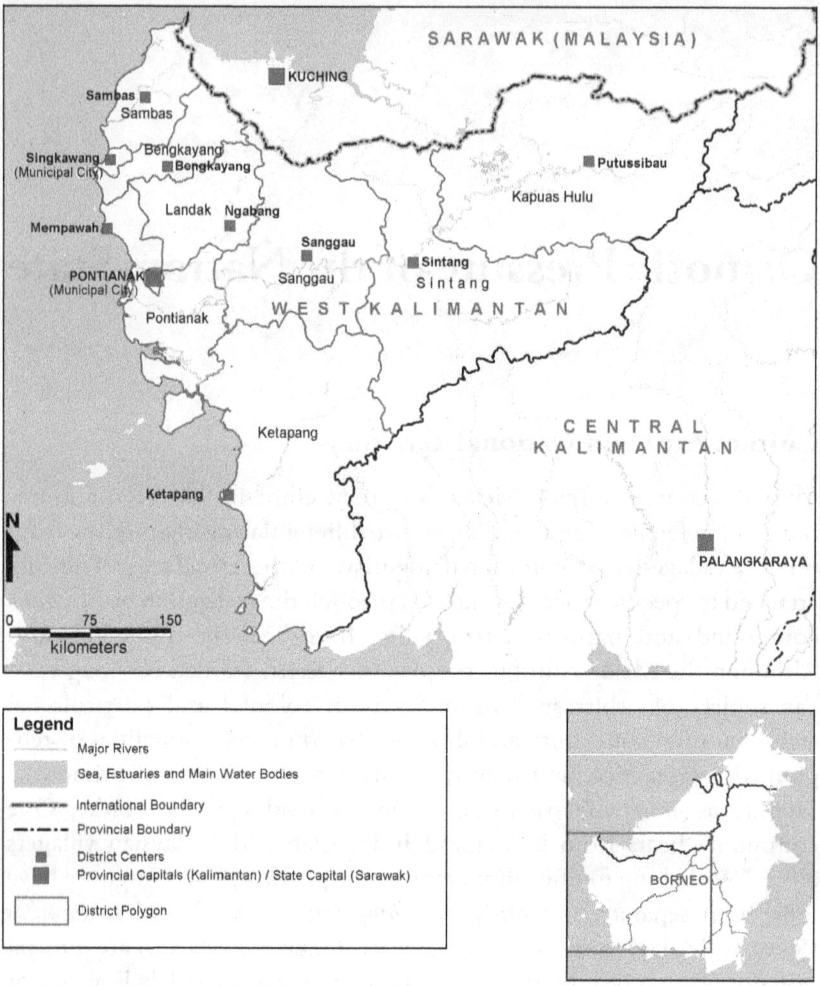

Fig. 11 West Kalimantan Provinces

which includes Telok Melano, covers a long stretch of territory from the Kunyit River (Sei Kunyit, see Fig. 12) to Lundu. The absorption of the Malaysian communities into the Kuching-based socio-economic network following the construction of a paved road between Sematan and Kuching and subsequent human interaction, expanding kinship relations, and changing population composition have gradually produced a collective amnesia among Malays whose homelands are across the national border.

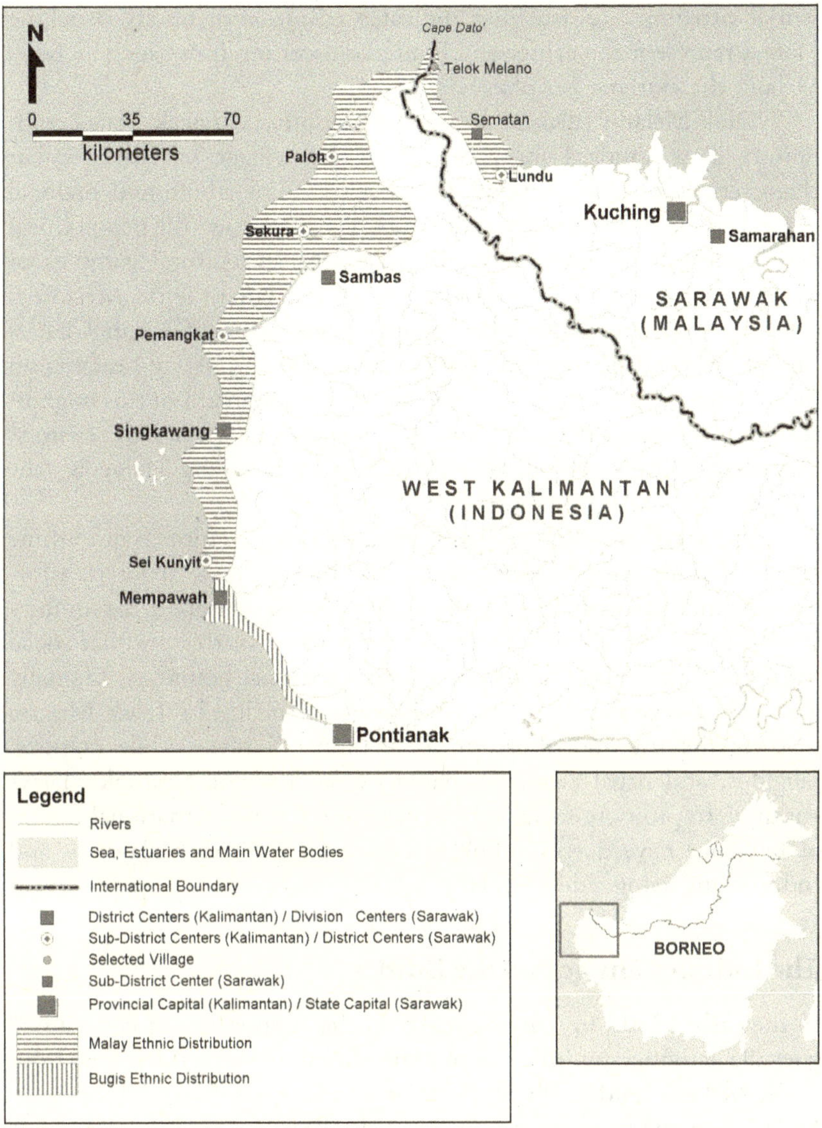

Fig. 12 Malay/Bugis Cultural Area

The other Malay cultural complex in this region is that of the Sarawak Malays, which became firmly established in Kuching and its vicinity over the course of colonial history (Chapter 5). Along a spectrum of Malay geo-culture in the national terrain of Sarawak, where spatial proximity to Kuching indicates ethnic authenticity, Kuching Malays represent the center and borderland communities such as Telok Melano the extreme periphery.[1]

Telok Melano villagers do not use any other Sarawak Malay community as a standard for comparison. The village has the peculiar characteristic of being a point of convergence of ethnic and national space. It is located at the extremity of two areal entities: the geo-political nation-state of Malaysia and the Sambas Malay cultural complex of western Borneo. From the perspective of the latter, Telok Melano is a tiny enclave created by the colonial engineering of Rajah Charles Brooke, who encouraged the settlement of Sambas Malay peasants on the colonial Sarawak frontier. Telok Melano is a remnant of this migrant community, which protrudes into and remains in Malaysian territory. The villagers themselves describe their home as "hujung Malaysia" (the end of Malaysia) in this borderland.

The social standing of Telok Melano in the national and ethnic terrain, doubly peripheral in nature, has undergone a major transformation since the early 1980s when an Indonesian migrant community emerged within walking distance of the village. In this peculiar social field where the village boundary is also a national boundary, the daily life bears transnational character. The everyday life in Telok Melano involves the use and abuse of the national border. While cultural, religious, and ritual elements shared by Sambas and Sarawak Malays continue to promote social cohesion, national and international frames of reference have deeply influenced location work of Malaysians and Indonesians living side by side.

The Indonesians across the Border

In the early 1980s, in conjunction with the suppression of communist guerrilla activities, an influx of migrants began to settle just across from Telok Melano border. The community of Temajuk was established by Malay migrants from forty overcrowded villages in the coastal districts

[1] More specifically, local dialect reflects degree of recognized difference. Kuching Malays say that Lundu people speak like birds, while Lundu Malays differentiate themselves from the Malays in Sematan by subtle variations in intonation, accent, and vocabulary, as well as ritual practice. The Malays of Sematan similarly use linguistic and ritual differences to distance themselves from Telok Melano villagers 35 kilometers away.

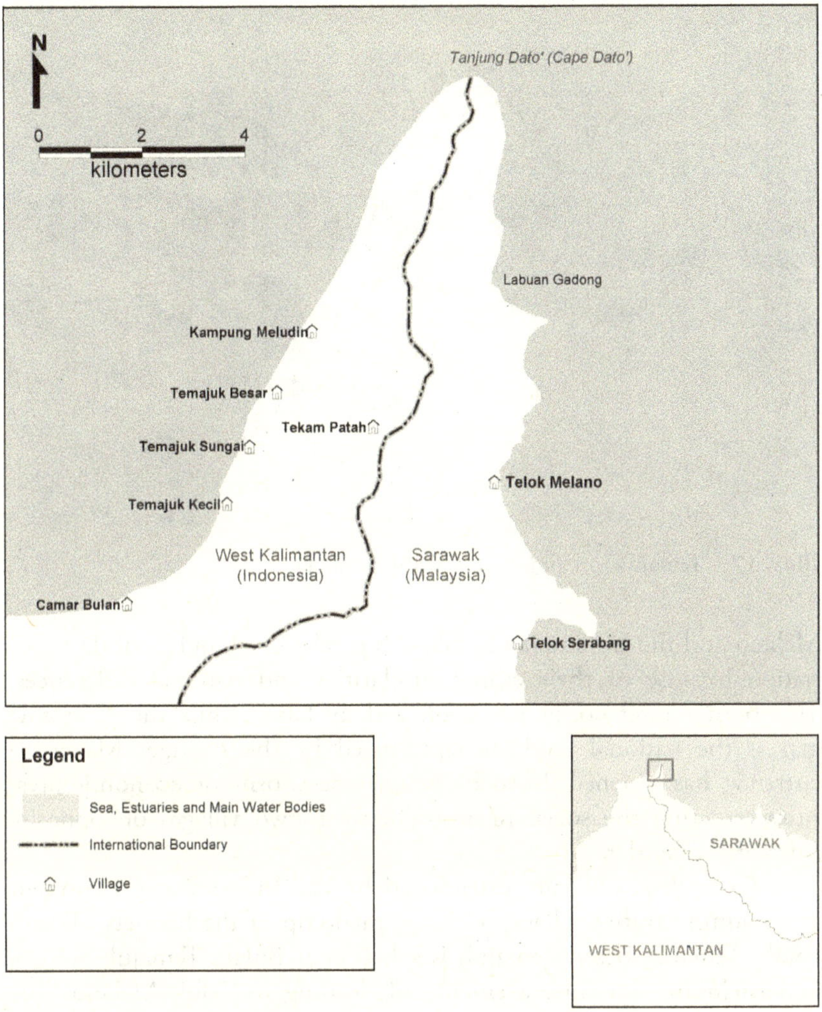

Fig. 13 Cape Dato Borderland

of Sambas, West Kalimantan. After communist activities were finally subdued through a series of arrests and surrenders in 1988, the migration of Sambas Malays to the frontier adjacent to Cape Dato accelerated. Temajuk rapidly grew into six hamlets with 1,300 residents.

Telok Melano village became a gateway for Indonesians entering Malaysian territory, and a police station in Telok Melano began to function as an immigration post. More importantly, daily social interaction in the form of trade and informal visits developed between Telok

Illus. 17 Temajuk, an Indonesian frontier village

Melano and the Indonesian hamlets, but relations require subtle negotiation because of their ethnic similarities and national differences. Transborder interactions occur on a daily basis, while the economic gap at the national level, as represented by the stronger Malaysian currency, has widened. In such circumstances, osmotic economic pressures structure the social relations between two villages on opposite sides of the border.

Temajuk is officially categorized by the Indonesian government as an administrative village, a *dusun*, made up of the hamlets (Tekam Patah, Temajuk Besar, Temajuk Kecil, Camar Bulan, Temajuk Sungai, and Meludin) that line a small path leading to Telok Melano. The closest hamlet to Telok Melano is Tekam Patah, right on the Malaysia-Indonesia border. The walk from Telok Melano to Temajuk Kecil takes approximately two hours, and Camar Bulan is another hour away. Temajuk is linked by an unpaved road to Paloh, the administrative center of Paloh District. Sambas, to the south, is a nine-hour walk from Camar Bulan. From Paloh, access is easier to other Indonesian coastal towns such as Sekura, Sambas, Pemangkat, Mempawah, and Pontianak, the state capital of West Kalimantan. These towns are all connected by land transportation.

Temajuk was formed by individually-motivated chain migration from Paloh and its vicinity. This spontaneous form of migration is called *spontan*, in contrast to the government-led *transmigrasi* (transmigration). Temajuk Kecil was formed by H. Syafari Bintolo and ten households from Teba on 22 March 1981. This was followed by the opening of Temajuk Besar by Pak Tapa and his followers. Prior to 1982, there were no permanent dwellers in Temajuk, as people went back and forth between the frontier and their home villages. In 1982, seven households settled down, and permanent population grew to 20 households in 1983, 165 in 1987, and 284 in 1992. As of 2001, there were 1,331 residents, in 334 households.

According to residents of Temajuk, economic difficulty in their home villages led to their migration. Initially they faced a series of obstacles. Many members of the Pasukan Gerilya Rakyat Sarawak (PGRS) — often referred to as "clandestine communists" — operated in the vicinity of Temajuk, and this military threat only disappeared after 1988. Also, the distance from Paloh and other communities and the rough waters off Cape Dato made it difficult to obtain daily necessities, and food shortages during the *landas* monsoon season have remained a problem.

Temajuk villagers often refer their houses *pondok* (temporary huts), and many still maintain houses in their home villages in Paloh and Jawai. People in Temajuk Besar, Temajuk Kecil, Camar Bulan, and Meludin who maintain dual residency are best described as circular migrants. During *Hari Raya*, the important Muslim holiday at the end of the fasting month, Temajuk is deserted and quiet because most residents go home for family gatherings.

Temajuk has the air of a typical frontier village. There is no electricity or piped water. In front of the houses remain large half-burnt tree trunks, a reminder of the pioneers' efforts in clearing thick forests. The area was once covered with primary forest and with old secondary forest utilized by the forefathers of Telok Melano villagers to cultivate hill rice. In 1981, a path was hacked out between Temajuk Kecil and Temajuk Besar, connecting the village to Malaysian territory. Upon the advice of security officers (HANKAM), Temajuk villagers started to sell logs in the neighboring Malaysian market for cash income, rather than burning or letting them rot.

When I first visited Temajuk, I often saw men carrying heavy chain saws, and the sawn timber they left to dry along village paths. Although most settlers had been coastal wet-rice cultivators, in their new home they chose logging in search of fast cash. During the dependence of the Temajuk economy on logging, the majority of Temajuk residents were not initially engaged in agriculture. None of the Indonesian government's agricultural schemes was implemented in Temajuk village. Some residents tried to cultivate cash crops, such as pepper, by obtaining seedlings from Telok Melano, but these efforts often failed because of a lack of agricultural expertise. Even cultivating staple foods such as hill rice and cassava was not an easy enterprise in Temajuk because wild boars often destroyed the crops.

Tekam Patah, whose compound of 50 households spreads right across the border, has established a symbiotic relationship with Telok Melano. The newest among the five village clusters of Temajuk, Tekam Patah was opened in the late 1980s by migrants from Sarang Burung Danau in Jawai District of Sambas. As in the other villages, the residents are all Sambas Malays, with the exception of three male Dayaks, and there is a strong tradition of village solidarity based on kinship relations existing in the home village. When its residents migrated to Temajuk, Sarang Burung Danau's population exceeded 1,000, and population pressure led residents to move. In contrast with Temajuk's other hamlets, many Tekam Patah villagers have sold their houses and lands in Sarang Burung Danau, and even during festive seasons, most residents remain in Tekam Patah and celebrate the holidays in their frontier homes. Another difference between Tekam Patah and the other hamlets is its reliance on cultivated crops and a lack of dependence on exploitative logging. The residents have planted cassava and bananas along with coconut trees and pepper vines. The presence of the latter cash crops, which require several years to bear fruit exemplifies the long-term perspective of Tekam Patah's people. For their survival until these crops in production, these villagers engage in hill rice cultivation. The advice of their neighbors in Telok Melano has contributed in no small way.

Borderland Symbiosis

Human traffic across the border reestablishes socio-economic ties that were badly disrupted by military confrontation between Malaysia and Indonesia in the 1960s and communist insurgency in the 1970s and 1980s. The transnational networks have been revitalized, and the Telok Melano-Temajuk nexus has become an important point of articulation for Malays in western Borneo.

There is no immigration checkpoint on the border between Telok Melano and Temajuk. In the village compound of Telok Melano, a police station monitors the flow of people across the border. Indonesians who enter Malaysia at Telok Melano are supposed to report to this police station to obtain permission for temporary entry. On their return from other towns in Sarawak, police officers sporadically check their belongings. If a substantial quantity of imported goods such as cigarettes is found, they may be confiscated. Malaysians who intend to visit Indonesia through Telok Melano report to the same police station, recording name, address, and ethnic identity on the police form. If Malaysian travelers wish to go further into Indonesian territory than Temajuk, to Paloh or Tanah Hitam, for instance, they report to the village headman of Temajuk Kecil to complete the necessary paper work. Unregulated economic transactions between Malaysians and Indonesians are permitted only among the inhabitants of Telok Melano and Temajuk, who can transport and sell their cultivated products across the border.

Table 14 The Number of Border Crossings between Malaysia and Indonesia, Recorded at the Telok Melano Police Station between 1989 and 1994

Year	*Malaysia to Indonesia*	*Indonesia to Malaysia*
1989	75	–
1990	139	–
1991	136	–
1992	202	1,683
1993	78	933
1994*	4	255

Note: * as of 19 May 1994.

Source: Police Station, Telok Melano.

The above table shows the number of crossings between Malaysia and Indonesia, recorded at the Telok Melano police station between 1989 and 1994. The figures do not include the everyday crossborder traffic of local residents of Telok Melano and Temajuk, and of Indonesian merchants and kinsmen who visit so frequently that they become familiar figures who do not report officially to the police. Thus the figures are not a true reflection of the actual number of people who cross the international border.

After the formation of Temajuk in the early 1980s, a new kind of social symbiosis developed between the two Malay communities. Daily interaction is dense both in the field of economic exchange

Illus. 18 Temajuk villagers coming to Telok Melano for threshing rice

and in ritualistic reciprocal relations. A frequent exchange of goods and services, for instance, takes place on occasions such as weddings, funerals, and the Islamic religious ceremonies of *Hari Raya* (Celebration Day of Fasting) and *Hari Raya Haji* (celebrated in conjunction with the annual pilgrimage to Mecca). The Malays of Telok Melano and Temajuk often participate in each other's rituals because there are no religious or customary differences.

The main components of Hari Raya and Hari Raya Haji are the prayer for God's blessing, performed at the village prayer house, and the "open house", during which people visit each other's homes freely. In the early morning of the first day, Indonesian children come to Telok Melano and visit homes (*naik rumah*) to enjoy specially prepared dishes and sweets. In the afternoon of the first day, more Indonesian visitors come to the Malaysian village. All visitors are welcomed and served several kinds of cakes, and drinks such as coffee and tea. On the second day of Hari Raya, many Telok Melano villagers return the visit, going on foot to Tekam Patah and even further into Indonesian territory. They are also served cakes and drinks. Hari Raya customs in Temajuk are more or less the same; the only differences are that Indonesian cakes are baked, while Malaysian ones are steamed, and in Indonesia the cakes are much sweeter and the drinks unsweetened. These Hari Raya visits are based on kinship, friendship, and patron-client relationships. The regular exchange of communal feasting strengthens these dyadic cross-border relationships.

Weddings, which usually take place at the beginning of the May-to-July dry season, are also important rituals that involve a substantial exchange of goods and services between Malaysians and Indonesians. Wedding ceremonies are followed by large-scale feasts with several hundred attendees. It is not uncommon to find Indonesians, usually those who work regularly in Telok Melano, helping with the cooking and other preparations. Later, many Indonesians come down to attend the feast. Four or five dishes, including chicken, deer meat, and fish, are served to all guests. Such feasts are rare treats that require good planning, a lot of money, and a large workforce. Guests usually contribute a few Malaysian ringgit to help cover the cost. Similarly Telok Melano villagers attend Indonesian weddings, wearing their best clothes and giving cash to the newlywed couple.

Finally, reciprocity is observed between Indonesian and Malaysian villagers during funerals. News of a death is delivered immediately across the border. For example, on hearing of the death of a daughter of an Indonesian couple who regularly work for a Telok Melano entrepreneur, the patron's family quickly went to the house in Tekam Patah with a large sack of rice to be served to guests at the wake and funeral. Others went across the border to deliver a supply of coconuts, essential for Malay cooking. Not only goods but also a great deal of labor was offered by Malaysian villagers. One of the Malaysians said, "As a Malay, I have to render help, otherwise no one comes and helps when I die."

It should be pointed out that reciprocal relationships across the border are limited to these rather specific ritual occasions. In Telok Melano, the rituals such as *kenduri arwah* (in memory of deceased family members) and rituals associated with preventing illness, averting evil, house building, and house warming are usually attended only by Telok Melano villagers, who are informed by formal or informal invitation. Indonesians occasionally participate in these rituals, but invitees are usually limited to residents of the same village.

There is also village-level cooperation between Telok Melano and Tekam Patah for the maintenance of bridges linking the two communities. As the traffic volume between them increased, there was a greater need for new bridges over several streams in the borderland. The people

Illus. 19 Malaysia vs. Indonesia: an international football match between Telok Melano and Temajuk

of both communities agreed that Telok Melano should provide chain saws, gasoline, and nails and that Tekam Patah should prepare lumber. When the materials were ready, they worked together. And when the bridges need repairs, they work together again. Cross-border *gotong royong* (communal work sharing) has thus become a regular practice because residents cannot obtain government assistance for inter-village projects that extend beyond the national territory.

Osmotic Pressure of the Nation-State

Although ritual occasions and community-level *gotong royong* between Temajuk and Telok Melano are two-way interactions, the movement of goods and people largely goes in one direction: from Indonesia to Malaysia. Just as osmotic pressure is determined by the difference in concentration of a liquid between two organs, the difference between two national economies determines the direction of the movement of people and goods across the international border. The relative value of goods is not constant, and can change as they cross the social threshold where nation-states meet. The strength of one national economy and currency relative to the other drives the movement of low-cost goods and also promotes the formation of a low-cost labor. The devaluation of labor provides the basis for the devaluation of personhood, which is reflected in the amount of bridewealth paid to Indonesian spouses in Malaysian territory.

Currency

Pak Johari is an Indonesian trader who often visits Telok Melano. A skinny man in his 40s, he comes to Telok Melano daily or every second day during the dry season, traveling more than ten kilometers from Temajuk Besar and Tekam Patah to Telok Melano. Pak Johari procures a variety of Indonesian products at a shop in Temajuk Sungai and sells them in Telok Melano (hair-pins, perfume, soap, mirrors, shampoo, talcum powder, vitamin pills, ointment, mosquito coils, lighters, matches, candies, cookies, needles and thread, headache medicine, dried fish, cigarette papers, yeast, Indonesian *kretek* (clove) cigarettes, brown coconut sugar, and various other items). He carries his stocks in a cardboard box tied to his bicycle. He accepts payment either in Malaysian ringgit or Indonesian rupiah and also sells on credit. Buying on credit is common, and a substantial number of residents of Telok Melano are in debt to Pak Johari. When they see him riding his bicycle in the village compound, they ask him to stop and open his box. The women and girls, who do not have many opportunities for consumption, playfully take things out of the box, ask prices, bargain and joke with the trader, and often throw things back into the box. On his way home, Pak Johari buys bottles of home-made coconut oil from Telok Melano villagers to sell in Temajuk, where coconuts are a scarce commodity.

Another way Indonesian goods come into Telok Melano is through agent-to-agent transactions. Unlike the sporadic trade undertaken by individual traders, this type of exchange involves fixed relationships between Indonesian suppliers and Malaysian distributors. Several Temajuk traders come to Telok Melano on a regular basis and leave Indonesian cloth (*kain*), *sarong batik*, underwear, and children's clothes with their sub-agents, usually housewives, who are responsible for setting the retail price and selling the goods in the village. The total price of each consignment of goods is fixed and will be paid to the Indonesian traders when they return with new supplies, usually a month or two later. The Malaysian agents are not obliged to sell all the goods and can return unsold articles to their suppliers, with their price subtracted from the total. The village agents make as much profit as possible by adding their own margin to the original price. In Telok Melano, three women function as village agents. Their Indonesian suppliers include a teacher from Temajuk and merchants who come to Lundu and Sematan via another border crossing point at Tebudu.

Less frequent, but no less important in providing access to commercial goods from the outside world, are the visits of traders from the Natuna Islands and Java. Natuna traders who enter Malaysian territory via Temajuk, started visiting the Cape Dato area long ago, and through them Telok Melano has long functioned as an important commercial link to Kuching (Harrisson 1970: 234–7). The Natunas have also been linked by kinship relations to Telok Melano and through commerce with Santubong, which is close to Kuching. The Natuna Islands are known for salted fish, dried fish, and mats made of screw palm (*pandanus*). Natuna *pandan* mats are much appreciated for their beautiful designs and high quality, and are used only for important guests or on special occasions such as Hari Raya.

Indonesian traders from Java visit the Cape Dato area even less frequently than traders from the Natunas. One trader I met sold clocks with two motifs — one depicting the Crucifixion for Christian Dayaks and the other with a scene of Mecca for Muslims. This man traveled across West Kalimantan, visiting Dayak longhouses and Malay villages, and then reported to the police checkpoint at Telok Melano for entry into Sarawak. The presence of these traders indicates that Java-based petty trade networks extend as far as the frontier of Borneo.

There is yet another way of merchandizing Indonesian goods in Telok Melano. One young village man goes to Temajuk Sungai one to four times a week to buy Indonesian *kretek* cigarettes, rice, laundry soap, and other items to sell at his wife's grocery shop in Telok Melano. He has his own motor bike, which gives him a great advantage in crossing the border and back bringing Indonesian goods. A pack of Gudang Garam, the most popular Indonesian cigarette among men in the area, sells for M$2.00 at his shop. He buys these cigarettes at a shop in Temajuk Sungai for Rp 1,300 per pack or approximately M$1.60. At the time of our research (when the Malaysian ringgit floated at approximately 2.60 to the USD), the value of the ringgit was rising against the Indonesian rupiah; thus payment in Malaysian currency was always welcomed by Indonesian shopkeepers. The exchange rate was often determined rather arbitrarily in the borderlands. I recorded *de facto* exchange rates of Rp 700 to M$1 in Temajuk Besar;

Illus. 20 A border point at Cape Dato with Temajuk and Telok Melano villagers side by side

Rp 650 to M$1 in Tekam Patah; and Rp 800 to M$1 in Telok Melano. Telok Melano villagers sometimes increase the price of Malaysian ringgit during a village festival or *Pesta Sempadan* (Border Festival). On such occasions, when many Indonesians come to visit and Malaysians open food stalls, the village exchange rate is fixed at Rp 1,000 to M$1. Visiting Indonesians have to pay more in rupiah if they are not carrying ringgit.

Compared to the Indonesians, who eagerly participate in cross-border petty trade, few Telok Melano villagers initiate commercial exchange with Indonesians. Although the six Temajuk hamlets are much closer than the nearest Malaysian town and can be reached over-land throughout the year, the geographical proximity and marketing opportunity has had little impact on the stagnant economy of Telok Melano. To understand why cross-border petty trade is pursued only by a few economically marginalized Malaysians, we have to look at the practical reason why Telok Melano folks shun profit making through transactions across the border — their lack of enthusiasm for Indonesia's currency. Indonesians selling commodities in Malaysia receive ringgit, a much stronger currency. For both Indonesians and Malaysians, saving money in rupiah is a risky business, for the value of Indonesian currency has been highly unstable. The official exchange rate was approximately Rp 750 (to M$1) in 1992, Rp 1200 in 1994, and Rp 3,000 at the height of Indonesian monetary crisis of 1997.

For Indonesian villagers in the borderland, accumulating savings in ringgit is a good defensive strategy against the diminishing value of their own currency, while the use of rupiah is fairly limited even for borderland Malaysians. The rupiah is not accepted in daily commercial transactions among Telok Melano villagers. Any Indonesian currency earned through petty trade is thus useable only in Temajuk to purchase cigarettes, brown coconut sugar, mosquito coils, and other Indonesian commodities. While Malaysian ringgit is an all-purpose currency in the vicinity of the border, the use of Indonesian rupiah is essentially confined to Indonesian territory.

One of the few cross-border peddlers in Telok Melano is Kak Mariam, who makes regular trips to Temajuk to sell vegetables, fruits, coconut oil, and second-hand clothes. She lives near her vegetable gardens, which are approximately 200 meters from the border gate, and she often takes her vegetables as far as Camar Bulan by bicycle. Selling vegetables door to door in Temajuk for Indonesian currency, she once made Rp 80,000 in two weeks. In Telok Melano, where the average monthly cash income is between M$150 and M$200 (well below the national poverty line of M$250), Rp 80,000 (over M$100) is substantial.

Telok Melano's agricultural surplus is also brought to Temajuk during the fruit season. A bundle of *rambutan* fruits, after given free to fellow villagers, can be sold to Indonesians for Rp 1,000. Fruit had no market value at all before Temajuk was established, except for *durian*, which commands a high price (M$3–M$5) even in Telok Melano. Now the surplus is customarily sold in Temajuk by middlemen, who push their bicycles heavily loaded with foodstuffs into Indonesian territory.

Pak Mat is one such peddler in Telok Melano. Born in Miri, in northern Sarawak, to a Malaysian father and an Indonesian mother, he is married to an Indonesian woman from Temajuk and used to live on the Indonesian side of the border. The fact that he was born in Malaysian territory to a Malaysian father gave him Malaysian citizenship, and he retained his Malaysian Identification Card even after he moved to West Kalimantan with his Indonesian mother. This made it possible for him to settle in Telok Melano with his family about four years ago. Initially it was not easy for him to adjust to the village and earn his living. As a newcomer, he does not own any farmland, and has to rent small agricultural plots from Melano landowners. His cacao and pepper trees will take several years to bear fruit, and to support his wife and five children in the meantime, he sells surplus fruit in Indonesian villages on behalf of Telok Melano villagers, taking advantage of his Indonesian accent, Indonesian wife, and familiarity with the Temajuk people. He visits the Indonesian villages regularly, often making painstaking trips three times a day on a bumpy, narrow path. The profits are usually shared equally by the tree owners and the landowners.

Those who engage in petty trade with Indonesians are socially marginalized in Telok Melano. Kak Mariam, whose house is adjacent to the border, seldom visits the village compound of Telok Melano, and she is one of the most peripheral Malaysian nationals in Telok Melano village. Pak Mat is no less marginalized; as an ex-resident of Indonesia with a heavy Sambas accent, he is more Indonesia-oriented than other Telok Melano villagers.

Devaluation of Labor and Bridewealth

The relative appreciation of the Malaysian ringgit and depreciation of the Indonesian rupiah affected not only commodity transactions but also social and economic relations between the borderland communities. Like commodities, labor flows strictly in one direction — from Indonesia to Malaysia. Many Indonesians seek employment opportunities in Telok Melano, which is perennially short of labor, and receive cash payment in ringgit. Their employment is arranged individually, without the involvement of brokers. Indonesians from Temajuk are employed to clear secondary forest for swidden agriculture, do weeding, harvest pepper and cacao, and do household chores. These odd jobs are seasonal and sporadically available. For instance, at pepper harvest time, Malaysians often have trouble finding Indonesian workers since the demand for pickers is quite high. Each employer tries to maintain a small pool of regular laborers with whom they have prior experience, and a number of Telok Melano villagers have loosely structured patron-client relationships with Temajuk Indonesians.

One employer is a Telok Melano widow whose two children are away for schooling and work; she always has trouble finding adequate labor for her meager rice fields. She paid M$42 to an Indonesian man to clear and burn off secondary jungle for swidden rice fields. Later, she hired two Indonesian women to weed for three days, paying them M$4 per day, and providing simple food. One month later, the same two women from Temajuk were hired again for weeding. On another plot, she hired an Indonesian man whose wife works for her regularly to clear the field for the planting of pepper vines. Because the employer does not have much cash income, she suggested payment in the form of fertilizer, a packet of coffee, 1 kg of sugar, and M$10. The relationship between this widow and the Indonesians is the loosest type of patron-client relationship, with minimal obligation on the side of the employees. The widow constantly faces the disappointment of broken promises, unfulfilled duties, and requests for extra-payment. She was furious, for instance, when after many requests her pepper field was left uncleared of undergrowth, and on another occasion when an Indonesian laborer used all her herbicide on his own plot.

A few relatively affluent Telok Melano villagers maintain more stable patron-client relationships with Indonesians from Tekam Patah. Pak Yusof returned a decade ago to Telok Melano from Sematan, where he worked as a carpenter. He is a descendent of a pioneering immigrant from Dutch Sambas. As one of the first settlers, his grandfather, a Dayak from Landak who later converted to Islam, cleared a large tract of virgin forest to plant hill rice, and Pak Yusof inherited part of this holding. Now he operates the largest agricultural fields in Telok Melano, used mostly to grow pepper and cacao. His family owns more than 500 pepper vines, which generate more than M$10,000 yearly, and a substantial number of cacao trees. In addition to cash crop production, his family owns a boat, engines, and a dragnet, which are used at sea for seine fishing (*mukat*). Part of the dragnet's catch is usually divided among the helpers, with a larger share going to the boat/engine owner, and the remainder is sold to villagers.

Pak Yusof regularly hires both male and female Indonesian laborers from Tekam Patah, and three to six of them are working for this family at any given time. They come to Telok Melano almost every morning (some stay overnight) to help the family with washing and cooking, picking pepper seeds in harvest season, and pulling the dragnet for fishing. The pepper vines owned by the Yusof family produce about 2,000 kg of seeds yearly. If left unattended, ripened seeds will fall or be eaten by birds. It is thus crucial to have enough workers for the labor-intensive pepper picking. Dragnet fishing requires at least seven people, and usually three of whom are Indonesians.

Illus. 21 A Tekam Patah villager picking peppers for a Telok Melano employer

Although the profit from pepper cultivation and fishing is substantial, so is the expense of maintaining this labor force. Pak Yusof's wife cooks 2 kg of rice every day for her family and its workers. Monthly payments can reach up to M$125 per worker, a substantial sum in a village where the average income does not exceed M$200. It needs to be reiterated that the relationship between the village entrepreneur and the Indonesian workers is not one of strict dominance/subordination. The Indonesians are not bonded laborers, nor are they in debt; they come to work only when they wish, although mutual trust is a factor. Malaysian employers often complain about Indonesian workers not showing up to work as promised. Some also claim that Indonesian employees would never stop chewing betel and chit-chatting after lunch unless they were asked to resume work.

In addition to the resident villagers, three absentee landowners also recruit Indonesian and Malaysian laborers during the pepper harvest. The Malays in Sematan who purchased land from village landowners occasionally commute to the village to take care of their large pepper gardens on the hill adjacent to the village compound.

The following table shows the daily wage variation recorded in Telok Melano village and in Sematan town in 1994. There is a clear difference in wage levels between Malaysians and Indonesians, as well as a general decline in wages as the work site gets closer to the border. The highest amount is M$9.00, paid to Malaysians in Sematan. When Telok Melano villagers work for fellow villagers and for the Malay pepper garden owners from Sematan, they usually receive M$6.00 per day and lunch. Indonesian workers receive far less.

Table 15 The Average Wage for One-day's Pepper Picking in Telok Melano and Sematan

Employer	*Work Site*[2]	*Employee*	*Wage (per day)*
Melano/Sematan	Melano	Indonesians in Temajuk	M$3.50 (lunch provided) M$4.00 (without lunch)
Melano/Sematan	Melano	Malaysians in Melano	M$6.00 (lunch provided)
Sematan	Sematan	Malaysians in Sematan	M$9.00

According to the Telok Melano villagers, the average payment for one day's work as an odd-job laborer in Temajuk rarely exceeds Rp 1,0.00 (approx. M$1.30). Despite the low wages paid to Indonesians relative to the Malaysian standard, there is a constant labor flow from across the border.

Wealth reflects social relations. When the commodification process takes place in the borderlands between two nation-states with an asymmetric economic relationship, a relative valuation — and devaluation — of people and things also takes place. In Telok Melano, an interesting case of commodified labor becoming decommodified is seen when an individual changes communal affiliation from Indonesian to Malaysian. The decommodification of labor occurs as the person is

[2] The pepper gardens where the Indonesians and Melano villagers work under contract are located in Telok Melano and the inland area between Telok Melano and Telok Serabang. In this figure, these gardens are together described as "Melano".

incorporated into a local community in which labor becomes unique and reciprocal but not marketable. For instance, Pak Mat, the ex-Temajuk resident and peddler depicted in the previous section, was socially marginal to Telok Melano; but once his village membership was certified by the village headman, he was entitled (and obliged) to take part in *gotong royong* (communal work sharing) activities such as firing swidden fields and padi planting. *Gotong royong* is only for community members, and no monetary transaction is involved. Unlike his former neighbors in Temajuk, whose labor is obtained through payment in Telok Melano, Pak Mat now takes part in reciprocal relations with Telok Melano villagers. As he shed his Indonesian past and became a member of the Malaysian village, the status of his labor changed in accordance with his new affiliation.

Another cross-border linkage is created by marriage, and a devaluation of Indonesian spouses, as reflected in the amount of bridewealth paid to them, is commonly observable in the borderland. Six Indonesians from Sambas who are married to Telok Melano residents live in the village. The Indonesian spouses, five women and one man, all in their 20s, have applied for Malaysian citizenship, although the process is expected to take years to complete. Kinship ties with Indonesians that were largely forgotten during the colonial and post-colonial periods are being reestablished through such marital alliances.

Because of its geographical isolation from other Malay communities, endogamy was common in Telok Melano until recently. Most villagers had no choice but to find a spouse within the village. Recently, however, more options have become available. Young men who feel ready to settle down with their own family make a trip to the coastal villages of Sambas to *cari cewee* (look for girls). The trip may take three months or more as the young men visit families of Indonesians who have married and settled in Telok Melano. No one goes to Kuching or other urban Malaysian centers to seek a spouse. Occasionally someone goes to such places for work and happens to meet a future partner there, but it is generally believed that no Malay women from Sematan and Lundu, let alone Kuching, would want to live in distant Telok Melano. The bridewealth, the necessary payment to a bride in a Muslim wedding ceremony, is M$120 in Malaysia, while M$50 is said to be sufficient for an Indonesian woman. Likewise, at the engagement, a Malaysian man usually pays M$3,000 or more to a Malaysian bride's family for the wedding reception and other necessities (*belanja dapur*), while a young man from Telok Melano typically pays only M$300 for marriage to an Indonesian girl. Some Telok Melano youths have gone through an official Muslim wedding ceremony (*nikah*) at their Indonesian bride's village and have simply taken their wives back to Telok Melano after a certain period.

Spectrum of Differences

While symbiotic relationships in economic, ceremonial, and kinship domains have emerged among Telok Melano and Temajuk people in the borderland, belonging to different nation-states generates inevitable tension. Membership of the Malaysian or Indonesian nation-state entails quite different social positioning in the state system, and involves a gap in wealth. In the peripheral economy, Malaysia's greater economic power allows its citizens to enjoy the higher value of their currency and to mobilize the inexpensive Indonesian labor at their disposal. According to Telok Melano residents, before the pepper bubble in 1997 (to be discussed in Chapter 8), Temajuk (especially Tekam Patah) villagers were willing to trade their labor for a few secondhand clothes. At lunch break after weeding grass in the field or doing household chores, they are said to be happy with a meal of plain rice and *sambal belacan* (salty shrimp paste) provided by their employers. Telok Melano people refer to Temajuk men and women, who often have large families and little means of subsistence, as *orang susah* (people living in hardship).

Within Sarawak, Telok Melano villagers occupy a low stratum of the Malaysian national economic hierarchy. In the borderland, they enjoy a relative advantage and attribute the characteristics of low status to their Indonesian neighbors. For example, Telok Melano villagers frequently talk about the theft of marketable crops such as watermelons, durians, or peppers, and generally blame Temajuk villagers. Victims sometimes know who the offenders are, but their identities are never revealed. Instead, precautionary measures are taken to fend off robbers. During durian harvest season in particular, tree owners keep vigil in a nearby hut to scoop up fallen fruit. Sometimes rifle shots are fired to scare away thieves. Coconuts, too, are often stolen from Telok Melano land, but a close watch on fallen coconuts and the detection of theft on the spot is practically impossible as most trees are outside the village compound. Because coconut palms are abundant in Telok Melano, a few stolen coconuts has never turned into a serious problem, but ill feeling remains.

Indonesian men having casual relationships with Telok Melano women have caused some unhappiness in the village. A few women have children fathered by Indonesian husbands from the Sambas region who went back to Indonesia after a short sojourn in Malaysian territory. Some of these Indonesians already had families at home. One man pretended he was single and married a Malaysian woman in a formal ceremony in Telok Melano, but subsequently left this wife and a baby to return to his family in Indonesia. Some Telok Melano villagers say that Temajuk is a lawless place with no marital duties or responsibilities, that men take as many wives as they please, and that they dump older wives who have lost their sexual attractiveness. Although Malaysian Muslim men are also permitted to marry up to four wives under Muslim law provided they can support all the families and the prior wives give consent, no Telok Melano villagers have done so.

Telok Melano villagers also comment on the strong sense of regional identity that marks Temajuk villagers, often mentioning the Sambas Malays' strong adherence to local dialect: "Indonesians from Temajuk continue to speak their own dialect with a heavy Sambas accent, even when alone surrounded by one hundred Malaysians." In contrast, some of Telok Melano villagers, upon entering a Tekam Patah compound, adapt their speech to match that of the Indonesians.

The Indonesians across the border are said by Telok Melano villagers to possess *semangat kuat* (strong spirit or will). Temajuk villagers show greater group identity than Telok Melano villagers. Their sense of being Sambas Malays and Indonesians is a source of pride. That this ethnic nationalism often takes the form of anti-Malaysian sentiment surprises Telok Melano villagers, especially when tension emerges during international football matches or other festivities where young people from both countries have fun. For instance, five Telok Melano youths attended an international karaoke singing contest held at a village meeting hall at Temajuk Kecil. They were having a good time with the Indonesians, listening to Indonesian popular songs sung by Temajuk youths. However, when one Telok Melano boy stood up and started singing a Malaysian popular song, something totally unexpected happened. The Indonesians started to leave the hall one by one. When the song was finished, there were no Indonesians in the hall; only the singer's Malaysian friends were left, puzzled by the actions of their hosts. It was not because the boy was unpopular among the Indonesians. In fact, he was friendly with many of them and often crossed the border for fun. According to one Malaysian who was there, these

Indonesians simply did not like to listen to Malaysian music sung by a Malaysian villager in their homeland.

Indonesian songs, by contrast, are popular in Telok Melano. During our research, the most popular tune, sung by almost all the villagers, was the Indonesian "Cinta Merah Jambu". The cassette tape of this song came from an Indonesian shop in Paloh. Villagers simply loved the song and sang it on such occasions as the annual school festival and a village karaoke contest, as well as at home and in their gardens. It never appeared on the Malaysian pop chart on radio or TV, but it was a big local hit among the Telok Melano villagers.

The Temajuk villagers' sense of Indonesian identity, or *semangat kedaerahan* (territorial or regional spirit), extends to the cultural and political arena. It is often expressed in a Java orientation, an inclination to locate their cultural heritage in the old Javanese kingdom of Majapahit. At wedding ceremonies, Temajuk brides and grooms wear Javanese-style ceremonial attire, and attendants wear the Javanese *blangkon* (a ceremonial rimless skullcap). At funerals, they proudly claim to recite the Koran in an authentic Javanese way.

Compared to Telok Melano villagers, their attachment to nation-state is strong. The walls of small village shops display posters of national heroes (*Pahlawan Nasional*) who contributed to Indonesia's independence and nation building, and a small number of Temajuk households display pictures of President Suharto and his wife. Such everyday nationalism is not apparent in the daily life of Telok Melano, where there are few pictures of the Malaysian Agong (King), Prime Minister Dr. Mahathir, or high-ranking politicians of the Sarawak state government, except on the walls of the policeman's home, the police station, and elementary school classrooms.

Indonesian superiority is also felt quite strongly by Telok Melano villagers in the realm of spiritualism and esoteric knowledge. *Ilmu* is magico-religious power, and its possessors are both respected and feared. That "Indonesians possess strong magic and are good at using it" is firmly believed in Telok Melano. For instance, one Telok Melano man in his early 40s is paralyzed and unable to talk. He looks as though he barely survived a severe stroke. This man used to be one of young village leaders and was famous for his skill in ship building — until he became a subject of Indonesian black magic. According to villagers, he was quite hostile to people from Temajuk, making fun of their poverty and speaking derisively about them in public. One day he suddenly lost his ability to speak, and his legs and arms became

Illus. 22 International Koran recital by Telok Melano and Tekam Patah villagers

paralyzed. Now he sits all day long at the entrance of his house watching the seashore. His mysterious sickness is believed to have been caused by the black magic of an Indonesian who felt humiliated by his words and sought revenge.

While *ilmu* as magico-esoteric power is seen as an attribute of aggressiveness and the outlaw character of the Indonesians, it is also related to their religious and scientific knowledge and their world view. In the realm of religious knowledge and devotion, Temajuk elders are generally regarded as better Koran reciters than those of Telok Melano. In religious ceremonies which both sets of villagers attend, the Indonesians elders lead with strong and precise chanting of Koranic verses, while the Malaysians follow in a low monotonous tone. The images held by Telok Melano villagers of Temajuk Indonesians, as "aggressors", "outlaws", and "possessors of magico-esoteric power (*ilmu*)", are the same images held by other Sarawak Malays of Telok Melano villagers themselves. Because of their geographical location adjacent to the border and their social interaction and kin relations with Indonesians, they are often regarded by Kuching Malays as essentially Indonesian.

Just as our Kuching Malay friends gave us a Muslim amulet for protection against the *ilmu* of the borderland inhabitants (Chapter 4), a Kuching Malay teacher stationed at the village elementary school was warned repeatedly before moving to Telok Melano that he should "Be careful in dealing with the village folks who are good at black magic." Upon returning to Kuching for the holidays, he spoke the way the villagers do, for example, adding a specific affix to nouns and verbs and using vocabulary not used by Kuching Malays, and immediately became the object of laughter among his friends. This teacher was one of the few people who quickly understood the object of our stay in Telok Melano and helped us by commenting on differences in custom and ritual between Kuching and Telok Melano. His viewpoint was that of a Malay born and raised in Kuching, who somewhat distanced himself from the locals. He often attributed the difference between them to Indonesian influence in Telok Melano, pointing out that the locals had long mixed with Indonesians.

Nation and Culture

This chapter demonstrates that the geographically linear boundary between Malaysia and the Republic of Indonesia and the national identities that have emerged on either side of it are not simply imposed upon western Borneo by the governments found there. Local communities in the borderland have constructed a boundary that they use for classifying and valuing people and things. By attending to social transactions between Malaysia and Indonesia in the borderland of western Borneo, this chapter has looked into how the value of commodities, labor, and personhood depreciates when they move across the international border. The decrease in value, which I call devaluation, stands for the reduction in the worth of things and people as their *use value* is transformed to *exchange value* through transnational mobility.

This chapter has not discussed transnational economic processes in the matrix of supply-and-demand theories. Rather it focuses on the issue of value, that is, the change in the value of commodities, labor, and personhood in the borderland where multiple power relations are clearly manifest among communities, ethnicities, and nations. Telok Melano and Temajuk are just two of many communities of parallel ethnicity that exist side by side along the border between Malaysia and the Republic of Indonesia that stretches from Cape Dato in the west to the Sebatic Island between Sabah and East Kalimantan. Since the emergence of their respective nation-states, Malays on both sides of the border have experienced processes of inclusion and exclusion. They are incorporated into their respective nation-bound economic systems, but because of their isolation from political and economic centers often lack the basic social services rendered by states. Inadequate infrastructure — especially a lack of roads connecting borderlands to markets — denies villagers access to the national network of commodity distribution. Inhabitants at the periphery therefore resort to locally specific strategies, as exemplified by the socio-economic symbiosis that has developed between Telok Melano and Temajuk, both socio-economically alienated and marginalized communities.

But symbiotic relationships and the sharing of religion and ritual do not avert the inevitable tension generated by membership in different nation-states. Social interaction depends upon a subtle balance of gain and loss, as well as pride, trust, and affinity. In an area where the community boundaries coincide with those of nation-states, local residents utilize communal as well as national affiliation to maximize gains and minimize costs. It is misleading to suppose that only the nation-state determines the value of commodities, labor, and personhood. Rather, local communities make use of the nation-state. Sarawak Malays in Telok Melano and Sambas Malays in Temajuk consciously differentiate things and people in the borderland as exchangeable commodities. When original use value is transformed into exchange value, commodities become the subject of local classification as well as discrimination. Once detached from the classificatory system of a single nation-state, the values of things, labor, and rights-in-person are redefined, partly in accordance with the system of classification in the other nation-state. Differences between national economies, manifested for example in currency exchange rates, are important ways of separating border zone communities.

From the time of Durkheim and Mauss (Durkheim and Mauss 1963), the moral hierarchy of things and people has been a major subject of inquiry. For anthropologists concerned with economic exchange, culture has also been a pivotal frame of reference. The issue of value and the value equivalence of commodities have been examined in relation to locally specific cultural coding as well as idiosyncratic systems of classification and discrimination (Appadurai 1986, Kopytoff 1986, Parry and Bloch 1989). While commodification homogenizes value, the essence of culture is discrimination (Kopytoff 1986: 73).

Through an analysis of relative value in things and people in a borderland, this chapter adds the crucial frame of reference of nation to the conventional examination of the process by which a collectively shared cognitive order is generated. It would be misleading to suppose that a cultural system is the single determining factor in the cognitive process. The effect of other factors on the formation of worldviews, such as accelerated transnational commodity flows and migration, requires attention. I argue that nation as a basic frame of reference, rather than culture, has become increasingly significant in the process of valuation and devaluation of things and persons. Transformations in the nature of commodities and people as they move across national boundaries have a profound effect on the process of classification of the world. At the same time, people's cognitive systems also greatly affect the commodification process. This dialectical process can only be examined within the context of power relations and their manipulations.

CHAPTER EIGHT

Borderland Development

Cape Dato Revisited

The movement of commodities and labor between Telok Melano and Temajuk reflects attitudes toward the national currencies of the two places. Malaysians in Telok Melano adhere to their own currency, but Indonesians across the international boundary accumulate Malaysian ringgit as well, creating asymmetric power relations between the border communities. The relative value of labor is determined by the relative value of the national currency in the international foreign exchange market; the Malaysian villagers, taking advantage of their stronger currency, underpay fellow Malays (who happen to be Indonesian).

But Indonesians also reap advantages from the situation. The residents of Temajuk regarded the downturn of the Indonesian economy during the last phase of President Suharto's leadership favorably because, as residents of the borderland, they had peculiar access to Malaysian ringgit. Saving ringgit was safe and profitable for Temajuk villagers because its value was rising relative to their own. In this sense, Indonesians migrating to the national periphery adjacent to the border escape the spatial limitations of a national economy as determined by the compulsory use of a single currency within the national territory. Many villagers openly said they hoped the Indonesian economy would continue to decline, thereby enhancing the value of their ringgit savings and earnings against their own currency.

When I returned to Temajuk in August 2002, I found that the Indonesian villagers of Tekam Patah had made a substantial profit from trading pepper to Malaysian middlemen from Telok Melano. At the height of the Indonesian monetary crisis (*crismon*) in 1997, the Indonesian economy was in recession, the price of daily necessities had risen

Illus. 23 Hari Raya at Pak Jayadi's house (1994)

dramatically, but villagers in the region were enjoying an unexpected bubble economy.

For example, Pak Jayadi migrated from Jawai to Tekam Patah in 1987 with only Rp 7,500 in his pocket. After almost ten years of struggle, he received a boost from the Indonesian economic crisis. He was then cultivating fields yielding up to 1.5 tons of pepper annually. In 1997, the value of the rupiah declined to Rp 3,500 against the ringgit. In that year, one kilogram of white pepper fetched 23 ringgit on the Malaysian market, and one of black pepper 16 ringgit. Pak Jayadi had previously sold pepper to Malaysian middlemen at exchange rates in the range of Rp 750 (1992) and Rp 1,200 (1994), but the rate increased to Rp 3,500 in 1997. One ringgit brought a value in rupiah 4.7 times higher when compared to 1992. Pak Jayadi subsequently achieved overnight success, acquiring a concrete house, an electricity generator and two motorcycles. By 2002, more than two-thirds of Tekam Patah's 50 households owned their own generators and some families had three motorcycles.

An economic community united by a single currency is a basic social grouping. The residents of Telok Melano and Temajuk are divided by national currencies because nationality and national currency are meant to coincide with national space. Such places, however, can give rise to new and flexible, transnational economic interactions based on the strategic use of currency.

This chapter extends the ethnography of the borderland in western Borneo from the level of a village to that of a border arc between Sarawak and West Kalimantan. The purpose is to update the examination of the contemporary dialectics between the states and local societies at the periphery of national space.

Jalan Tikus to *Jalan Gajah*: From Rat Paths to Elephant Paths

The following map shows malaria-infested "black areas" (*kawasan hitam*) in southwestern Sarawak identified by government health officials, which occur sporadically along the Sarawak border. Villagers often suffer from sudden bouts of severe headaches and shivering, despite the state's regular spraying of anti-mosquito pesticide in all houses. On the Malaysian side, people say the reason such areas are concentrated near the border is that malaria-infected Indonesians enter Sarawakian territory and are bitten by mosquitoes that spread the parasite to Malaysians. The spots on the map coincide with the communities along the border that have long functioned as pipelines between the two nation-states. These border communities are ethnically specific: one serves as a link for the transnational traffic of Malays, another does so for Ibans along the border that stretches from Cape Dato on the Sarawak-West Kalimatan border to Sebatic Island between Sabah and East Kalimantan. There are many such places like this linked by the flows and movements of people, goods, diseases, and ideas. The Telok Melano-Temajuk border zone is one of such hubs connecting Malaysia and Indonesia.

As the economic gap between Indonesia and Malaysia widened, the two countries studded the border with official immigration posts and customs houses that monitor official flows of traded goods and documented laborers. The Cross Border Agreement of 1984 proposed the opening of ten points of entry and exit (*Pos Lintas Batas*) along the Kalimantan-East Malaysia border: Paloh, Sanjingan, Sungai Aruk, Saparan, Jagoi Babang, Sidding, Bantan, Merakai Panjang, Nanga Badau,

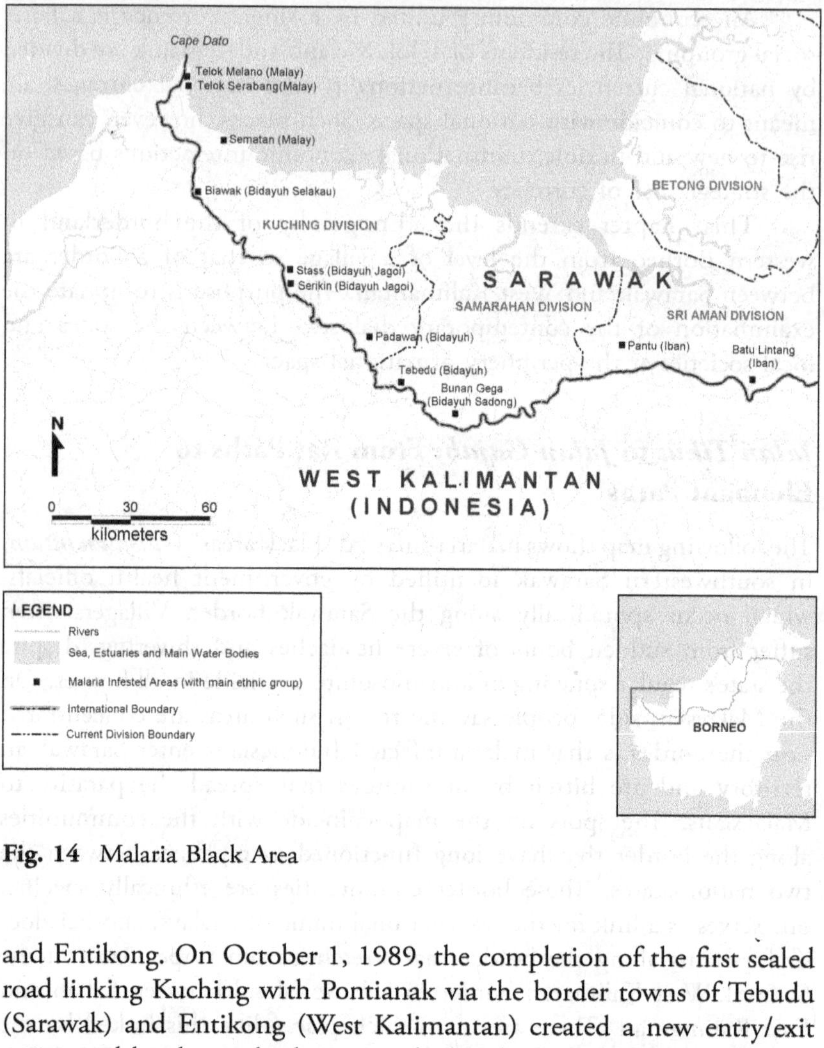

Fig. 14 Malaria Black Area

and Entikong. On October 1, 1989, the completion of the first sealed road linking Kuching with Pontianak via the border towns of Tebudu (Sarawak) and Entikong (West Kalimantan) created a new entry/exit point, and border trade there increased in leaps and bounds. Between 1988 and 1990, customs revenue jumped sharply on a volume of trade that increased nearly seven-fold from previous decades (Sarawak Development Institute 2001: 12).

In addition to new entry/exit points such as the one at Tebudu-Entikong, many traditional trading hubs have been upgraded to official checkpoints. Cape Dato, lacking road connections to the outside, remains one of the most isolated at these locations. Sematan is gazetted by the Sarawak government as a landing point for timber coming from West Kalimantan.

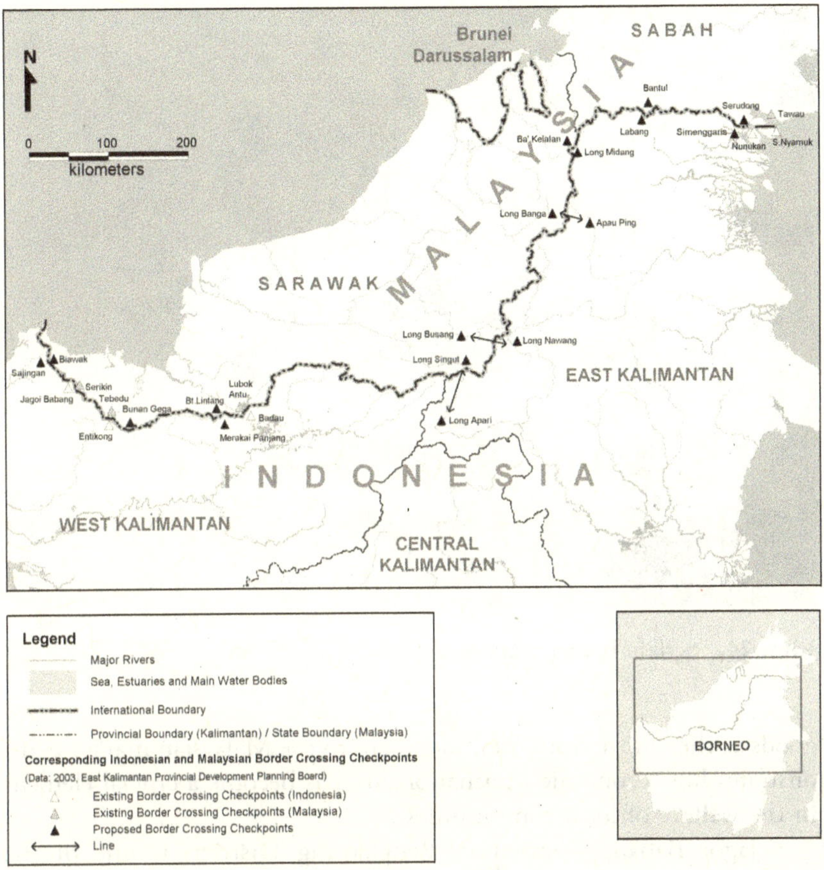

Fig. 15 Border Checkpoints

As hubs for local cross-border traffic were transformed into official border posts, small paths traditionally called "*jalan tikus*" (lit., rat paths) were replaced by larger roads that facilitate greater traffic. Traditional *jalan tikus* later became "*jalan gajah*" (elephant paths) connecting border towns to the capital cities of Pontianak and Kuching and other major towns in Kalimantan and East Malaysia.

Economic transactions and social relations are closely interlinked, as shown by the symbiosis between Temajuk and Telok Melano. The commodification process in borderlands between nation-states with asymmetric economies entails a relative valuation and devaluation of things and people, and changing national affiliation of commercial

Illus. 24 Serikin border market

goods as they move from the Indonesian to the Malaysian market demonstrates how economic transnationality has become a crucial element in the welfare of local communities.

Jagoi Babang, located in Bengkayang District, is one of the Indonesian communities whose economy is dependent on the border trade with Malaysians across the international boundary (see Fig. 8). Bengkayang District, consisting of five villages and 22 hamlets, shares the border with southwestern Sarawak. The community currently comprises 11 Bidayuh sub-dialect groups, including the majority Jagoi Dayak. The road connection with the state capital, Pontianak, is fairly good, but the city is a 254-kilometer drive away.[1] It is only a four kilometer ride costing five ringgit on an Indonesian motorbike from Jagoi Babang to Serikin, a Malaysian Jagoi Dayak village. Serikin in turn can be reached by car from Kuching in less than one hour. The proximity of the Malaysian market and the separation from

[1] Pontianak to Singkawang, 145 km; Singkawang to Bengkayang, 70 km; Bengkayang to Seluas, 91 km; Seluas to Jagoi Babang, 18 km; Jagoi Babang to Serikin, 4 km.

the Indonesian distribution network make the national affiliation of Jagoi Babang ambiguous because local residents are closely tied to the Malaysian economy.

On the Malaysian side, the unpaved road from Bau to Serikin is being upgraded to a paved road, and new bridges are also under construction alongside the old ones as the Sarawak government prepares for increasing traffic along this route. Serikin itself contains many well-built houses, and villagers there derive substantial income from leasing plots to Indonesian traders opening stalls. Indonesian motorbikes come and go with passengers and goods, their youthful drivers acting as porters bringing items from Indonesian territory. The market is full of Indonesian products. Music CDs, VCDs and DVDs, kitchenware and utensils, leather shoes, rice, dried shrimp, dried squid, hats, toys, cloth, floor mats, and Balinese stone carvings are displayed in simple wooden stalls. Many of the Indonesian traders stay overnight on Saturdays, waiting for weekend shoppers from Kuching who come to Serikin's regular Sunday market. Most customers are Kuching Malays, while Chinese purchasers are generally traders buying Indonesian goods. I was frequently called "taukay" by Indonesians, who mistook me for a Chinese shopowner. On the roadside, signs warn of restrictions on the sale of wild animals, and at one checkpoint, a Malaysian officer asked me whether I had purchased rice.

On the Indonesian side, the adjacent communities of Jagoi Babang have also benefited substantially from the border trade:

> The borderland villagers of Jagoi Babang are extremely well-off. The majority of villagers have gas cooking stoves [propane gas cylinders are obtained from Serikin], VCD players, and motorbikes. Some even possess automobiles. The village is strategically located adjacent to Sarawakian territory, where for the villagers-cum-petty traders, only a Cross Border Pass is required to enter Malaysia. With the pass, they are allowed to go as far as Bau and stay in Sarawakian territory from one week to one month. Those who wish to go to Serikin only are not required to go through immigration. Many Jagoi Babang villagers maintain kin relations with their Dayak counterparts in Serikin. The daily interaction is dense. For them, the international boundary is just a village boundary. Both Malaysian ringgit and Indonesian rupiah circulate and are easily converted. (Interview with the District Chief of Jagoi Babang)

The transnational flows of people and commodities are not a recent phenomenon. Jagoi Babang has served as an economic hub between Sambas and Sarawak since the 1950s at least. The following is the recollection of a Sambas resident who smuggled rubber sheet into colonial Sarawak via *jalan tikus* connecting Jagoi Babang and Serikin:

> Smuggling activities from Sambas to Sarawak were already taking place in the 1950s, mainly in the form of illegal sales of rubber and timber. Rubber fetched a higher price in Sarawak (Rp 20/kg) compared to local market prices (Rp 6/kg). Rubber sheets (approximately 50 kg per person) were transported by foot, following a footpath from Sambas that leads to Serikin or Biawak. The journey took three to four weeks. Rubber was also exchanged for pepper, which could later be resold in Sambas at a higher price. People living closer to the border were involved in timber smuggling, and some men from our village worked as tree cutters. Timber was usually sold to the Chinese on the other side of the border. Smuggling activities declined during and after the Konfrontasi period in the 1960s when the border areas were heavily patrolled on both sides, and many smugglers were arrested. (Interview with a villager of Sain Rambi, Sambas)

Another border-crossing inspection post, which pairs Entikong (Indonesia) and Tebudu (Malaysia), also functions as a crucial commercial hub. After its official opening in 1987, an influx of Indonesian commodities started to enter Sarawak. The subsequent development of Entikong-Tebudu trade provides more economic benefits to West Kalimantan than to Sarawak. In 1998 the trade surplus reached three million US dollars owing to the depreciation of the Indonesian rupiah (Fariastuti 2000: 10). For instance, the rise in cross-border trade of traditional agricultural commodities increased from 25 per cent in 1996 to 40 per cent in 1998, and export values of black pepper and cocoa increased from 4 and 8 per cent respectively in 1996 to 29 and 22 per cent in 1998; the total value of exports traveling via Entikong Post reached USD2,980,000 in 1996 and USD3,100,000 in 1998. The actual amounts could be much higher owing to the impossibility of recording all traditional trading activities along the border (Fariastuti 2000: 10).[2]

Many traders at Entikong told me that the weak Indonesian rupiah was the basis of their business, and it is clear that the outflow

---

[2] "Traditional trade" is defined as "an external trade carried out by people living in the border districts and having Border Crossing Passes (Pas Lintas Batas)". In contrast, international trade must comply with export and import rules.

Illus. 25 Entikong/Tebudu border check point

of commodities from Indonesian territory, both documented and undocumented, will continue as long as the depreciated rupiah renders a profit to local people, who are marginalized from the Pontianak-based commercial network. The opening of the Entikong Post did not eliminate illicit cross-border trade. The most common smuggled goods are cigarettes, rice, bird's nests, clothing, household items, and hewn timber (Sarawak Development Institute 2001: 11).[3]

Transnational Flow of Labor

In addition to the cross-border movements of agricultural products and natural resources into Malaysia, the mobilization of labor has become increasingly crucial for Malaysian industries and for peripheral

[3] The illegal trade of forest resources causes environmental damage and reduces local capacity to sustain economic development. The wood processing industry in West Kalimantan has already run out of timber, causing workers to be laid off (Personal communication with Dr. Fariastuti of Universitas Tanjungpura).

Indonesian peasant communities structurally drawn into Sarawak's production system. Lying on the geographical periphery of the Republic of Indonesia, West Kalimantan has become part of the economic infrastructure of Sarawak, and Indonesian labor is indispensable for the development of Sarawak's economy. So-called "3 D" jobs (dirty, difficult, and dangerous) are filled by Indonesian migrant workers in sawmills, at construction sites, and on oil palm and acacia mangium plantations. Indonesian women work in households and coffee shops.

People from Sambas regency have long found employment in timber-related industries. Out-migration began in the 1950s and increased in the mid-1970s after the military presence put a halt to contraband rubber trading across the border. Labor initially migrated to other parts of West Kalimantan, especially went to logging areas near Pontianak and Ketapang. The people of Sambas have since become well known for their proficiency at the felling and hauling techniques required by the logging industry. During the 1970s, labor migration to Sarawak was common, largely oriented towards logging sites and FELDA (Federal Land Development Authority) oil palm plantations, and local logging companies recruited Sambas Malays for operations in Riau and Sumatra.[4] In this decade and the one that followed, migrant labor from Sambas mainly consisted of adult males, but female workers began to work outside Sambas during the 1990s. At present, the destinations of labor migrants have expanded to include plywood factories, sawmills, as well as oil palm and acacia mangium plantations in Kuching, Sibu, Bintulu, and Miri. Along with Javanese contract workers from east and central Java, Sambas Malay workers constitute the majority of the work force in these places.

According to a labor agency based in Sambas, which regularly sends local Malays to Sarawak's timber companies, the number of Indonesian laborers (TKI, *Tenaga Kerja Indonesia*) sent to Malaysia peaked between 1990 and 1995, when an average of 700 workers per month were mobilized from Sambas. Even after the Asian economic crisis set in, the agency still managed to send 120–30 workers monthly from

[4] The Federal Land Development Authority (FELDA) is Malaysia's largest palm oil producer, and indeed the world's largest. Originally created in 1956 to channel financial assistance to state governments for land development programs, FELDA's role was later expanded to include the task of implementing land development programs throughout the country.

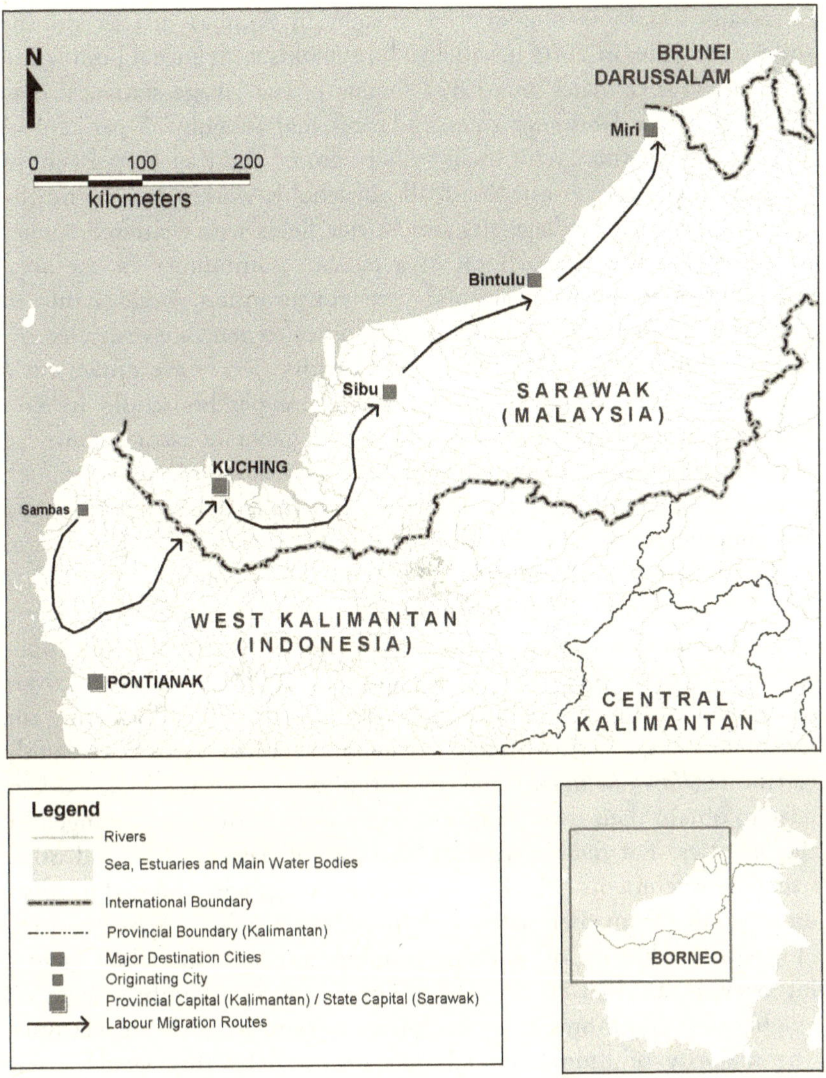

Fig. 16 Sambas/Sarawak Labor Migration

Sambas in 1997. In 2003, 150–200 laborers were sent each month. Present labor regulations in Malaysia limit the contracts of Indonesian workers to a maximum of four years, but Indonesian laborers who wish to continue working after finishing their contracted term routinely obtain new identification papers and re-enter Sarawak.

Sain Rambi is one of 180 villages in Sambas district on the Indonesian side; in 2003 it had 660 households with a total population of 2,834 (1,437 males and 1,397 females). The village statistical data for 1999 (*Data Monografi Desa*) indicates that roughly 75 per cent of all household earners were small-scale peasants, and that 40 per cent of them were landless. A quarter of all households worked for the nearby rubber factory. The village sits amidst rice fields with scattered rubber trees and has the typical look of a peasant community in the area, and residents grow rice for their own consumption. Besides rubber, they have no major agricultural commodities to generate cash income, unlike neighboring Tebas, where citrus fruits (*jeruk*) are grown on a large scale. The average monthly expenditure per household in Sain Rambi is Rp 300,000–400,000, and people generate extra income for household expenditure through supplementary economic activities such as fishing, operating motor taxis (*ojek*), petty trade, rubber tapping, and for landowners selling cash crops such as maize and coffee. Workers at the nearby rubber factory earn Rp 400,000 per month.

Labor recruitment agents come directly to Sain Rambi village and offer candidates a choice of companies and destinations. Male applicants must pay Rp 600,000 in advance (in 2000), a sum that covers Malaysian work permits and transportation. The cost of preparing the documents required to obtain a passport — birth certificate, family certificate (*Kartu Keluarga*), and passport photo — is extra. Male workers have to obtain their own passports, while work permits are arranged by the agencies. For female workers, the cost of passport fees and other necessary documents (M$300) is paid by the agencies and deducted six months later from their salaries. Applicants must be at least 18-years-old, with no history of violating immigration law. The labor agent I interviewed said that 80 per cent of families in Sain Rambi village and neighboring communities expect their children to work in Malaysia. The majority of Indonesian laborers recruited by this agency come from Sambas, Tebas or Pemangkat and surrounding areas. Recruiting agencies from other areas (Pontianak and Singkawang) also operate in Sambas, around 600 Sambas Malays are sent to Malaysia each year.

Recruitment is usually a collective process. Approved TKIs are transported by the agencies to the border post at Entikong in groups of between 50 and 200. Immigration procedures are handled by the agencies, and the laborers are put onto separate buses at Tebudu according to their work destinations (for example, Kuching, Sibu, Bintulu, or Miri). Passports are handed to individuals at the border

Illus. 26 Sambas Malay workers at a Japanese plywood factory in Bintulu

posts and collected again at their destinations. While they remain in Sarawak, Indonesian laborers only hold photocopies of their passports, employment IDs, and other documents.

Most ex-laborers in Sarawak view the working conditions in reputable sawmills and plywood factories and some oil palm plantations as good. The average working day is 12 hours in two shifts, and the

Table 16 The Home Regions of Factory Workers Employed by a Japanese Plywood Factory in Bintulu, Sarawak

Region	*Number of Workers*
Java	
Central Java	9
West Java	3
Kalimantan	
South Kalimantan	1
West Kalimantan	17

Table 17 The Home Villages of the Factory Workers from West Kalimantan

Village	*Number of Workers*
Jawi	5
Tebas	4
Galing	4
Pemangkat	1
Pontianak	1
Selobat	1
Telok Keramat	1
Total	17

pay is M$13 (a basic eight-hour daily wage of M$7, plus overtime of M$5). Every day, M$3 is deducted as a "levy" to be returned to the worker upon completion of a two-year contract. With the ringgit trading at approximately 2,200 rupiah, the monthly wage is equivalent to Rp 550,000, and Indonesian workers earning the amount are usually able to bring home M$6,000 after two years of work. For young women working fulltime at a local *warung* (casual restaurant) and café in Sain Rambi, the monthly wage is approximately Rp 150,000. After their return, many workers use this money to buy consumer goods such as motorcycles, or carry out home renovations.

The migration of Indonesian labor across the international boundary is an essential element in the development of the economy of Sarawak. The states, both Malaysian and Indonesian, created a broad zone of deterritorialized borderlands, where Malaysian employers and the Indonesian workers, especially Foochow entrepreneurs and Sambas Malays, work side by side. The economic gap between Indonesia and Malaysia widened after the Asian economic crisis of 1997, and the weak rupiah was responsible for massive flows of resources out of Indonesia. When out-migration is tolerated by the state and local institutions emerge to support it, a nation's people become a labor reserve for foreign production systems. When agricultural commodities and natural resources are also incorporated into the cross-border exchange, the expansion of capitalist production is further augmented.

With the development of commodity markets and timber-related industries in Sarawak, outflows of labor became an integral feature of the rural societies of West Kalimantan. Sawmills, plywood manufacturers, and plantations are heavily dependent on Indonesian labor recruited from the region's peasant communities. The flow of workers has been supported by the opening of official immigration posts and the construction of road networks directly connecting local villages with Sarawak's main economic hubs of Kuching, Sibu, Bintulu, and Miri.[5]

The agricultural frontier of the Brooke white rajahs has become an industrial frontier, thanks in part to resourceful Indonesia. The increased number of Indonesians crossing the border to earn Malaysian wages gave rise to a proposal to build a "border industrial zone" on the Malaysian side of frontier where Indonesian workers could commute to work every day. Malaysian companies would thus bear no responsibility for the welfare of their employees, for dormitories, recreational facilities, recruitment personnel and so forth. Some Indonesian local officials reacted positively to this concept, and were willing to build a vocational school on the Indonesian side to supply quality labor for Malaysian industry.

The widening gap between Indonesian and Malaysian wages, accelerated by a decline of the Indonesian rupiah in international exchange markets, makes the proposal realistic.[6] In August 2005, Sarawak's first training center for Indonesian maids was officially launched near the Tebudu/Entikong border crossing. Malaysia's Public Health and Environment Minister officially opened the center at Bandar Mutiara Tebudu, a town 100 km from Kuching (*Sarawak Tribune*, 24 August

---

[5] There are important works by Indonesian and Malaysian scholars on the borderlands of Borneo. For the detailed account on the border zone between Kalimantan and Sabah/Sarawak, conducted by Indonesian researchers specialized in anthropology, economics, political demography, political ecology, and history, see Riwanto Tirtosudarmo and John Haba (2005). For the ethnographic description of Sarawak-East Kalimantan border relations, see L. Jayl, D. Chew, and I Ketut Ardhana (2004). See Dave Lumenta (2008) for the historical analysis of cross-border movement of Apau Kayan Kenyah in Central Borneo.

For the comparative analysis of borderland with broader theoretical implications, see Martinez (1986) and Van Schendel and Baud (1997). For the recent case studies of borderlands in Southeast Asia, see Horstmann and Wadley (2006).

[6] The border zone between West Malaysia and Singapore, for instance, has long functioned as a labor reservoir for Singapore, while multinational corporations utilize inexpensive Indonesian labor on the Indonesian island of Batam just off Singapore. The transnationally mobilized Indonesian workers are structurally parallel to Mexicans working in San Diego/Tijuana border industrial zone (cf. Ishikawa 1993).

2005). The first batch of 60 Indonesians learned how to take care of disabled persons, senior citizens, and children, and how to conduct routine housework. Trainees also received language lessons in Malay, English and Mandarin. The center can handle up to 150 trainees per month, and courses last between one to three months.

Border Connection

In addition to labor, the exploitation of natural resources receives governmental attention along the frontier. In 2003 the BIMP-EAGA Malaysia Business Council, taking its cue from the development of Thailand and Malaysia's joint oil and gas resources, initiated a study for joint cooperation between Sarawak and Kalimantan in order to explore potential resources in the borderlands, anticipating that enormous mining and timber resources had been left untapped in both countries.[7] There has been regular dialogue between Kalimantan and Sarawak aimed at identifying opportunities for joint development of the border area (*The Borneo Post*, 20 February 2003).

In June 2005 the Indonesian Government announced a Kalimantan oil palm mega-project. The idea was to develop the world's largest oil palm plantation in a five- or ten-kilometer band along the border between Indonesia and Malaysia. To finance the USD567 million project, the Indonesian President and Chamber of Commerce and Industry met with the Chinese government and interested entrepreneurs from the private sector. The oil palm project, launched in Indonesia under the banner of "bringing prosperity, security and environmental protection to the Kalimantan border area", included plantation sites covering 1.8 million hectares, about half the size of the Netherlands.[8]

---

[7] The BIMP-EAGA stands for the Brunei Darussalam-Indonesia-Malaysia-Philippines East ASEAN Growth Area, which comprises the entire sultanate of Brunei Darussalam; ten provinces in the Indonesian islands of Kalimantan, Sulawesi, Maluku, and Irian Jaya; Sabah, Sarawak, and Labuan in Malaysia; and Mindanao and Palawan in the Philippines. The vision for the BIMP-EAGA is the development of the East ASEAN subregions and the uplift of the people residing in those areas through the potential of regional economic cooperation.

[8] The following account on the Kalimantan oil palm mega roject is based on the report "The Kalimantan Border Oil Palm Mega-project", AIDEnvironment, Apr. 2006, commissioned by Milieudefensie – Friends of the Earth Netherlands and the Swedish Society for Nature Conservation (SSNC) <http://www.foe.co.uk/resource/reports/palm_oil_mega_project.pdf>.

Fig. 17 Planned Border Plantation Belt

The anticipated massive increase in demand for biofuels and continued growth in consumption of edible oils have led the Indonesian government to calculate that future global demand for oil palm production is unlimited, and that the development of the Kalimantan-

Sarawak-Sabah border area will attract investors from India, Malaysia and China. The project aimed to promote security, bridge the gap in prosperity between Kalimantan and Malaysian Borneo, address illegal logging along the border, create 50,000 jobs for Javanese workers, and produce biofuel for domestic consumption and export. The oil palm plantation was to produce 2.7 million bunches of fresh fruit annually from 2010 onwards, while rubber plantations in the zone were to produce 135,000 tons of rubber sheet annually. In its initial stage, the project focused on the Sambas, Sintang, Bengkayang, Sanggau and Kapuas districts in West Kalimantan.

The plan gave rise to a campaign and lobbying effort by NGOs, Indonesian media and foreign diplomats that forced the Indonesian government to revise its position on the project. Indonesia's President, Susilo Bambang Yudhoyono, acknowledged that conservation concerns had to be taken into account. However, despite the possible cancellation of the mega-project, palm oil companies have already moved into the border area, and plans to develop Kalimantan border area remain alive. The Indonesian government still expects to authorize the development of three million hectares of new oil palm plantations, comprising two million hectares along the Kalimantan-Malaysia border and one million hectares elsewhere, to meet the domestic and global demand for biofuels. To deal with growing criticism against extensive exploitation of the remaining forest area, the definition of the border zone was changed from the original of 5 to 10 km to 100 km.

Apart from the continued push to expand oil palm plantations, the Indonesian government will pursue strong development in ten growth areas[9] along the border, with priority given to logging, forest plantations, mining, agriculture, marine fisheries, plantations, industry and tourism.[10] The Temajuk-Aruk border belt, where Temajuk village sits adjacent to Telok Melano, is designated as an economic niche for logging, marine fishing, plantations, industry and tourism. In order to

[9] These "growth areas" are Temajuk-Aruk (Sambas Regency), Jagoi Babang (Bengkayang), Entikong (Sanggau), Jasa (Sintang), Nanga Badau (Kapuas Hulu), Nunukan-Sebatik (Nunukan), Long Apai-Long Pahangai (West Kutai), Long Midang (Nunukan), and Long Nawang (Malinau).

[10] Kebijakan Spatial dan Strategi Penembangan Kawasan Perbatasan Kalimantan-Sarawak-Sabah, Directorate General of Spatial Planning, Ministry of Public Works, Indonesia, 5 July 2005.

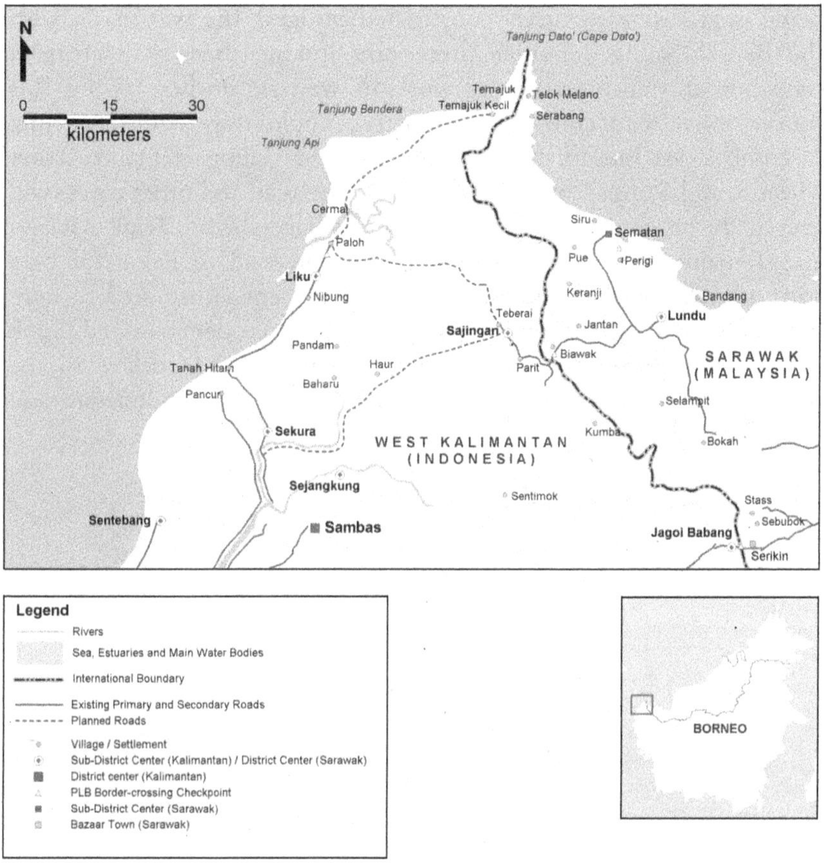

Fig. 18 Planned Roads to the Cape Dato Area

support the development project, the government is constructing a road network connecting border regions to the state capitals of Kalimantan. Construction is underway on seven routes in West Kalimantan, covering 2,856 km.

On a short trip from Sambas to Sajingan in March 2006 I saw road construction between Sajingan (the twin village of Biawak, Sarawak) and Paloh, and between Cermai and Temajuk. Between Sajingan and Galing, there were numerous heavy machines working on *kerangas* (Sundaland heath) forest (see Appendix). Basic leveling was complete for the greater part of the route but surfacing was not. On the Malaysian side of the border, the road between Biawak and Lundu was also being upgraded with newly constructed bridges. The two roads, with the Biawak/Sajingan border checkpoint linking them, will create a trans-border transportation network in western Borneo. Using this transnational road connection, a person could travel from Kuching to Sambas, via Lundu, Biawak/Sajingan, and Galing. Temajuk, Telok Melano, and Sambas (and subsequently Pontianak and other cities) will eventually be connected as well. Young villagers from Telok Melano and Temajuk have already begun to use the road to Paloh for bike trips. On the Sarawak side, the state government is rumored to have proposed the construction of a new road between Sematan and Telok Melano, but Telok Melano still remains an isolated enclave in the midst of an expanding transnational network crossing Indonesian and Malaysian territory.

Conclusion

The neglect of a spatial understanding in works of historical ethnography was a prime motivator for my research. Each chapter of this book, utilizing different time scales and geographical frames, has examined the processes at work in the borderlands of western Borneo, considering mercantile and capitalist development, relationships between the national and the transnational, and the location work of border communities and the state. This final chapter recapitulates the relationships among nation-state, transnationalism, and power.

Structural Power and Organizational Power

To examine the borderlands of western Borneo as a field of dynamic tension where labor is mobilized, deployed, and organized for production, it is useful to draw upon concepts of *organizational power* exercised in the state's spatial encroachment and consolidation, and *structural power* organizing and orchestrating the various operating units for organizational power at work (cf. Wolf 2001: 383–97). The borderland of western Borneo is a point of articulation between the two forces, the one responsible for the formation of production sites and markets both for commodities and labor and the other for the capitalist expansion that links the periphery of maritime Southeast Asia with global economic forces.[1]

Organizational power is concerned with how individuals are deployed and social fields arranged for production. The classic plural

[1] In *Iranun and Balangingi* (2002), James Warren examines historical processes where commodity chain, labor mobilization, and colonialism in the Sulu-Mindanao region led to global economic-cultural interconnectedness and interdependencies.

society was a colonial example of the exercise of this power, where multiple ethnic groups became enmeshed in the system of colonial production. In British Malaya, for example, Chinese labor was typically mobilized for tin mining, and Indian labor for rubber plantations. Operating units such as mine sites and plantations growing rubber, tobacco, pepper, and gambier, as observed in the borderland of Lundu District, were supported by colonial policies, and labor was controlled by plantation owners, entrepreneurs, labor recruiters, and colonial officials. Everyday supervision of work, the sale of produce, eating, drinking alcohol, and even gambling are examples of how operating units circumscribed the actions of others. This kind of organizational force is also at work in the present-day economic regime where the flexible accumulation of capital is underway, along with transnational labor mobilization. Offshore production arrangements, as in the colonial past, occur in niches where organizational power operates. The arena of the operation is varied; from coconut plantations to plywood factories and ultimately to the territorial state.

Structural power is a force derived from global capitalism that emerges when capitalism engages local social formations. It creates operating units, a process closely related to the emergence and transformation of community, labor and commodity markets, and in the case of the borderlands under analysis the territoriality of the state itself. Structural power in the form of colonialism, internationalism, transnationalism, and globalization structures political economy and labor processes on the ground. This mode of power "not only operates within settings or domains but also organizes and orchestrates the settings themselves, and that specifies the distribution and direction of energy flows" (Wolf 2001: 384).

The border zone of western Borneo offers a useful window to observe how a nation-state becomes a territorial as well as a transterritorial entity under organizational and structural power. With a special focus on the making and implementation of policy, and the reaction of local society, we have looked at a geographically specific, empirical case study along the jungle frontier in Borneo in order to examine the identity of national space.

National Space and Transnationalism

The making of national space by the Brooke government began with the alchemy of land administration. A series of laws made land previously under the jurisdiction of Brunei Sultan and local Dayak chiefs *terrae nullius*, unoccupied land. Under the second rajah, all unoccupied land, now the property of the government, became available to "Sarawak subjects" for commercial production, but reverted to the state if left uncultivated. With the state directing the energy of the people into the cultivation of commodities, Chinese and Malay workers, under the leadership of *taukay* and *nakoda* entrepreneurs respectively, were allowed to enter Sarawak, leading to the formation of an ethnically segmented colonial society adjacent to Dutch West Borneo territory. These arrangements created numerous operating units for organizational power within state territory, where two distinctive processes of social grouping occurred: the formation of Chinese estates with continuous transboundary inflows of Chinese laborers and of Malay communities that incorporated Sambas Malay laborers-cum-settlers. The way these flows of labor were handled differed from one ethnic group to another, as the examination of the formation of Malay and Chinese communities in Chapter 1 showed.

Once the production system became operational, the government attempted to ensure that community members and especially laborers remained within the colonial space, and that commodities produced there generated tax revenues when traded across the territorial boundary. To clarify and confirm the affiliation of labor and of agricultural or forest produce, Sarawak authorities created a series of ordinances regulating the movement of people and dutiable commodities. These regulations covered compulsory possession of passports, the arrest and extradition of criminals who crossed the border, the pursuit and arrest of runaway coolies, control of border crossings during outbreaks of disease, regulation of the opium trade, restrictions on cross-border swidden agriculture, and registration of cultivated land. Another series of regulations dealt with naturalization, marriage registration, and spousal support and child rearing with intention to make mobile locals sedentary.

The advent of rubber cultivation changed the way people on both sides of the border interacted. The operating units, where both organizational and structural forces were at work, became transnational as well as global. The International Rubber Regulation Agreement of 1934 disrupted cross-border trade, and the implementation of this agreement was epochal because it linked the international market to rubber merchants and to smugglers in the borderlands of western Borneo, with the latter exploiting cross-border trading to increase profits.

The imperial cooperation of the interwar period of internationalism in the 1930s resulted in the formation of a new social field where local agency utilized micro transnationalism at the national margin.

Trans-border trading of rubber in the borderlands of western Borneo became the major industry of Lundu District during the 1930s. After the Japanese occupation, with economic chaos on the Indonesian side during and after Indonesia's independence from the Dutch, a wide range of commodities, including tobacco, gold, poultry, textiles and sawn timber were smuggled into Sarawak, a process that continued during the 1950s and early 1960s. This movement of goods, which began as a response to imperial restriction on rubber production and trade, was made possible by Chinese traders who created their own arrangements operating alongside and sometimes in competition with the British and Dutch colonial apparatus. For the first time in the history of the borderlands of western Borneo, the organization power of the Chinese commercial networks challenged the state and the structural power of imperial internationalism.[2]

A crucial change in the nature of transnational flows in the borderlands of western Borneo took place in the late 1980s, when the labor force on the Indonesian side became the subject of deployment by the Sarawakian industries. Uninterrupted transnational flows of labor required systematic organization of recruitment, immigration, and transportation, and the arrangements adopted to control labor flows in western Borneo caused a fundamental transformation of border society. Once production got underway, a regular supply of labor from Sambas in West Kalimantan became necessary for the factories, which operated 24 hours a day and 365 days a year. With the establishment of an Indonesian labor market for timber-related industries and agro-plantations in Sarawak, Indonesian border society in Kalimantan became part of the infrastructure underlying East Malaysia's industrial expansion.

Transnational mobilization for production is an important element in social dynamics on both the local and supra-local level. In the late nineteenth century, Malay traders and Chinese entrepreneurs transformed the frontier of colonial Sarawak into plantation zones that utilized foreign labor. A century later, Malaysian timber and plantation industries are employing labor from the Sambas region of West

[2] The importance of attention to the organizational power of the Chinese commercial networks was suggested by George Souza. I am also grateful to Sidney Mintz for suggesting new approaches to research on market and marketplaces.

Kalimantan and other parts of Indonesia. Although the mode of labor deployment and the organizations and institutions involved vary from time to time, the direction of labor flow is the same.

From the time when J.H. Boeke developed his notion of a dual economy, Indonesia has been a primal case where two separate economic systems have coexisted, one geared to local subsistence needs and the other to wage labor (Boeke 1953). On the Indonesian side, the state does little to limit the movement of people and goods. The current flows of both documented and undocumented commodities and labor are a modern manifestation of older transnational commodity and labor flows. The Dutch divided Indonesian rural society into two labor sectors, one for subsistence-oriented agriculture and the other for plantation-based commodity production. Under the current international division of labor, the colonial element in the production of agricultural commodities has been replaced by foreign capital. Production sites are located abroad, while rural agricultural communities generate and maintain steady outflows of labor.

Contemporary transboundary flows of labor, capital, and technology are accelerated through the articulation of organizational and structural power. The state's apparatus for establishing new niches for labor and resource mobilization is deeply tied to global arrangements for new kinds of industrial production, such as oil palm and acacia plantation, with green agendas for the global energy crisis and climate change. The transnationalism being formulated by Malaysia and Indonesia requires deliberate organizational action to systematize cross-border flows of labor and resource with the participation of a wide range of private entrepreneurs and public sectors.

Spatial Modernity, New and Old

My final remarks concern the relationship between transnationalism and the nation-state as a territorial entity. The examination of social dynamics at the state margin raises questions about whether it is possible to treat the national and the transnational as polar opposites. I have argued that the emergence of national territoriality in the Weberian sense and the inflows and outflows of people and commodities across the porous border are mutually constitutive in nature. Borderland history shows a resonance between the two that is the basis for the construction and evolution of national space. In other words, the spatiality of the state is molded by the flux of people and goods, and generates policies and practices that respond to these flows. The appearance and maintenance of national space entails a dialectic between border society and the state, and understanding the relationship between them requires locating both outside the realm of conventional models of state-society juxtaposition and of societal inclusion of the state.

The historical and ethnographic study of the borderlands of western Borneo suggests that the nation-state and transnationalism are not mutually exclusive. The functionality of the state has been strengthened by the development of transnationalism and vice versa. As national boundaries become more rigid, differences between nation-states increase, and these imbalances stimulate trans-border flows. As seen in the case of Telok Melano-Temajuk interactions, without the socio-economic difference between Malaysia and Indonesia (for example, in the strength of the currency and the valuation of labor), the national space and its boundary would mean little in the borderland.

Recent decades of socio-economic development along the border in western Borneo have strengthened the state's involvement in transnational projects through policies that have deliberately aimed at utilizing border niches for national development. Transnational flows of labor and natural resources were formerly tolerated because they had no negative consequences for entrepreneurial and national interests elsewhere. The borderland is now a location where state-driven development is creating a new state-society dialectic. The state's control of the national boundary, both in practice and as image, is gradually taming the borderland.

The physically porous border in western Borneo has become a social field characterized by disparities between a set of polities, exploited by people on both sides of the border through intentional transgressions of the boundary. Residents of the border zone both deny and acknowledge national space. The realization of territoriality occurs when its denial leads the state to implement policies calling for the enclosure of such transgressions. The dialectical process between state policing and the adaptive transnationalism of local society contributes to the genesis of nation space, and state and society exercise a multiplier function. Clarifying this process offers a way to understand how two seemingly contradictory social movements — the construction of national space and the simultaneous deconstruction of a state boundary through parochial transnationalism — operate as general features of a borderland.

Besides security concerns, a point amply explored in the earlier chapters, economic networks extending over the national boundary are one of the prime factors generating and maintaining a boundary between the nation-states. Markets, both international and local, and borderlands need each other. Commodity and labor markets make use of fundamental differences between two nation-states. The prime force behind the creation and maintenance of the borderland as a socio-economic interface has been mercantile wealth and capitalism. Trans-border transactions are a force behind the emergence of a geopolitical membrane, where an economic osmotic pressure determines the direction of commodity and labor, and the value of personhood. During the first century after the declaration of a national space by Charles Brooke, the mercantile exchange through the Malay and Chinese networks was the main component of transnationalism in the region. In recent years the development of road networks in both territories has facilitated new transnational flows. Since the 1980s the borderland has been the niche for transnational deployment of labor supporting the development of timber-related industries and agro-plantation businesses. The speed and volume of transnational flows are subject to fluctuation of market prices and foreign exchange rates, production demand, the supply of resources, and changes in the international economic climate. The state-sponsored expansion of transnational transportation networks and the opening of border checkpoints have made the borderlands a new social field where cross-border flows support both national projects and official transnationalism under the control of the state.

Contrary to the image of an all-powerful leviathan, the state in this part of maritime Southeast Asia has always been weak, particularly in the borderlands. The zonal *mandala*-like character of the territoriality of the sultanates was inherited by the colonial geo-body of the Sarawak kingdom, which had a porous border and was in constant need of transnationalism for its survival. The geo-body gradually took shape within the new frontiers. A physically unrecognizable boundary on a low mountain range in virgin rainforest, the absence of transportation networks, extremely low population densities and a small number of officials made it impossible for the state to inscribe clear-cut territoriality, whether on the ground or on the mental map of people. As local villagers of Telok Melano repeatedly stated during my fieldwork, "the state border was a new thing. It came after our grandfathers and grandmothers started living here". The spatial boundary of the state has been essentially external to their lifeworld, unless they find the meaning and utility.

Observing the current spatial compression of communication, trade, and movement of people, scholars recently began to identify a new phase of spatial modernity. But this is not new at all in borderlands. People have lived in a transnational world since the age of commerce, when the networks of merchant wealth embraced territories far greater than the colonial maps, and the trans-sovereign mobility of peasants and merchants was the norm rather than an exception.

Facing transnationalism in everyday life, we increasingly feel that the nation-state is not the sole or the dominant principle for connecting people. "Is the state really powerful?" For borderlanders in places such as Telok Melano, this is an age-old question, and the answer has always been obvious. For them the state, both colonial and postcolonial, has been an exogenous institution. They have observed the genesis of national space in their village compound and in the forest, but their spatial identity or mental map differs from that of the national school atlas.

Social and natural resources have become the subject of state mobilization and management, and the total system of capitalism is incorporating the last frontier across the border. How will the residents of borderlands cope with the transition from mercantile transnationalism to state-led capitalism? Will people be totally drawn into the larger system of controlled transnationalism to accept its impact and become its agents, or will they find another way of re-entering and re-exiting national space? There is much to learn from the location work of the people on the border, whose entry into transnational modernity precedes that of people living within the confines of a single nation-state.

APPENDIX

Agriculture in Telok Melano

Swidden Cultivation

This appendix is the description of slash-and-burn cultivation conducted by the Sarawak Malays. The account of land-adaptation by the Malays of Telok Melano reveals that locally specific ecological adaptation is understood by looking at locally specific historical processes. A history of the adaptive strategy of a hinterland village from the 1880s to 1990s illustrates the nodes of articulation between history and ecology in the borderland under analysis.

Clearing Undergrowth and Felling Jungle

In the western region of the Kuching Division of Sarawak, Telok Melano and the neighboring village of Telok Serabang are the only Malay peasant communities where the swidden cultivation of hill rice is practiced. There is just one small irrigated plot, where a family is experimenting with wet rice (*padi paya*) cultivation. It should be noted that the sandy soil of the borderland area is classified as *kerangas*, an Iban word for poor soil not even suitable for extensive shifting cultivation. Telok Melano villagers have used such land for generations.

The commencement of the agricultural year in Telok Melano is not marked by a special natural phenomenon, such as the rising of the Pleiades at dawn in the case of the Iban (Freeman 1955: 40), nor by village consultation or agricultural rites. However, the agricultural cycle proceeds at about the same time each year since there are two distinct seasons in that part of Borneo, wet and dry.

Swidden rice cultivation in Telok Melano consists of five phases: clearing undergrowth and felling jungle, firing fields, planting *padi*,

Illus. 27 A scaffold for cutting down a tree

weeding, and harvesting. The process of clearing undergrowth (*tebas*: v.f. *nebas*) and felling bigger trees (*tebang*, v.f. *nebang*) begins in late July and continues through early September. Only when *nebas* is completed does *tebang* begin. Villagers distinguish three kinds of forest land. Primary forest is called *hutan tua* (literally "old forest"). Secondary forest (*jerame*) is classified into two categories according to its age: *jerame tua* is old secondary forest, usually more than six to seven years old, and *jerame muda* is younger secondary forest. The duration of clearing and felling operations depends on the type of forest and size of the swidden field (*umah*). It takes an adult approximately one week to clear the undergrowth of one acre of secondary forest, while felling trees (*tebang*) takes another week. *Nebas* and *tebang* are monotonous and backbreaking work, carried out manually with *akar upak*, sticks for lifting the bottom part of the undergrowth, and *parang*, or machetes.[1] *Nebas* involves cutting ferns whose roots are tightly entangled with other weeds and can be done by women as well by men.

After cultivation and fallowing, *jerame* appears as a patchwork or mosaic of fields in various stages of regeneration. For instance, a large plot of cultivated land cleared by five villagers during the 1993 agricultural season had mixed-*jerame muda* growth (aged one year, three years, and five years) and *jerame tua* growth (aged six to eight years and more than ten years) side by side. In old *jerame* of, say, ten years, when trees reach 15–20 cm in diameter; they are cut down with 10–15 *parang* strokes.[2] Cutting vines encircling trees is another tedious task. They must be removed completely, or a cut tree may remain half-fallen, suspended in a vine mesh.

Clearing *hutan tua* is called *rimba* and is far more labor intensive. In order to fell approximately 7,500 square meters of primary forest, Pak Tuah, in his 40s, worked a week to clear the undergrowth and a whole month to fell trees manually with an ax (*kapak*).[3] Clearing undergrowth is less troublesome than it is in secondary forest, because the dense forest canopy suppresses the growth of weeds and ferns. To fell the bigger trees, a temporary scaffold is built to give access to the upper trunk, which is smaller in diameter and easier to work with. A tree one meter in diameter can be felled in 30 minutes. Then big branches are cut from the trunk to speed drying. Even a skilled and industrious villager can fell only three trees a day.[4]

The intensive labor associated with *rimba* discourages many villagers. In 1992, six men opened *hutan tua*. In 1993, only two did so. The plots opened in 1993 were on a steep hill about 20 minutes' walk from the village compound. The remaining 25 villagers who opened swiddens that year worked on relatively young secondary forest. No one cleared *hutan tua* in 1995.

---

[1] With a chainsaw, one acre of *jerame* can be cleared in a day or two. During my research in Telok Melano, however, I observed only one instance in which a chainsaw was used for *tebang*. The cost of the chainsaw and the fuel necessary for its operation — one day's operation in felling primary forest uses one gallon of gasoline costing M$6 — largely precludes their use in swidden operation.

[2] For cutting trees of more than 30 cm in diameter in the secondary forest (*jerame*), villagers still use the word clearing (*nebas*), not felling (*tebang kayu*).

[3] In addition to *kapak*, *bliong* was used for chopping down trees.

[4] If a chainsaw is used, felling a bigger tree takes less than ten minutes.

Clearing undergrowth and felling the jungle are tasks carried out by individual families. Villagers do not organize work-sharing groups for the purpose, and they seldom hire outside labor for their own swidden farms. The lack of rotational work-sharing among households and the high cost of hiring outside labor deter over-exploitation of both *jerame* and *hutan tua* for swidden cultivation in Telok Melano. The under-exploitation of agricultural fields is also closely related to the stagnation of cash crop production in the village, an issue that will be discussed below.

Firing Fields

A good burn of felled *hutan tua* or *jerame* is a prerequisite for a good *padi* harvest. The success of the burn solely depends on good weather after felling the forest. It takes about two weeks for fallen *jerame* to dry, and in the case of *hutan tua* at least one month, to get a good burn. Inadequate burning results in both quick regeneration of weeds and backbreaking work to remove half-burnt tree trunks and branches from the field. The firing is carried out in August and September at the end of the dry season (*musim panas*), usually after a long drought (*kemarau*).[5]

Before setting the fire, a *rintis* (path/ditch) needs to be cut around the field. Dry branches and weeds are removed from this zone to prevent fire spreading to adjacent cultivated fields and forest. Firing requires careful reading of the wind. It is usually begun about noon. In the morning, the wind is usually still, so villagers wait until midday, when *angin laut* (a sea breeze) starts blowing from the east. Firing should be completed before 2 o'clock, when the wind suddenly changes to *angin barat* (a breeze from the west).

Unlike clearing the forest, firing is carried out by a team of men and women, young and old, who have different tasks. Some set fires with *sutoh*, large torches made from coconut leaves and bamboo; some extinguish fires at the edges of fields by beating the flames with the lower stems of coconut trees; and some are "fire fighters" (*orang bomba*),

---

[5] In 1994, the first firing was done on 23 August and the last in late September. Firing that year turned out to be quite successful thanks to an exceptionally long drought. Between mid-August and mid-September, which is the most crucial period for firing, it rained only five times including short, insignificant showers.

Illus. 28 Setting fire by *sutoh* (coconut palm torch)

who carry herbicide spray tanks filled with water. The fire is set at several different places by men walking backward against the wind. They shout "hoo, hoo" at the top of their voice. This is not a warning signal to fellow villagers but rather meant to encourage the spirit of the wind.[6] Fire setters must face the backs to the wind, otherwise they would be chased by the blazing fire.[7]

Planting Padi: Dibbling and Sowing

After the firing, villagers wait for rain, which will soften the dry earth. If the burning has gone well, the process of sowing is greatly simplified. If not, unburned brushwood must first be cleared. Planting involves two procedures, dibbling and sowing. Usually men dig holes on the field with a dibble-stick (*tegal*; v.f. *negal*), and women follow behind dropping seeds into the holes.

---

[6] A small ritual called *Sembahyang Hajat* is also carried out to call the wind when firing a plot. The same ritual is conducted to quiet waves at the sea or to ask for rain during a drought.

[7] There have been several casualties in neighboring villages due to the neglect of this basic rule.

Illus. 29 *Jerame* after firing

Illus. 30 Dibbling and sowing

The following details were collected on an occasion when seven women and five men worked to plant *padi*. The operation was completed in four hours. The size of the field was about 0.5 ha and the amount of *padi* planted was 23 *gantang* (69 kg). The work was done as *gotong royong* (work-sharing) affair organized by several households, the only stage of agricultural labor Telok Melano villagers share, going to one household's field the first day, another's the second day, and so on in succession until all participating households' fields have been planted. Each host family provides homemade cakes and beverages to all workers. If planting is not finished on the given day, the task is finished by the individual household.

Table 18 Dibbling and Sowing

Dibbling	
Number of dibbling holes per square meter (average)	16
Number of holes dibbled in one minute (average per person)	42.2
Number of holes dibbled in one minute (range)	36–51
Depth of holes	6–9 cm
Diameter of holes	4–6 cm
Sowing	
Number of seeds per hole (average)	20.7
Number of seeds per hole (range)	13–31
Number of holes sown per minute (average)	35.2
Number of holes sown per minute (range)	22–45
Distance (approx.) of hand from hole	30 cm
Number of holes sown per handful of seed (average)	11.2
Number of holes sown per handful of seed (range)	8–17

Thirteen kinds of *padi* seed are cultivated by Telok Melano villagers: *padi hitam*, *padi ruwan*, *padi Sematan*, *padi narjas*, *padi melawi*, *padi mokok*, *padi sanee*, *padi bajak*, *padi kunpang*, *padi pulut*, *padi serendah*, *padi putih harus*, and *padi berat kasar*. Cash crops of cucumber, pumpkin, and corn are interspersed on the same land with *padi*. These are harvested before the *padi* ripens.

Weeding

One of the least pleasant chores for swidden cultivators is weeding. The rainy season (October–March) begins around the time of *padi* planting. Rain is necessary for the growth of *padi*, but it also promotes the rapid growth of weeds. Young secondary forest, especially if it has been used recently for cultivation, is especially prone to the invasion of *lalang* (*Imperata sp.*) and other fast-growing weeds.[8]

Immediately after burning is finished, this most irksome task should begin. Clearing the undergrowth, felling the jungle, firing the fields, and planting the *padi* are standard procedures which every household must perform in order to move to the next phase. Weeding, however, is not an absolute requirement, though desirable, especially in the months of November and December, which are critical for the growth of young *padi*. One finds wide variations among Telok Melano families in the time and effort invested in weeding. Villagers say, "Mun lalang kuat, beras sik manis" ("if weeds are thick in the field, the rice will not be sweet"), but not all practice frequent weeding.[9]

Unlike the Ibans (Freeman 1955), villagers in Telok Melano use only a machete (*parang*) for weeding. The short-bladed bush-knife is not found here. While weeding, villagers often make a fire, using rubber latex as a starter. They say the smoke drives away vermin, although its effectiveness is questionable.

Harvesting

An entire month between early March and early April is devoted to harvesting rice in Telok Melano. Every day people come back from their fields with harvested *padi* in their baskets and spread them on mats for drying. No ritual marks the commencement of harvesting, and the whole business is done individually, although villagers know exactly who has started and completed.

The ears of *padi* are cut manually with a small hand knife, *ketam*, which has a thin blade of tin set firmly in the center of a wooden handle. The handle is held upright in the palm of the hand, with the blade protruding slightly from between the second and third fingers;

[8] The *lalang* in our kitchen garden grew 30–40 cm in 10 days in mid-February 1994.

[9] In a rather neglected plot quite far from the village compound, approximately 900 square meters, weeding was done on a total of 6 days (Nov. 13, Nov. 27, Dec. 5, and Dec. 29–31) between seeding in late October 1993 and harvesting in late March 1994. The last weeding in December was carried out on three consecutive days by two Indonesian women hired for M$4 a day with lunch.

Illus. 31 Cutting off ears of rice by *ketam*

the stem of the *padi* plant is grasped between the two upper fingers and the thumb a short distance below the lowest node of the panicle; then, by exerting slight tension and sudden pressure with the fingers, the stem is severed.

Reaping at normal speed yields some 40 panicles per minute. This speed is greatly reduced if the crop has ripened unevenly, since reapers have to choose only the ripe panicles and take care not to step on unripened *padi*. Cutting panicles and putting them in a basket tied to the waist is hard and monotonous labor. *Padi* ears dampened by rain are hard to sever, so that reaping is usually carried out under the blazing sun.

Harvested *padi* panicles are immediately spread out to dry on woven mats made from *apong* (*Nipa fruticans*) or on plastic sheets. When dry, they are threshed by treading. Villagers stand on the mat and repeatedly gather up panicles with the instep and inside of the foot and ankle. In this process of *tinjak padi* (stepping on rice), the grain (*ampak*) is gradually separated from the branches of the panicles.

Separated *ampak* is next winnowed. Due to damage by birds, mostly sparrows, a significant number of *ampak* will be empty,[10] and

[10] The farm that I worked with my adopted mother had more than five per cent empty *ampak*.

these have to be sorted out before storing. Winnowing consists of the skillful tossing of grains in a large circular basket. Gradually, the empty husks are tossed over the edge of the basket, leaving behind a heap of sound *padi.* The other method of winnowing observed in the village is to tip the grains down onto the mat from the basket raised above the head of the bearer. When the wind is strong enough, the empty husks are blown away from the main stream of sound *padi.* Repetition of this action results in a heap of rice on the ground with light empty husks scattered around. The *padi* grains are again dried in the heat of the sun before final storage. When the grains are dried under the blazing sun, one day is enough to remove excess moisture.

Land Use and Productivity

Clearing undergrowth and felling the forest is the most labor-intensive phase of swidden *padi* cultivation. Under normal circumstances, villagers in Telok Melano prefer to use secondary forest because it is usually nearer to the village and easier to work than *hutan tua.* However, repeated use of the same fields results in rapid weed growth and a drastic decline in productivity. Swiddens are thus usually cultivated for one or two years and then left fallow. The fallow period depends on the individual cultivator, but it is usually between one and eight years.

Due to the coastal setting, cultivated fields in the vicinity of the village compound are quite sandy. The soil locally called *tanah segup* is planted only with coconut, pineapple, and watermelon. Inland cultivated fields, though of slightly better soil quality, tend to contain some barren sand as well. Fields often contain either small rocks or clayey soil of high viscosity. Continuous utilization of this poor quality land results in a rapid decline in soil nutrition. Thus, villagers who cultivate *padi* on soil of inferior quality usually use a plot for only one year, then leave it fallow. In some cases villagers use fields reclaimed from *hutan tua* for two consecutive years, but the harvest drastically declines in the second year.

Two crucial factors affect the *padi* yield: the number of *padi* seeds (unhulled rice) planted, and the productivity of the swidden field. Most previous assessments of *padi* yield conducted among Dayak shifting cultivators have been based on average yield per acre. In the course of fieldwork in Telok Melano, I realized that assessment calculated on this basis did not make much sense because the results vary greatly according to the total amount of seed planted, the quality of the soil, the density of weed growth, the number of holes dibbled and the number of *padi* grains placed in each hole. Two adjacent rice fields I observed, for example, differed in the amount of seed planted. Both were located in *jerame* on a hillside. In one, a 2-acre plot, 23 *gantang* (69 kg) of rice was planted by *gotong royong*. In the other, a 1-acre plot, 20 *gantang* (60 kg) rice was planted by family members. Thus, the ratio of *padi* input *per acre* between these two fields is almost 2:1. The table below shows the great variation in the amount of rice planted *per field* in the 1993 season (figures given in *gantang*, which equal three kg).[11]

Table 19 The Amount of Rice Planted per Field, 1993

Villager	*Gantang of Seed Planted*	*Type of Swidden*
Pak Tuah	10[1]	Primary forest
Pak Dunan	20	Old secondary forest
Abu	9	Old secondary forest
Pak Juli	20	Old secondary forest
Pak Putih	14	Young secondary forest
Pak Lon Mat	101	Young and old secondary forest
Pak Saii	30	Young secondary forest
Pak Rena	14	Secondary forest
Haji Muren	11	Secondary forest
Pak Bogo	28	Old secondary forest
Pak Sute	20	Old secondary forest
Gondol	10	Old secondary forest
Mak Ngah	2.5[2]	Young and old secondary forest

Notes: [1] On average (total of 40 in 4 fields).
[2] On average (total of 5 in 2 fields).

According to villagers, one *gantang* of planted rice seeds yield one *guni besar* (100 kg) of unhusked rice.[12] This traditional estimate of rice input/output ratio appears optimistic in light of today's actual yields. The following table summarizes *padi* yields in the 1992 season (unhusked rice harvested per *gantang* planted), showing that the yield in no case exceeded the traditional 100 kg/gantang ratio and in most cases was far lower.

[11] For the discussion on the measurement of productivity based on harvest ratio, see Tanaka 2002.

[12] *Guni* (sack) *besar* (big) is a large plastic bag used for keeping agricultural produce.

Table 20 *Padi* Yields, 1992

Villager	*Ratio*[1]	*Padi Planted*[2]	*Yield*	*Net after Husking*	*Swidden Type*
Pak Putih	50 kg	40	2,000 kg	1,000 kg	Secondary forest
Pak Saii	10 kg	20	600 kg	300 kg	Young secondary forest
Pak Rena	100 kg	14	1,400 kg	700 kg	Old secondary forest
Pak Tuah	78 kg	13	1,000 kg	500 kg	Primary forest
Pak Mail	100 kg	3	300 kg	150 kg	Old secondary forest
Mak Ngah	50 kg	2	100 kg	50 kg	Young secondary forest
	38 kg	3	115 kg	57.5 kg	Young secondary forest

Notes: [1] Yield of unhusked rice/*gantang* planted.
[2] Gantang.

In today's Telok Melano, only one out of 39 households maintains 100 per cent self-sufficiency in rice every year. A few others are nearly self-sufficient, although they rely on rice purchased at Sematan or Temajuk (Indonesia) for one or two months before the harvest. According to the caretaker of the village-owned electric husking machine, the yearly consumption of unhusked rice is about 350 to 400 kg per household. The majority of families in Telok Melano produce about half that amount, which means they rely on commercial rice for half the year.[13] The factors responsible for the diminishing yield will be discussed along with the current condition of cash crop production.

Cash Crop Cultivation

The production of export-oriented commodities is a fairly recent development in Telok Melano. The shift toward cash crop production in this remote community began under agricultural schemes supported by Sarawak's Department of Agriculture in the late 1980s. Government assistance increased after Telok Melano was selected as a model village for the Agricultural Department Project (ADP) in 1991. In the process of implementing various schemes, the villagers received generous in-kind grants that include seeds and seedlings (pepper, rubber, rattan, cacao, clove, fruit trees, and corn), livestock (goats

[13] Ten kg of rice costs M$15 at Sematan market and Rp 8,000 in Temajuk (approximately M$11). Indonesian rice brought in from Temajuk is sold at a village shop in Telok Melano for M$1.50 per kg.

and rabbits), and farm inputs (fertilizers, pesticides, and herbicides). In addition to these schemes, young people participated in incentive programs, such as agricultural courses at the Semangok Agricultural Center in Kuching.

Excluding those who work for the police and the Samunsam Wildlife Sanctuary, most villagers' monthly income ranges from M$200 to M$300; the highest is about M$800 and the lowest M$50 (1991 Report of the Agricultural Office, Sematan). By government standards, many thus fall below the poverty line, having a monthly income of less than M$250. Pepper and cacao provide the most important income for many villagers, a source that is necessarily subject to the fluctuation of commodity prices in the international market.

Until the late 1980s, when the subsidy programs were first implemented by the Department of Agriculture, Telok Melano's contact with the export-oriented market economy was limited to the occasional sale of copra and forest produce such as rattan and *engkabang*. Since then, Telok Melano has had experience with the cultivation of the following cash crops.

Rubber

In the 1920s Chinese and Dayak peasants responded to the regional rubber boom and shifted from pepper to rubber, but coastal Malays failed to take advantage of this crop. The first rubber was planted in Telok Melano in 1953, but the price of rubber fell sharply in the late 1950s. When the price of rubber sheet fell to as low as 30 cents per *kati*,[14] villagers lost interest. Rubber trees planted in the late 1950s and early 1960s still stand near the village compound, mostly untapped in the intervening years. In 1994, a large-scale rubber scheme implemented by the Kuala Lumpur-based Rubber Research Institute of Malaysia (RRIM) provided 24 households with 450 high-yielding rubber seedlings each.[15]

Cacao

Cacao is another new cash crop in Telok Melano. In the 1980s, a few villagers planted cacao on their own initiative. Many trees were planted

[14] 1 kati = 600 grams.

[15] This was a five-year project providing a total of M$3,090 of in-kind grants to each participant.

under the cacao subsidy scheme in 1991, when 13 applicants received 1,100 seedlings each. After two additional schemes, there were 20 cacao cultivators, each tending more than 1,000 trees.[16]

Pepper

There are three successful pepper cultivators in Telok Melano, all originally from Sematan town, with yearly incomes ranging from M$4,000 to M$10,000. All started planting with their own capital. For other villagers, a government subsidy is the only way to get started, and free fertilizer and pesticide are granted only if a recipient maintains a minimum of 200 vines in good order. Between 1987 and 1991, 29 villagers received the subsidy. By 1993, however, 19 of them had lost their trees. Under new subsidy schemes in 1993 and 1994, ten villagers tried pepper cultivation again.

Coconut

For many years, coconut was the only export-oriented commodity produced by Telok Melano. In the early 1960s, when one *gantang* of rice cost M$1, the price of copra was still relatively high: M$10 (for first grade) and M$8 (for second grade) per *pikul* (60.48 kg). At that time, several Chinese started planting coconut trees at Samunsam. Returning after the military confrontation with Indonesia, the first thing villagers did for a living was collect coconuts from their gardens, which had become thickly covered with *lalang*.

However, the market price of copra declined after Konfrontasi. Many evacuees found no reason to return to their villages to resume coconut cultivation and resettled elsewhere. Those who returned had no choice but to sell copra at Sematan market. After government subsidy programs began to diversify cash crop production, many villagers turned their back on copra. Its price at Sematan market was too low to warrant the hard labor required to produce it, and it ceased to be a worthwhile venture. By the 1993 season, when its selling price was only M$0.40/kg at Sematan bazaar, only four households produced copra for sale.

---

[16] To be entitled to receive subsidies such as fertilizers and herbicides, an applicant has to maintain at least 1,000 trees.

Illus. 32 Removing husks with a *sui* for copra production

Approximately six coconuts are needed to produce one kg of copra, and the several stages of processing are all done manually. First, coconuts are collected from the garden, often in the bush. The husk is removed with a *sui* or *kapak*, the hard inner shell is split, and the meat is removed with a sharp knife. The meat is then sun-dried for several days. Not only the low price of copra but also the village's physical isolation from Sematan market and the high cost of transportation prevents Telok Melano cultivators from generating a profit from the crop. To illustrate, 100 kg of dried copra requires approximately 600 coconuts. Selling the 100 kg of copra generates M$40, which barely covers the cost of fuel necessary to travel to Sematan and back. The majority of Telok Melano villagers still own coconut trees and use the nuts for cooking and making oil. Practically everyone in the village produces coconut oil for home consumption, which has become a luxury for most urban Malays, who purchase commercial oil made from peanuts and oil palm.

***

Traditional swidden *padi* cultivation and new cash crop production are often conducted in one set of operations in Telok Melano. Cash commodities such as rubber, cacao, and clove are usually planted in a swidden plot after the *padi* harvest. In 1994, a subsidy of 450 rubber seedlings was given to 24 villagers by the Department of Agriculture. Among the recipients, 19 opened secondary forest and planted *padi* with the intention of planting the rubber seedlings after harvest.

This agricultural practice — *padi* planting and subsequent cultivation of a long-term cash crop on the same plot — is regarded as "malpractice" by officials of the Agricultural Department. For instance, cacao, which originated in the South American thick-canopy jungle, needs to be surrounded by shading trees. Young cacao seedlings, if planted on a former rice field with no surrounding trees, are exposed to the blazing sun and often lose the tips of their leaves in the heat. Furthermore, Telok Melano planters are not concerned about the spacing of cash crops and simply plant crops randomly in a former *padi* field. Cacao trees, however, need to be properly spaced. If the spacing is too great, weeds immediately proliferate, the thick undergrowth deprives the soil of nutrients, and moisture from the weeds promotes the spread of disease to the vulnerable cacao trees.

Since the latter half of the 1980s, especially after Telok Melano was selected as ADP (Agricultural Department Project) model village, the villagers have received generous amounts of seedlings, herbicides, and fertilizers for cash crop production. The ADP program was scheduled to end in 1995 after the preferential implementation of various schemes for five years. At the time of our research, Telok Melano peasants had become very much dependent on government subsidies. The withdrawal of in-kind assistance, especially of fertilizer and herbicides, would greatly change the landscape of agriculture in Telok Melano, where cash crop cultivation had not yet reached the level at which villagers were willing or able to purchase agrochemicals themselves. Without agrochemicals, the ecological niche of Telok Melano, where weeds regenerate quickly and poor soil predominates, will overwhelm villagers' labor input on their cultivated land. Without sufficient weed control or nutrients, cash crop production, which has not rooted firmly in Telok Melano, is likely to be replaced by capital-free, labor-intensive swidden agriculture.

Social Relations of Shifting Cultivation

Opening the forest for *padi* and subsequent use of the cultivated field for cash crop production will remain common practice among Telok Melano villagers. When cultivated fields and usufruct become the subject of trans-generational transmission, the practice results in some confusion. Land ownership and usufruct are clearly differentiated by Melano villagers, as are "inheritance" and "succession to land title". Like other societies in Borneo where swidden agriculture is practiced, land title is granted to the person who first clears the primary forest for hill rice cultivation. The mode of land transmission to descendants is two-fold. The first is the inheritance of *jerame* (secondary forest), where the cultivated land is divided equally among the offspring of those who cleared the land. The divided lands are registered officially when officials of the Department of Land Survey come to the village for this purpose.[17]

Equal inheritance is the norm: all siblings regardless of gender and seniority have an equal right to inherit property from a parent. This practice, coupled with cognatic kinship system, can lead to the fragmentation of land property over several generations. However, in Telok Melano, a second system of land transmission, based on usufruct, often prevents it from being fragmented. Under the usufruct system, all descendants have a right to cultivate the secondary forest opened by their apical ancestor. Inherited land is not divided among them, but utilized under communal management. This usufruct system functions especially in swidden rice cultivation, where land is left fallow after being used for a year or two.

Under this kin-based system, the land called *tanah peninggalan alur X* (the land left by the late Mr./Ms. X) is utilized by X's descendants only for cultivation (*makan sama*, literally "eat together"). One can clear and cultivate the land with the consensus of all legitimate usufructuaries. In actual practice, when hill rice is cultivated on communally managed *jerame*, casual notice to the eldest kin member suffices

---

[17] Actual survey and documents may not be indispensable for the official recognition of land possession among villagers.

to commence clearing. The usufruct operation prevents land from being fragmented by equal inheritance and also functions to avoid land disputes among descendants.

Table 21 Long-term and Short-term Crops in Telok Melano

Long-term Plants	*Years before Bearing Fruit*	*Life Expectancy (years)*
Durian	7–8	30–50
Mango	3	30
Clove	3–4	30
Engkabang	10	30–40
Langsat	10	30
Coconut	5	80
Short-term Plants	*Years before Bearing Fruit*	
Cacao	4	
Pepper	2–3	
Corn	1 term only	
Banana	1 term only	
Peanut	1 term only	
Watermelon	1 term only	

Source: Villagers of Telok Melano.

Communal land management by kin members, however, does not always keep a holding intact. *Tanah peninggalan* can be converted into privately owned property when a member of the usufruct sharing group clears *jerame* and cultivates certain kinds of crops — *tanaman jangka panjang*, or long-term plants. The above table lists the long-term plants which function to establish private ownership of cultivated land in Telok Melano. It is worth noting that cash crops, such as pepper and cacao, promoted by the agricultural schemes do not function to establish the private ownership of land. Cacao and pepper are regarded as short-term crops, although the villagers do not actually know their life expectancy. This is partly because these cash crops are relatively new to the village and have an ambiguous status in terms of importance and life expectancy. This is also a reason why, despite subsidy schemes, these income-generating crops are often neglected or quickly abandoned.

There is another mode of land use based on *pinjam* (borrowing) or *numpang* (free riding). *Pinjam/numpang* enables the usufruct of land to be lent to non-relatives, that is, non-members of the *tanah peninggalan*-holding group. *Pinjam/numpang* is based on mutual agreement between lender and borrower of the usufruct of *jerame*. The borrower is required to inform the lender of the kind of plant to be cultivated and the duration of usage in an official letter bearing the signature of the village head or the sub-District Officer in Sematan. However, this procedure is rarely followed. When the usufruct agreement expires, the cultivated land should be returned to the lender together with cultivated plants on it. Though a borrower usually cultivates hill rice and short-term plants such as corn, banana, peanut, watermelon, and pineapple, there are cases when cash crops such as pepper, cacao, and rubber are planted on the borrowed land. In the latter cases, the usufruct agreement lasts many years, but it is strictly applicable to the present generation. Thus, the land with cash crops will be returned to the owner of the *jerame* if the borrower and his/her spouse pass away.

This system of usufruct benefits the lender in two ways. First, the lender obtains a cleared field ready for the cultivation of cash crops if the borrower plants *padi* and returns the plot after harvest. Second, the owner may acquire cash crops along with the returned land when the agreement expires. These benefits are often manipulated by usufruct possessors. For instance, in 1993, a villager lent the usufruct of his *jerame* to an Indonesian woman to plant hill *padi* for one year. He intended to use the land she cleared for rubber cultivation under the agricultural scheme the following year. Thus by lending his usufruct, the land owner prepared for the next year's rubber cultivation without lifting a finger.

Bibliography

Abbreviations

SG	The *Sarawak Gazette*
SG-LDMR	Lundu District Monthly Report, The *Sarawak Gazette*
LDR	Lundu District Report (The Sarawak Museum)
LDQR	Lundu District Quarterly Report (The Sarawak Museum)
SGG	The Sarawak Government Gazette

Abang Yusuf Puteh. 1996. *River of Dry Tears*. Kuching: Shobra Publications Sdn. Bhd.

———. 1996. *The Malay Mind*. Kuching: Shobra Publications Sdn. Bhd.

———. 1996. *The Malay Culture of Sarawak*. Kuching: Shobra Publications Sdn. Bhd.

———. 1998. *Malay Politics and Perabangan*. Kuching: Shobra Publications Sdn. Bhd.

Abdul Majid Mat Salleh, Hatta Solhee and Mohd. Yusof Kasim. 1988. "Socio-economic Development in Sarawak; Policies and Strategies for the 1990s", Proceedings of a seminar held at Kuching, Sarawak, October 10–12, 1988. Kuching, Sarawak: Angkatan Zaman Mansang (AZAM).

Aikawa, H. 1944. *Tonan Asia no Shigen to Gijutsu* [Natural Resources and Technology in Southeast Asia]. Tokyo: Mikasa Shobo.

Alvarez, R.R. and G.A. Collier. 1994. "The Long Haul in Mexican Trucking: Traversing the Borderlands of the North and the South". *American Ethnologist* 21(3): 606–27.

Anderson, B. 1991. *Imagined Communities: Reflections on the Origin and Spread of Nationalism*, revised and extended edition. London; New York: Verso.

Andriesse, J.P. 1972. *The Soils of West-Sarawak (East Malaysia)*, Memoir 1, Department of Agriculture, Sarawak, East Malaysia, Soil Survey Division Research Branch. Kuching: Government Printing Office.

Appadurai, A. 1986. *The Social Life of Things: Commodities in Cultural Perspective*. Cambridge; New York: Cambridge University Press.

———. 1996. "The Production of Locality", in *Modernity at Large: Cultural Dimensions of Globalization*. Minneapolis: University of Minnesota Press.

Bala, P. 2002. *Changing Borders and Identities in the Kelabit Highlands: Anthropological Reflections on Growing Up near an International Border*. Dayak Studies Contemporary Society Series, No. 1, Universiti Malaysia Sarawak, The Institute of East Asian Studies. Kuching: Lee Ming Press Company.

Balakrishnan, G. (ed.). 1996. *Mapping the Nation*. London; New York: Verso.

Balibar, E. 1991. *Race, Nation, Class: Ambiguous Identities/Etienne Balibar and Immanuel Wallerstein*. London; New York: Verso.

Bampfylde, C.A. and S. Baring-Gould. 1909. *A History of Sarawak under its Two White Rajahs 1839–1908*. London: Sotheran.

Barlow, C. 1978. *The Natural Rubber Industry: Its Development, Technology, and Economy in Malaysia*. Kuala Lumpur: Oxford University Press.

Barth, F. 1969. *Ethnic Groups and Boundaries: The Social Organization of Cultural Difference*. London: Allen and Unwin.

Beccari, O. 1904. *Wandering in the Great Forests of Borneo*. London: Archibald Constable.

Benjamin, G. and C. Chou (eds.). 2002. *Tribal Communities in the Malay World*. Netherland and Singapore: IIAS and ISEAS.

Benjamin, G. 2002. "On Being Tribal in the Malay World", in *Tribal Communities in the Malay World*, ed. B. Geoffrey and C. Chou. Netherland and Singapore: IIAS and ISEAS.

Bhabha, H.K. 1990. "Introduction: Narrating the Nation", in *Nation and Narration*, ed. H.K. Bhabha. London: Routledge.

Blume, C.L. 1843. "Toelichtingen Aangaande de Nasporingen op Borneo", in *De Indische Bij*, ed. van G. Muller. Leyden: H.W. Hazenberg en Comp, pp. 103–76.

Boeke, J.H. 1953. *Economics and Economic Policy of Dual Societies Exemplified by Indonesia*. New York International Secretariat, Institute of Pacific Relations.

———. 1966. "Dualism in Colonial Societies", in *Indonesian Economics*. Hague: W. van Hoeve.

Braudel, F. 1966. *La Méditerranée et le Monde Méditerranéen a l'époque de Philippe II*, 3 vols. Paris: Armand Collin.

Chatterjee, P. 1986. *Nationalist Thought and the Colonial World: A Derivative Discourse?* London: Zed Books.

———. 1999. "Anderson's Utopia". *Diacritics* 29(4): 128–34.

Chew, D. 1990. *Chinese Pioneers on the Sarawak Frontier 1841–1941*. Singapore: Oxford University Press.

Cole, J. and E. Wolf. 1974. *The Hidden Frontier: Ecology and Ethnicity in an Alpine Valley*. New York: Academic Press.

Cooper, A.M. 1968. *Men of Sarawak*. Kuala Lumpur: Oxford University Press.

Cooper, F. and A.L. Stoler (eds.). 1997. *Tensions of Empire: Colonial Cultures in a Bourgeois World.* Berkeley: University of California Press.

Cramb, R.A. 1988. "The Commercialization of Iban Agriculture", in *Development in Sarawak: Historical and Contemporary Perspectives*, ed. R.A. Cramb and R.H.W. Reece. Monash Paper on Southeast Asia 17, Center of Southeast Asian Studies, Monash University.

Dave Lumenta. 2008. "The Making of a Transnational Continuum: State Partitions and Mobility of the Apau Kayan Kenyah in Central Borneo, 1900–2007", PhD Thesis, The Graduate School of Asian and African Area Studies, Kyoto University.

Davidson, J.S. 2008. *From Rebellion to Riots: Collective Violence on Indonesian Borneo.* Madison: University of Wisconsin Press.

Davidson, J.S. and D. Kammen. 2002. "Indonesia's Unknown War and the Lineages of Violence in West Kalimantan". *Indonesia* 73: 53–87.

De Jong, W. 2002. *Forest Products and Local Forest Management in West Kalimantan, Indonesia: Implications for Conservation and Development.* Tropenbos Kalimantan Seroes 6, Wageningen.

Dickens, P. 1991. *SAS The Jungle Frontier: 22 Special Air Service Regiment in the Borneo Campaign, 1963–1966.* Kuala Lumpur: S. Abdul Majeed & Co.

Donnan, H. and T.M. Wilson. 1994. "An Anthropology of Frontiers", in *Border Approaches: Anthropological Perspectives on Frontiers*, ed. H. Donnan and T.M. Wilson. Lanham: University Press of America.

Durkheim, E. and M. Mauss. 1963. *Primitive Classification.* London: Cohen and West.

Drabble, J. 1973. *Rubber in Malaya 1876–1922: The Genesis of the Industry.* Kuala Lumpur: Oxford University Press.

Fariastuti. 2000. "West Kalimantan and Sarawak Trade Relation", in *Borneo 2000: Language, Management, and Tourism*, ed. Michael Leigh. Kuching: Universiti Malaysia Sarawak and Sarawak Development Institute.

———. 2002. "Mobility of People and Goods across the Border of West Kalimantan and Sarawak". *Antropologi Indonesia* 67: 94–104.

Foucault, M. 1980. "Questions on Geography", in *Power/Knowledge*, ed. Colin Gordon. New York: Pantheon Books.

Frank, A.G. 1964. *Capitalism and Underdevelopment in Historical Studies of Chile and Brazil.* New York: Monthly Review.

Freeman, D. 1955. *Iban Agriculture: A Report on the Shifting Cultivation of Hill Rice by the Iban of Sarawak.* London: Her Majesty's Stationery Office.

———. 1970. *Report on the Iban.* London: Athlone.

Furnivall, J.S. 1939. *Netherlands India: A Study of Plural Economy.* Cambridge: Cambridge University Press.

———. 1944. *Netherlands India: A Study of Plural Economy.* Cambridge: Cambridge University Press.

———. 1948. *Colonial Policy and Practice: A Comparative Study of Burma and Netherlands India*. Cambridge: Cambridge University Press.

Galaty, J. 1982 "Being 'Masai': Being 'People-of-Cattle': Ethnic Shifters in East Africa". *American Ethnologist* 9(1): 1–20.

Gellner, E. 1983. *Nations and Nationalism*. Oxford: Basil Blackwell.

Gereffi, G. and M. Korzenirewicz. 1994. *Commodity Chains and Global Capitalism*. Westport, London: Praeger.

Greenblatt, S. 1991. *Marvelous Possessions: the Wonder of the New World*. Chicago: University of Chicago Press.

Gupta, A and J. Ferguson. 1992. "Beyond 'Culture': Space, Identity, and the Politics of Difference". *Cultural Anthropology* 7(1): 6–23.

Harrisson, T. 1970. *The Malays of South-West Sarawak before Malaysia: A Socio-Ecological Survey*. East Lansing: Michigan State University Press.

———. n.d. "The Malays of South-west Sarawak before Malaysia". *Sarawak Museum Journal* (Museum File).

Harvey, D. 1996. *Justice, Nature and the Geography of Difference*. Oxford: Blackwell.

Heine-Geldern, R. 1956. *Conceptions of State and Kingship in Southeast Asia*. Cornell University, Southeast Asia Program, Data Paper No. 18.

Heyman, J. 1991. *Land, Labor, and Capital at the Mexican Border*. Flagstaff: University of Arizona Press.

———. 1994. "The Mexico-United States Border in Anthropology: A Critique and Reformulation". *Journal of Political Ecology* (1): 43–65.

Hong, E. 1987. *Natives of Sarawak: Survival in Borneo's Vanishing Forests*. Penang: Institut Masyarakat.

Horstmann, A. and R.L. Wadley (eds.). 2006. *Centering the Margin: Agency and Narrative in Southeast Asian Borderlands*. New York: Berghahn Books.

Ishikawa, M. 2005. "The Story of Nakoda Hitam: Her Life and Ventures at Maritime Crossroads at the Turn of the 20th Century". *The Sarawak Museum Journal* 61, no. 82 (New Series): 247–62.

Ishikawa, N. 1993. "The Frontline of Circular Labor Migration and Community Studies" (in Japanese). *Minzokugaku Kenkyu* [Japanese Journal of Ethnology] 58(1): 53–72.

———. 1997a. "Who is the Sarawak Malay?: Discourse Analysis of Ethnicity" (in Japanese), in *Minzoku no Seisei to Ronri* [The Logic of Ethno-genesis], ed. M. Uchibori. Tokyo: Iwanami Shoten.

———. 1997b. "Rubber Boom and Peasants on the Border: A Case from Western Borneo" (in Japanese). *Minzokugaku Kenkyu* [Japanese Journal of Ethnology] 61(4): 586–615.

———. 1998a. "Between Frontiers: The Formation and Marginalization of a Borderland Malay Community in Southwestern Sarawak, Malaysia, 1870s–1990s", PhD thesis, PhD Program in Anthropology, Graduate School and University Center, City University of New York.

———. 1998b. "A Benevolent Protector or Failed Exploiter?: Local Response to Agro-economic Policies under the Second White Rajah, Charles Brooke (1868–1917) of Sarawak", in *Japanese Anthropologists, Malaysian Society: Contribution to Malaysian Ethnography*, ed. A.B. Shamsul and T. Uesugi. Osaka: National Museum of Ethnology.

———. 1998c. "On the Value and Value Equivalence of Commodity, Labor and Personhood: the Use and Abuse of Nation-States in the Borderland of Western Borneo", Paper presented at the 4th International Symposium, *Population Movement in Southeast Asia: Changing Identities and Strategies for Survival*, Joint Research Project on Population Movement in the Modern World, September 17–19, 1998, Japan Center for Area Studies, National Museum of Ethnology, Osaka.

———. 1999a. "The Social History of Coconuts in Sematan, Southwestern Sarawak". *The Sarawak Museum Journal* 54(75): 239–51.

———. 1999b. "Cultural Borderland and Economic Borderland: A Report from Southwestern Sarawak" (in Japanese), in *Economy as Culture*, ed. K. Kawada. Tokyo: Yamakawa Shuppan.

———. 2000. "The Inscription of National Space: the Formation of State Territory in Southwestern Borneo" (in Japanese), in *The Logic of Areal Formation*, ed. Y. Tsubouchi. Kyoto: Kyoto University Press.

———. 2002. "The Memory of Villagers and the History of the Nation: Independence Movement and the Borderlands of Western Borneo" (in Japanese), in *Ethnic Mobilization and Political Leaders*, ed. E. Kuroda. Tokyo: Yamakawa Shuppan.

———. 2008. "Cultural Geography of the Sarawak Malays: a View from the Margins of the National Terrain", in *Representation, Identity and Multiculturalism in Sarawak*, ed. Wan Zawai Ibraham. Kajang: Persatuan Sains Social Malaysia.

———. 2008. *Kyōkai no Shakaihi: Kokka ga Shoyū o Sengensuru toki*. Kyoto: Kyoto University Press.

Jayl L., D. Chew, and I Ketut Ardhana. 2004. "Borders of Kinship and Ethnicity: Cross-border Relations between the Kelalan Valley, Sarawak, and the Bawan Valley, East Kalimantan". *Borneo Research Bulletin* 35: 144–79.

Kearney, M. 1991. "Borders and Boundaries of the State and Self at the End of Empire". *Journal of Historical Sociology* 4(1): 52–74.

Keyes, C. 1976. "Towards a New Formation of the Concept of Ethnic Group". *Ethnicity* 3(3): 202–13.

King, V. 1990. "Why is Sarawak Peripheral?", in *Margins and Minorities: the Peripheral Areas and Peoples of Malaysia*, ed. V.T. King and M.J.G. Parnwell. Hull: Hull University Press.

Kirchhoff, P. 1959. "The Principles of Clanship in Human Society", in *Readings in Anthropology* Vol. 2, ed. Morton H. Fried. New York: Thomas Y. Crowell.

Kopytoff, I. 1986. "Biography of Things: Commoditisation as Process", in *The Social Life of Things*, ed. A. Appadurai. Cambridge: Cambridge University Press.

Leach, E.R. 1950. *Social Science Research in Sarawak: A Report on the Possibilities of a Social Economic Survey of Sarawak.* His Majesty's Stationery Office for the Colonial Office.

________. 1954. *Political Systems of Highland Burma.* London: G. Bell and Sons.

Lefebvre, H. 1991. *The Production of Space.* Oxford: Basil Blackwell.

Leigh, M. 1974. *The Rising Moon: Political Change in Sarawak.* Sydney: Sydney University Press.

________. 2002. *Mapping the Peoples of Sarawak.* Kota Samarahan: Institute of East Asian Studies, Universiti Malaysia Sarawak.

Levi, G. 1991. "On Microhistory", in *New Perspectives on Historical Writing*, ed. P. Burke. Cambridge: Polity Press.

Lockard, C.A. 1987. *From Kampung to City: A Social History of Kuching, Malaysia 1820–1970.* Ohio University, Monographs in International Studies, Southeast Asia Series, No. 75, Athens: Ohio University Press.

Lockard, C.A. and Graham, E.S. 1992. *Old Sarawak: A Pictorial Study.* Kuala Lumpur: Dewan Bahasa dan Pustaka, Kementrian Pendidikan Malaysia.

Lomnitz, C. 2001. "Nationalism as a Practical System: Benedict Anderson's Theory of Nationalism from the Vantage Point of Spanish America", in *The Other Mirror: Grand Theory through the Lens of Latin America*, ed. Á.C. Miguel and F. López-Alves. Princeton: Princeton University Press.

Low, H. 1848. *Sarawak: Its Inhabitants and Production.* London: Bentley.

Lundu District Office. 1951. *Lundu District Quarterly Report* 3rd; July–September.

________. 1954. *Lundu District Quarterly Report* 3rd; July–September.

________. 1956. *Lundu District Office First Half Yearly Report*; January–June.

________. 1959. *Lundu District Second Half Yearly Report*; July–December.

Mackie, J.A.C. 1974. *Konfrontasi: Indonesia-Malaysia Dispute 1963–1966.* Kuala Lumpur: Oxford University Press.

Martinez, O.J. 1986. "Introduction", in *Across Boundaries: Transborder Interaction in Comparative Perspective*, ed. Oscar J. Martinez. El Paso: Texas Western Press and the University of Texas at El Paso.

Migdal, J.S. 1988. *Strong Societies and Weak States: State-Society Relations and State Capabilities in the Third World.* Princeton: Princeton University Press.

________. 2001. *State in Society: Studying How States and Societies Transform and Constitute One Another.* Cambridge: Cambridge University Press.

Migdal, J.S. (ed.). 2004. *Boundaries and Belonging: States and Societies in the Struggle to Shape Identities and Local Practices.* Cambridge: Cambridge University Press.

Mohammed Yusof Shibli. 1950. "The Descent of Some Kuching Malays". *The Sarawak Museum Journal* 2: 262–4.

Moor, J.H. 1837. *Notices of the Indian Archipelago and Adjacent Countries.* Singapore.

Moore, D. and J. 1969. *The First 150 Years of Singapore.* Singapore: Donald Moore Press.

Morris, H.S. 1953. *Report on a Melanau Sago Producing Community in Sarawak.* London: H.M.S.O.

Muir, R. 1975. *Modern Political Geography*. London; New York: Macmillan.

Mundy, R. 1848. *Narratives of Events in Borneo and Celebes, Down to the Occupation of Labuan from the Journals of Sir James Brooke Esq.*, Vol. 1. London.

Nagatsu, K. 2001. "Pirates, Sea Nomads or Protectors of Islam? A Note on 'Bajau' Identifications in the Malaysian Context". *Asian and African Area Studies* 1: 212–30.

Naimah Said Talib. 1999. *Administrators and Their Service: The Sarawak Administrative Service under the Brooke Rajahs and British Colonial Rule.* Oxford: Oxford University Press.

Ongkili, J.P. 1967. *The Borneo Response to Malaysia, 1961–1963.* Singapore: Donald Moore.

Parnell, E. 1911. "The Tribute Paid in Former Days by the Then Dependent Provinces of Sarawak". *The Sarawak Museum Journal* 11 (Feb. 1911): 125–30.

Parry, J.P. and M. Block. 1989. "Introduction", in *Money and the Morality of Exchange*, ed. J.P. Parry and M. Block. Cambridge: Cambridge University Press.

Porter, A. 1967. *Land Administration in Sarawak: An Account of the Development of Land Administration in Sarawak from the Rule of Rajah Brooke to the Present Time (1841–1967).* Sarawak: Published by Authority.

Poulgrain, P. 1998. *The Genesis of Konfrontasi: Malaysia Brunei Indonesia 1945–1965.* Bathurst: Vrawford House Publishing; London: C. Hurst & Co.

Pringle, R. 1970. *Rajah and Rebels: The Ibans of Sarawak under Brooke Rule, 1841–1941.* New York: Cornell University Press.

Raffles, Sir Thomas Stanford. 1830. *History of Java* (2nd edition). London: J. Murray, vol. 1.

Rawlins, J. 1969. *Sarawak — 1839 to 1968* (2nd edition). Basingstoke, London: Macmillan Education Ltd.

Reece, R.H.W. 1988. "Economic Development under the Brookes", in *Sarawak: Historical and Contemporary Perspectives*, ed. R.A. Cramb and R.H.W. Reece. Monash Paper on Southeast Asia No.17, Center of Southeast Asian Studies, Monash University.

———. 1993. *Datu Bandar: Abang Hj. Mustapha of Sarawak.* Kuching: Sarawak Literary Society.

Ricklefs, M.C. 1974. *Jogjakarta under Sultan Mangkubumi, 1749–1792: A History of the Division of Java*. London, New York: Oxford University Press.

Ritchie, J. 2000. *Tun Ahmad Zaidi: Son of Sarawak*. Selangor: Pelanduk Publications.

Riwanto Tirtosudarmo and John Haba (eds.). 2005. *Dari Entikong Sampai Nunukan: Dinamika Daerah Perbatasan Kalimantan Malaysia Timur (Sarawak-Sabah)*. Jakarta: Pustaka Sinar Harapan.

Rosaldo, R. 1988. "Ideology, Place, and People without Culture". *Cultural Anthropology* 3(1): 77–87.

Röster M. and T. Wendl (eds.). 1999. *Frontiers and Borderlands: Anthropological Perspective*. Berlin: Frankfurt am Main.

Rush, J. 1990. *Opium to Java: Revenue Farming and Chinese Enterprise in Colonial Indonesia, 1860–1910*. Ithaca: Cornell University Press.

Sahlins, P. 1988. "The Nation in the Village: State-building and Communal Struggles in the Catalan Borderland During the Eighteenth and Nineteenth Centuries". *Journal of Modern History* 60: 234–63.

________. 1989. *Boundaries: The Making of France and Spain in the Pyrenees*. Berkeley: University of California Press.

________. 1990a. "Natural Frontier Revisited: France's Boundaries since the Seventeenth Century". *American Historical Review* 95: 1423–51.

________. 1990b. "The Use and Abuse of the Nation: the French Cerdagne during the 18th and 19th Centuries". *Critique of Anthropology* 10, nos. 2 & 3: 73–95.

Sanib Said. 1985. *Malay Politics in Sarawak 1946–1966: The Search for Unity and Political Ascendancy*. Singapore: Oxford University Press.

________. 1991. *Yang Dikehendaki: Biografi Yang Di-pertua Negri Sarawak Tun Datuk Patinggi Hj. Ahmad Zaidi Adruce Mohd. Noor*, Persatuan Sejarah Malaysia Cawangan Sarawak, Kuching.

Sarawak Development Institute (SDI). 2001. *Study on the Economic Linkages between West Kalimantan and Kuching*, Kuching, Sarawak.

Schneider, J. 1995. "Introduction", in *Articulating Hidden Histories: Exploring the Influence of Eric R. Wolf*, ed. J. Schneider and R. Rapp. Berkeley: University of California Press.

Scott, J. 1998. *Seeing Like a State*. New Haven: Yale University Press.

________. 1999. "State and People Who Move Around". *IIAS Newsletter* 19.

________. 2009. *The Art of Not Being Governed: An Anarchist History of Upland Southeast Asia*. New Haven: Yale University Press.

Smith, A. 1971. *Theories of Nationalism*. New York: Harper and Row.

Soja, E.W. 1989. *Postmodern Geographies: The Reassertion of Space in Critical Social Theory*. London: Verso.

St. John, S. 1862. *The Life in the Forest of the Far East*, vol. 1. London: Smith Elder.

Steinberg, D.J. and D.P. Chandler (eds.). 1988. *In Search of Southeast Asia.* Honolulu: University of Hawaii Press.

Tagliacozzo, E. 2005. *Secret Trades, Porous Borders: Smuggling and States Along a Southeast Asian Frontier, 1865–1915.* New Haven; London and Singapore: Yale University Press and NUS Press.

———. 2001. "Border Permeability and the State in Southeast Asia: Contraband and Regional Security". *Contemporary Southeast Asia: A Journal of International and Strategic Affairs* 23: 254–74.

Takumusho [Overseas Development Agency, Japan]. 1938. *Sarawaku Oukoku Jijyo* [A Report on the Kingdom of Sarawak]. Kaigai Takushoku Jigyo Chosabu [Department of Overseas Development Research].

Tambiah, S.J. 1976. *World Conqueror and World Renouncer.* New York: Cambridge University Press.

Tanaka, K. 2002. "Crop-Raising Techniques in Asian Rice Culture: Resemblance to Root and Tuber Crop Cultivation", in *Vegeculture in Eastern Asia and Oceania*, ed. S. Yoshida and P.J. Matthews. JCAS Symposium Series 16, The Japan Center for Area Studies (JCAS), National Museum of Ethnology, Osaka, Japan.

Thongchai Winichakul. 1994. *Siam Mapped: A History of the Geo-body of a Nation.* Honolulu: University of Hawaii Press.

Tsing, A. 1993. *In the Realm of the Diamond Queen: Marginality in an Out-of-the-Way Place.* New Jersey: Princeton University Press.

———. 1994. "From the Margins". *Cultural Anthropology* 9(3): 279–97.

Trocki, C.A. 1990. *Opium and Empire: Chinese Society in Colonial Singapore, 1800–1910.* Ithaca: Cornell University Press.

Turner, V. 1982. *From Ritual to Theater: the Human Seriousness of Play.* New York: Performing Arts Journal Publications.

Uchibori, M. 1984. "Transformations of Iban Social Consciousness", in *History and Peasant Consciousness in South East Asia*, ed. R.A. Turton and S. Tanabe. Senri Ethnological Studies 13. Osaka: National Museum of Ethnology.

Uljee, G.L. 1925. *Handboek voor de Residentie Westerafdeeling van Borneo.* Weltevreden: N.V. Boekhandel Visser and Co.

Vandergeest, P. and N.L. Peluso. 1995. "Territorialization and State Power in Thailand". *Theory and Society* 24: 385–426.

Van Schendel, W. and M. Baud. 1997. "Toward a Comparative History of Borderlands". *Journal of World History* 8(2): 211–42.

Van Schendel, W. and I. Abraham (eds.). 2005. *Illicit Flows and Criminal Things: States, Borders, and the Other Side of Globalization.* Bloomington: Indiana University Press.

Wadley, R.L. 2001. "Trouble on the Frontier: Dutch-Brooke Relations and Iban Rebellion in the West Borneo Boundaries (1841–1886)". *Modern Asian Studies* 35(3): 623–44.

________. 2003 "Lines in the Forest: Internal Territorialization and Local Accommodation in West Kalimantan, Indonesia (1865–1979)". *South East Asia Research* 11(1): 91–112.

Walker, J.H. 2002. *Power and Prowess: The Origins of Brooke Kingship in Sarawak*. Honolulu: University of Hawaii Press.

Ward, A.B. 1966. *Rajah's Servant*. Data Paper No. 61, Southeast Asia Program, Department of Asian Studies, Cornell University, Ithaca, New York.

Warren, J.F. 1981. *The Sulu Zone 1768–1898: The Dynamics of External Trade, Slavery, and Ethnicity in the Transformation of a Southeast Asian Maritime State*. Singapore: Singapore University Press.

________. 2002. *Iranun and Balangingi: Globalization, Maritime Raiding and the Birth of Ethnicity*. Singapore: Singapore University Press.

Weber, M. 1958. "Politics as a Vocation", in *From Max Weber: Essays in Sociology*, ed. H.H. Gerth and C. Wright Mills. New York: Oxford University Press.

Wilkinson, R.J. 1959. *A Malay-English Dictionary* (Romanised), Part I (A-K). London: Macmillan.

Williams, B.F. 1989. "A Class Act: Anthropology and the Race to Nation across Ethnic Terrain". *Annual Review of Anthropology* 18: 401–44.

Wilson, T. and D. Hastings. 1998. "Nation, State and Identity at International Borders", in *Border Identities: Nation and State at International Frontiers*, ed. T. Wilson and D. Hastings Cambridge: Cambridge University Press.

Wolf, E. 1999. *Envisioning Power: Ideologies of Dominance and Crisis*. Berkeley: University of California Press.

________. 2001. "Facing Power: Old Insights, New Questions", in *Pathways of Power: Building an Anthropology of the Modern World*. Berkeley: University of California Press.

Wolters, O.W. 1982. *History, Culture, and Region in Southeast Asian Perspectives*. Singapore: Institute of Southeast Asian Studies.

Zainal Kling. 1973. "The Saribas Malays of Sarawak", PhD Thesis, University of Hull.

Index